# Rethinking
# Information Work

# Rethinking Information Work

*A Career Guide for Librarians and Other Information Professionals*

Second Edition

G. KIM DORITY

 LIBRARIES UNLIMITED™
An Imprint of ABC-CLIO, LLC
Santa Barbara, California • Denver, Colorado

**Library of Congress Cataloging-in-Publication Data**

Names: Dority, G. Kim, 1950– author.
Title: Rethinking information work : a career guide for librarians and other information professionals / G. Kim Dority.
Description: Second edition. | Santa Barbara, CA : Libraries Unlimited, [2016] | Includes bibliographical references and index.
Identifiers: LCCN 2015033949 | ISBN 9781610699594 (paperback) | ISBN 9781610699600 (ebook)
Subjects: LCSH: Library science—Vocational guidance—United States. | Information science—Vocational guidance—United States. | Career development. | BISAC: LANGUAGE ARTS & DISCIPLINES / Library & Information Science / General. | LANGUAGE ARTS & DISCIPLINES / Library & Information Science / Administration & Management.
Classification: LCC Z682.35.V62 D67 2016 | DDC 020.23—dc23
LC record available at http://lccn.loc.gov/2015033949

ISBN: 978-1-61069-959-4
EISBN: 978-1-61069-960-0

20  19  18  17  16    1  2  3  4  5

This book is also available on the World Wide Web as an eBook.
Visit www.abc-clio.com for details.

Libraries Unlimited
An Imprint of ABC-CLIO, LLC

ABC-CLIO, LLC
130 Cremona Drive, P.O. Box 1911
Santa Barbara, California 93116–1911

This book is printed on acid-free paper ∞

Manufactured in the United States of America

This book is dedicated to my father, Roy Donahue, whose unconditional love, support, and encouragement instilled in me the confidence to become who I was capable of becoming, and an understanding that success was about not the amount of your paycheck, but rather the amount of your impact.

# Contents

# Acknowledgments

The first edition of this book was based on a course I developed at the University of Denver Library and Information Science graduate program called "Alternative Career Paths for Librarians." It was conceived as an exploration of all of the different paths one could pursue with an MLIS degree, and each year, it has expanded to incorporate new insights contributed by the previous class members. Thus, it is important to acknowledge the extraordinary contribution each group of students has made over the past 15 years to the body of knowledge presented here. I am deeply grateful to the students who have shared their questions, ideas, and experiences over the years, as they have led to deeper insights for all of us. As students in all of our many MLIS programs have gone on to become practitioners, they have contributed their unique skills and insights to the ever-changing LIS landscape and created new career paths in the process. Those of us in the profession as well as those who will enter it owe them our appreciation and applause.

In addition, I would like to acknowledge the tremendous support provided by the profession for the *idea* of alternative LIS career paths. A bit of an oddity when we first starting talking about them, alternative LIS career paths have now gained traction and are opening up expanding job opportunities in large part thanks to the willingness of librarians and other information professionals to test out new ideas and approaches. Thank-you to all of the fearless individuals who have scouted the territory for us and then reported back. We are in your debt.

As with the previous edition, this book draws on the knowledge I have gained from many, many wise and supportive colleagues throughout the years. Together, we have been exploring as many ways as we can devise for using LIS skills to create rewarding careers—with, no doubt, many more ways to come. Special thanks to Mary Ellen Bates, Marcy Phelps, and Scott Brown for your wise counsel and ongoing support here.

Lastly, I would like to thank my extraordinarily patient and insightful editor, Barbara Ittner, who not only helped me shape the original manuscript into a coherent whole but then also, flying in the face of good judgment and previous experience, was again willing to go through the process with me for a second edition. Barbara, you are patience and the triumph of faith over experience personified. And I am grateful.

# Introduction to the Second Edition

In 1977, Marc Porat coined the term "information economy" while working on his economics doctorate at Stanford. In 2014, Aaron Hurst, Dr. Porat's nephew, social entrepreneur, and founder of the Taproot Foundation, described what is perhaps our next defining phase, the "purpose economy." In his book *The Purpose Economy: How Your Desire for Impact, Personal Growth, and Community Is Changing the World* (Elevate), Hurst describes a new approach to work that is grounded in and reflective of the basic human need to be doing something worthwhile with our skills and knowledge. Purpose, he asserts, will increasingly become the driver of our careers.

That being the case, library and information science (LIS) professionals should be, as they say, in the sweet spot.

Few career paths offer the potential for creating meaning and purpose from our daily engagements as does information work. Information is a change agent; our skills enable us to be change agents who add value to lives, communities, organizations, and nations. We can do that as public, school, or academic librarians, as information specialists in for-profit and nonprofit settings, for government agencies, and for organizations of every type. We can help drive local economic development, instill confidence in a hesitant community college student, provide the market intelligence that lets a start-up succeed, or help a nonprofit attain the funding it needs or disseminate the knowledge those funds have enabled. And that's just a beginner list.

That's the good news.

On the other hand, launching, growing, or transitioning an LIS career has probably never been more of a challenge. Traditional libraries—especially public and school—are undergoing disruptive changes that affect who gets hired, what they get hired for, and whether or not those hires are required to be graduates of MLIS programs. Competition is fierce for plum jobs—defined as a full-time position that pays a decent salary, comes with benefits, and has at least some potential for growth and professional engagement. Unpredictability may be the new normal when it comes to LIS employment.

For example, the American Library Association's *State of America's Libraries Report 2015* finds that public libraries continue to be valued ("More than two-thirds of Americans agree that libraries are important because they improve the quality of life in a community, promote literacy and reading, and provide many people with a chance to succeed") and popular ("In 2012, there were 92.6 million attendees at the 4 million programs offered by public libraries. This represents a 10-year increase of 54.4% in program attendance.").[1] However, that increase in service and programs has not resulted in a corresponding increase in professional-level employment (45,115 in 2006, 46,808 in 2014).[2]

Public library circumstances have begun to improve with the strengthening economy as some states have restored at least a modicum of previously cut funding. A positive result is that the dire trend of libraries closing outright seems to have slowed ("The number of states reporting branch closures is down, from 10 states . . . to only five this year" [2014]).[3] However, stories like that of Missouri ("a 2016 budget that will cut state aid to libraries by a disastrous 79 percent . . .")[4] signal the reality of an unpredictable financial future for years to come, at best. The likelihood is that some public libraries will thrive, some will struggle, but entry-level, full-time "MLIS-required" positions will continue to contract due to shifting budget priorities and workplace structural changes.

School libraries and librarians are also prime targets during periods of budget cuts, often through "reorganizations" that allow state departments of education to avoid requirements for staffing middle and high schools with certified school librarians. (An indicator of the impact on this professional group is that when the first edition of *Rethinking Information Work* was published in 2006, the American Association of School Librarians [AASL] had 10,000 members; today, according to its website, it has closer to 7,000.[5])

Similarly, special libraries and librarians have seen their universe contracting at an estimated rate of 20 percent, according to Drs. James M. Matarazzo and Toby Pearlstein in their *Special Libraries: A Survival Guide* (Libraries Unlimited, 2013). The Special Library Association's membership numbers bear this out, going from a high of some 14,000 members to today's "more than 7,000," per its website. In fact, as described in Chapter 4, special librarianship jobs are increasingly transforming into embedded or integrated information professional roles, and the requisite skills are morphing into previously uncharted territories such as digital asset management; data gathering, organizing, analyzing, and synthesizing; and social media marketing.

Bottom line: traditional librarianship as a professional will probably continue to contract in job opportunities and transform itself in terms of the nature of the work. Special librarianship as it *was* practiced will also probably continue to contract (in terms of centralized enterprise libraries). However, for both disciplines, new information work opportunities and career paths are simultaneously expanding at encouraging rates.

By facing these realities, you'll be much better prepared to take maximum advantage of what some are calling today's career chaos, also known as the new normal. You'll realize you have many more choices than might have seemed evident at first glance, and you can start developing the skills and mind-set necessary to place yourself in the path of opportunity.

Where are those opportunities likely to lie? Think data management, digital archives, digital asset management, genealogy research, documentalist, user experience, content curation, compliance, information gamification, tech training, and maker spaces, among some of the increasingly popular job areas. This is just a starter list—possibilities are covered in greater depth in Chapter 4.

# Who This Book Is Written For

This book is written for any information professional (or soon-to-be) who has wondered, like me, in how many rewarding ways it might be possible to use LIS skills. When I graduated with my degree in hand years ago, I knew virtually nothing about what alternatives might exist—or be created—that would let me build a resilient and interesting career. I felt both lost and alone in my lack of knowledge, and quite foolish that I had gone through two years of grad school and somehow not managed to "pick up" this information somewhere along the way. I learned, however, that I wasn't alone—and, in fact, I hear from those I teach that this continues to be a major concern for a majority of MLIS students and grads. If you're among them, then this book is for you.

But it's also intended to meet the needs of mid-career practitioners concerned about job stability, LIS professionals exploring possible new ways to grow their careers, those considering how to restructure their careers to more positively support their other life priorities, and preretirement librarians considering launching encore careers (consultant? trainer?). In fact, the purpose of *Rethinking Information Work* is to help you create the career path that best meets your needs wherever you find yourself on the career spectrum—for both the immediate and long-term future.

# How to Use This Book

I've organized the chapters to correspond to the steps most of us are likely to take as we explore career options. Chapter 1 provides an overview of the LIS "landscape" and ways to think about its opportunities from a broad perspective. Chapter 2 provides a walk-through of career self-awareness, so that you'll be able to more effectively determine which choices are positive or negative for you, and why. Understanding your personal preferences will enable you to take a pass on avoidable and unnecessary career "detours" as you home in more confidently on the directions that best fit who you are.

Chapters 3 through 5 focus on specific types of LIS career paths. Chapter 3 provides an overview of the three traditional choices (school, public, and academic), noting their pros and cons and including voices from practitioners. Chapter 4 is designed to help you frame and explore the nontraditional options, providing both ways to consider alternative career paths and titles of potential jobs. And for those of you who know that what you're really interested in is going out on your own, Chapter 5 will give you the information you need to seriously consider independent work and whether this is right for you.

Chapters 6 through 10 will help you develop your own career strategy, giving you the key tools and tactics you need to create your best career opportunities. (In an uncertain job environment, knowing how to adapt and pivot may just be the greatest career security you can have.) Chapter 6 will help you understand how to identify and understand transferable skills, a key career asset, then show you how to translate those skills into non-LIS opportunities. Chapter 7 helps you make the most of the changes swirling through the professional (and beyond), while Chapter 8 focuses on how to build your professional equity—the anchor that will help you stay centered in the midst of those changes.

Chapter 9 is where you'll start assembling all the information we've covered into an action plan that's tailored for you—where your passions lie, the skills you may want to use, the opportunities you may want to pursue now or in the foreseeable future. It's where you'll focus on the steps necessary to get yourself from your starting point (here) to your next goal (there), as many times as you need or want to move forward into a new opportunity. Mastering this process will be what enables you to have the professional independence so central to control over your career and life.

That professional independence is also key to creating a resilient career, as explored in Chapter 10. How do you frame career opportunity? What actions support resiliency? What does taking charge of your own outcomes look like? This final chapter will help you develop your strongest, most authentic path to a resilient career.

## Preparing for What's Next

In the first edition of *Rethinking Information Work*, I asked the question who did we want to be, and how did we want others to think of us? My sense of information professionals included (and continues to include) words like energy, innovation, thought leadership, impact, engagement, passion, excitement, self-confidence, participation, entrepreneurial, collaborative, improvisational, and curious. I associate phrases like dynamic action, joy, contribution, laughter, politically astute, change agent, connected, adventurous, smart, and resilient with the LIS students and professionals I've had the good fortune to work with. Although I believe that to a great extent we're outgrowing many of our decades-old roles, I also believe that we can grow into amazing new roles barely imaginable today. How exciting is that?

In the chapters that follow, I hope the information, insights, and resources provided instill confidence in your ability to successfully navigate the career disruptions we'll all be facing, but most of all, I hope they help you find or create those opportunities that give you the greatest sense of purpose and engagement possible throughout the lifetime of your career.

A final note: since I've been writing about these concepts for a number of years in many environments, some of the material included here is drawn from those writings, while being updated for today's circumstances.

## Notes

1. "State of America's Libraries Report 2015," American Library Association, 2015, accessed at www.ala.org/news/state-americas-libraries-report-2015.

2. ALA Library Fact Sheet 2: Number Employed in Libraries, accessed at www.ala.org/tools/libfactsheets/alalibraryfactsheet02.

3. "State of America's Libraries Report 2015."

4. Rebecca T. Miller, "The Budget Dance: State Funding Is Not 'Low-Hanging Fruit,'" *Library Journal,* 140(9) (May 15, 2015): 8.

5. "About AASL," accessed at www.ala.org/aasl/about.

# 1
# Rethinking Information Work

*Adaptability creates stability.*
—Reid Hoffman and Ben Casnocha

We do information work.

We may work with the public creating maker spaces, work in corporations doing data analysis, work for nonprofits by supporting online information dissemination, or work for clients doing industry growth forecasts, among myriad other options. But in all cases, we are working with information on behalf of others.

Previously, when most of us graduated with our master's degree in library and information science (MLIS), we viewed our possible career paths within the framework of jobs we might land in the traditional spheres of librarianship. Many of us headed off for positions as school, public, or academic librarians, while a relative few pursued special library jobs. Today, these traditional career options still exist, although in somewhat reduced numbers, and are terrific career paths if they fit your skills, interests, aptitudes, financial requirements, and life stage at the time you follow them.

These traditional paths of librarianship can provide extraordinary, richly rewarding careers. However, for those whose interests or professional circumstances dictate other choices, it's reassuring to know that the traditional path is but one of *many* open to information professionals. That familiar MLIS (or MMLIS, MIS, or related) designation signifies that we possess a stunningly diverse skill set, one that can be deployed in an equally stunning number of places, positions, and opportunities. The challenge, however, comes in rethinking how we frame what we know, and *what we know how to do*, both for ourselves and for the employment world at large.

In my career, "doing information work" has given me the opportunity to set up a special collections library for a nonprofit; write several books; create web content to support marketing and public-information campaigns; create the first virtual library for online students; evaluate manuscripts for publishers; create an executive information service for a CEO; head up an LIS graduate program on an interim basis; create and teach a course in alternative career paths for LIS students and professionals; do freelance research projects for a broad range of clients; establish a consulting business focused on information strategy for businesses, government agencies, and nonprofits; and pursue a wide range of fascinating projects—including my most recent job as chief content officer for a psychology-focused online start-up.

Many friends and colleagues have had equally diverse careers. Take Christine Hamilton-Pennell, who has built a career that included research work related to school libraries at the Colorado Department of Education, teaching at the graduate level, doing freelance research, undertaking marketing consulting for libraries, developing web-based continuing education courses, developing a multimedia product, running a special library, developing a consulting expertise in the area of economic gardening, and coauthoring a long-running online Internet review site. She has been a presenter at national conferences on the topics of competitive intelligence (CI), planning and community development, and economic development, and worked as the economic intelligence specialist, Business/Industry Affairs, for the City of Littleton, Colorado. In a recent transition, Christine decided to take her career in yet another direction and became the librarian/information specialist for a leading Japanese-based medical devices firm.

Christine has done just about every type of information work available. Some of it has been within what we think of as traditional librarianship, while other projects have been well outside of it. In all circumstances, however, she has built—and then expanded on—a core group of skills central to being an *information professional*, which sometimes includes being a librarian.

Or consider the varied career of Michele Lucero Villagran. Formerly director of Client Development for LAC Group, Michele was responsible for both business development and client management (also known as client relationship management). She focused primarily on the company's law firm clients and prospective clients, not only acquiring new accounts but also making sure that existing clients were well served and, if appropriate, expanding their relationship to include additional LAC services. Beginning as the director of recruiting, Michele was promoted three times in her nearly three years with LAC Group, a testament to her willingness to take on new challenges and execute successfully.

In addition, Michele is an adjunct professor for Woodbury University in its graduate Organizational Leadership program and is also an adjunct in the University of North Texas (UNT) MLIS program (as well as being the California local program coordinator for the Greater Los Angeles and Northern California programs). Since graduating with her MLIS from UNT in 2004, Michele has also completed an MBA in strategic management from UNT and a master of dispute resolution from Pepperdine University's School of Law Straus Institute, and is currently a doctoral candidate completing her dissertation, *Examination of Cultural Intelligence within Law Firm Librarians in the United States: A Mixed Methods Study,* for her doctorate of education in organizational leadership.

Her route to her current roles? Ten years in public librarianship, then law librarianship, then work with legal publisher West, plus a stint with the Los Angeles Law Library, doing marketing and communications.

The takeaway here is that given the focus of most graduate programs, it's easy to assume that what we know is "librarianship." We may know cataloging, or readers' advisory services, or bibliographic instruction (BI), or how to build a dynamite academic library portal, or how to work with teachers to create terrific information-literacy modules. In fact, today's graduates probably know at least a good bit about each of these aspects of librarianship, as well as much more. They know how to "do librarianship."

But they—and we—also know something equally valuable. We all know how to do *information*. As LIS professionals, we know how to find it, evaluate it, organize it, maintain it, present it, and use it to deliver exceptional value. We can create information and deploy it, align it with strategic goals, and use it to support individual, organization, or community development. And this is just for starters.

LIS professionals are managing complex information projects, designing community information systems, taking the lead on extraordinarily sophisticated digitization initiatives, running geographic information systems (GIS) projects, helping launch cutting-edge information products and services, and creating online social communities.

They're using social media as an extension of web-based school libraries, embedding "on-demand" BI in online learning courses, and delivering virtual reference via text messaging and social media channels. They're answering questions 24/7 for online, for-profit companies, working with medical informatics, organizing data networks for online auction businesses, and doing collection development for database developers. They're moving into the emerging opportunities offered by such in-demand disciplines as "big data" structure and analysis, social informatics, and gamification for information, education, and behavioral change applications. LIS professionals can be found throughout the nonprofit, for-profit, government, and library worlds—sometimes, but less and less frequently, being called librarians.

If we reframe our skill set from "librarianship" to the larger and more encompassing "information work," then we have choices that can respond to changes in job markets, personal financial requirements, living arrangements, and other professional and life circumstances. We may be information professionals who happily choose to spend our entire careers in the library field, in traditional libraries. But if budgets continue to be cut, staffs continue to be downsized, and jobs become scarce in times of economic crisis, information professionals can *always* deploy their skill sets in new directions should they need or want to.

And therein lies the key to a dynamic career. The more broadly you consider your career and your professional skills, the more numerous—and rewarding—your career opportunities.

## Change Happens

Things change.

No matter how much our directors love us, no matter how great a job we do, circumstances, and management, change. Budgets get cut, people move on, organizations' priorities and staffing needs change.

Our working environments may change overnight, as the previously wonderful boss moves into the executive ranks, bringing in the replacement supervisor from hell. A flexible work schedule that fits you perfectly may be replaced with a more restrictive one that reflects the new management focus on a "tight ship." Or a change in leadership style at the top may result in fewer opportunities for growth and initiative throughout the rest of the organization.

Or the nature of the work we do and how we do it changes. Disruptive technologies and trends such as digitization, social media, instant messaging, and big data have changed forever what we mean by information collection, management, and dissemination. Our students are growing up in an integrated digital surround of information, communications, entertainment, and learning—and take for granted their 24/7 availability. Those of us who grew up before these technologies came online and went mainstream now find ourselves in a professional landscape bearing little resemblance to the one we trained for. And to draw on Alfred Toffler's assertion in his now-classic *Future Shock* (Bantam Books, 1970), we are facing an accelerating rate of change. When the first edition of *Rethinking Information Work* was published in 2006, I noted that "As has been pointed out by industry guru Barbara Quint, Google now fields more searches in a few *days* than the total received by the world's libraries in a *year*."[1] In fact, industry experts estimate that in 2006, there were about 23 million Google search per year; today that number is 3.5 billion searches *per day*, or roughly 1.2 trillion searches per year.[2]

Or the nature of libraries within their constituencies changes. This isn't necessarily a diminishment of the role of libraries, but may take them in new directions that push staffers outside their comfort zones. Perhaps expectations of what libraries are and can do rise as technologies advance. Or libraries may increasingly become critical lifelines for underserved populations, often without preparation or training or, frequently, funding. Or perhaps corporate libraries are asked to take on the more critical roles of analysis and strategic intelligence provider for their organizations—not only an unfamiliar and sometimes daunting responsibility for some, but also a terrific growth opportunity for more and more special librarians.

Or the nature of those leading the profession changes. We continue to graduate a passionate, smart, and dedicated group of recently minted information professionals pushing to step into leadership roles in an industry not necessarily known for embracing innovative new ideas, especially if accompanied by a lack of patience with dues-paying. Like the next generation of library users, many of these individuals have grown up in the electronic information surround, and their easy familiarity with emerging technologies is critical to the profession. Yet finding opportunities for these exciting new voices to be heard, and to mainstream these professionals into leadership roles, may require a willingness to rethink how library workplaces have traditionally been organized and managed.

Or we change. We outgrow a job we once loved, yearning instead for the exhilaration of a new challenge. We leave a job to follow a significant other to the opposite side of the country. We decide to seek part-time work to spend more moments laughing with our toddler or caring for an ailing parent. We discover a passion for history and begin to wonder about archives work. We realize belatedly that working on the reference desk is not the best job match for an introvert. We find that being able to afford a mortgage might be nice after all.

The reality is that we can't rely on an employer to pledge undying fealty—that is, lifetime employment—to us, because just like us, they have no idea what the future will hold. They may need to close our department, lay off staff because of mergers, cut our hours because of funding shortfalls, or transition us into positions that suit the organization's needs rather than ours. *None of this is personal*—it's simply how organizations, including libraries, work.

Things change, life changes, we change. And approached with the right attitude, that can be terrific. The trick is to find a way to create a career that can match us change for change, can keep up with our growth, can continue to offer us new opportunities and new challenges. The key is to understand that, in the long run, we are all self-employed.

And believe it or not, this is good news. Because if we understand that regardless of our current employment situation we are solely responsible for the well-being of our careers and paychecks, that means we can take control. We can focus not on lifetime employment but on lifetime *employability*.

## Lifetime Employment *vs.* Lifetime Employability

Lifetime employment may mean hanging on to a job, any job, rather than risk pursuing more rewarding career choices. Lifetime *employability* involves continually developing new ways to contribute value and grow professionally, and seeking out opportunities to do so.

In 1989, British organizational management specialist Charles Handy published a landmark book, *The Age of Unreason* (Harvard Business School Press). In it, he charted the effects of discontinuous change on Western economies and those who work within them. Especially applicable to information workers was Handy's description of portfolio workers, those individuals whose careers were built on their portfolios of projects rather than on decades-long work for one employer. William Bridges expanded on Handy's thesis with his *Jobshift: How to Prosper in a Workplace without Jobs* (Da Capo, 1995), a practical guide to creating a career based on ever-expanding skills rather than on finding an employer willing and able to guarantee a job for life.

More recently, Reid Hoffman (cofounder and chairman of LinkedIn) and Ben Casnocha published *The Start-Up of You: Adapt to the Future, Invest in Yourself, and Transform Your Career* (Crown Business, 2012). Their baseline premise? All of us need to embrace an entrepreneurial mind-set when it comes to our careers, considering them to be in "permanent beta." Translation: always stay focused on your competitive advantage, which is a combination of your assets, your aspirations, *and the market realities* (italics mine).

Handy, Bridges, Hoffman and Casnocha, and many others have made the point that in an era of school and municipal budget cutbacks, corporate downsizing, mergers and acquisitions (M&A), and outsourcing and offshoring, the only job security lies within ourselves—and in our ability to improvise our careers.

What does it take to ensure employability? First and foremost, it requires a sense of loyalty to your own professional goals. Although professional integrity mandates that we do our very best jobs for our employers and/or clients, we nevertheless must keep our own career goals moving forward at the same time.

The easiest way to practice this "enlightened self-interest" is to have your own career agenda firmly in place. This includes the strategies, tools, processes, and information resources that will support you as you:

- Respond to new opportunities within your library, organization, or community.

- Expand your skills to keep up with new technologies, disciplines, and processes.

- Demonstrate your ability to transition from an area of contracting opportunity to one of greater demand.

- Document a track record of initiative, innovation, and increasing responsibility.

- Develop a career that reflects who you are, what you value, and how you want to contribute, for as long as you want to do so.

Although information professionals are charting career paths in a work environment increasingly unpredictable, they're proving that lifetime employability, and the professional independence it provides, is indeed an achievable goal.

They're setting and executing research agendas, initiating new services built on emerging technology capabilities, participating in strategy teams, and applying their skills to information-business products, services, and start-ups. "Info pros" are being drawn into a brave new world with few road markers, fewer still established career paths to follow, and little guidance as to how to survive in this new workplace. Bottom line: in a trend that started small perhaps a decade ago, more and more of us are continuing to make it up as we go along. And we're starting to get pretty good at it.

Although occasionally (okay, often) unnerving, improvising a career in such a dynamic environment can also be incredibly rewarding, in every sense. No path to track means you're free to chart your own best route. No job description means you can create your own definition of how you contribute. No footsteps to follow means no assumptions of what can or can't be done—and the freedom to set expectations high enough to challenge yourself. No rigid pay grade means you can negotiate compensation that appropriately reflects your individual level of contribution. And the agility that comes with improvising your information career will be your key asset when it comes to building a resilient career.

What does it take to design a resilient career, one that allows you to successfully navigate the opportunities available to information professionals today—and tomorrow? And for that matter, what *is* a resilient career?

A resilient career is one that enables you to work for as long as you'd like, at work that you love, with an appropriate level of compensation and benefits. Ideally, it will offer you the level of challenge you thrive on, opportunities for learning and growth, and rewards of value to you, whether emotional, social, intellectual, financial, or all of these. And, when necessary, it should provide you with enough professional independence to leave an unhealthy work situation for a healthy one.

If we work at it, all of these goals are achievable. Through a combination of self-assessment, strategies, tools, processes, information gathering, and attitudes, you can design a career that closely reflects the type of professional life you'd like to have.

By creating your own professional agenda, you'll be able to focus your time and career energy on moving toward your goals . . . no matter where or how you're currently working. By rethinking information work as the broadest possible application of your skills, and then choosing how you'll deploy those skills for the greatest personal reward, you can redefine your universe of career possibilities.

## Career Competencies

What does it take to start moving your career in a direction that brings you work that will sustain you, financially and intellectually, for tomorrow and for a lifetime? As we'll see, it takes strategies and tactics, supported by tools and information. But first and foremost, it takes attitudes, expectations, and assumptions that work *for* you rather than against you. Among these are:

**An understanding of who you are, who you can be, and who you want to be.** Self-knowledge is a powerful tool. Without it, you can have no meaningful direction; with it, you can consistently identify what will support you on your path. Self-knowledge comes from exploring your preferences; thinking about what jobs, environments, and types of work make you the happiest; and understanding what determines success for you.

Having a better understanding of yourself in the context of your career also makes it easier to distinguish between your own goals and desires and the expectations others may have for what your career should be about. Not that they don't always have the best of intentions, of course. . . .

**A determination to accept reality.** Yep, librarians should be paid more. Yes, they should be treated with the respect their role in our society deserves. And there definitely should be more good, rewarding job opportunities and more potential for career growth in the profession. The reality is that salaries are probably not going to improve much in the foreseeable future. The general public rarely appreciates the extraordinary benefits libraries deliver at the level we would hope. Landing full-time jobs in traditional library settings may continue to challenge recent MLIS grads.

Neither wishing nor whining is going to change these realities. Only by facing them can you make useful choices and trade-offs among the options that *do* exist. That may mean living on a lower salary, moving to a different city, working in different environments where there's more flexibility, or higher pay, or more opportunity for growth. The key is that choices based in reality are the only ones that will actually get you unstuck.

**A focus on solutions rather than obstacles.** There are a million ways to say no: *we've never done that, we tried it before and it didn't work, that's not how we do things*. Or the famous and ever-popular *I can't see how that would work, who's going to pay for it, not my responsibility*, and my personal favorite, *are you nuts???* When someone poses a new challenge for you to deal with, it's easy to focus on all the potential obstacles and raise these as reasons not to move forward. But a solutions focus gives you the opportunity to use and demonstrate your analytical skills, your ability to think strategically, your project management capabilities.

By taking the initiative instead of ducking under the desk, you become a professional who has contributions to make and value to add. And your career efforts will focus not on the obstacles blocking your way, but on the solutions moving you forward.

**An understanding and acceptance of change.** We'll explore the impacts of change in greater depth in Chapter 7, but for now, the most important thing is to simply accept that change is nonnegotiable and your goal is to focus on the energy rather than the fear inherent in change.

In order to do this, you'll need to explore how you react to change. This will help you become comfortable with your change process and consequently more confident in dealing with the LIS profession's ongoing transitions.

**A willingness to adapt skills to the environment.** Whether in a business, a public library, an association information center, a government agency, or any of the other environments in which LIS professionals may find themselves, your ability to move easily among them depends in large part on your flexibility. Can you adapt to the language of your organizations, align your processes to support theirs, develop systems that use your knowledge to suit new goals?

How well you read environments and how effectively you transfer your skills to them determine how readily you succeed in new opportunities. The world is not going to adapt to us, we will need to be willing to adapt to it.

**A willingness to look for opportunity.** Opportunities are all around us, yet if not paying attention to them, we'll miss most of the moments when our careers—if not our lives—could have opened up.

French biologist Louis Pasteur asserted that "chance favors the prepared mind," and careers are no different. If your mind is focused on finding or creating opportunities, then you will be positioned to move quickly with new solutions or products or services when an opening arrives. Just as chance favors the prepared mind, opportunity favors the prepared skill set.

**An ability to anticipate.** The old assumption was that librarians waited to be asked. Their role was a passive, reactive one. No longer. LIS professionals must have an eye out for what will be needed next, and be there in advance. Often your most effective role is scout, riding ahead of the troops to see what's coming over the horizon. Your research and analysis skills uniquely equip you for this spot; you need only claim the ground.

"I think success lies at the intersection of preparation, determination, and opportunity," suggested Edward B. Stear in his now-classic *Online* article "Predicting the Future Is Important, Navigating the Future Is Essential."[3] Add to that intersection a focus on anticipating the needs of your clients, customers, colleagues, and communities, and you've ensured a key role for yourself as an LIS professional, no matter what your career path is.

**A willingness to take risks.** All growth involves risk. Every new opportunity demands that you move from what you know into the unknown, with all its potential risks. It's critical to accept the complementary relationship of risk and reward; doing so often determines whether you can continue to move toward your goals.

It's often said that men make decisions driven by a desire for gain, whereas women's decisions are based on a fear of loss. If we (men or women) remain mired in a bad situation based on this latter choice, then we've already lost. So learning how to take smaller risks in such a way that you're not paralyzed by fear means you'll have the confidence necessary for large, and well-thought-through, risks later.

**A commitment to continuous learning.** We graduate with an MLIS based on the information and learning universe—and its tools—of the moment. Within a few short years, the tools and technologies of that universe have changed, or unforeseen opportunities have taken our careers in new directions. Continuous growth calls for continuous learning; without it, we're stuck with yesterday's solutions.

Staying abreast of new ideas, processes, technologies, and tools is one of the most effective ways to ensure ongoing career resiliency, as well as your continued ability to contribute strategically to your organization.

**An enthusiasm and willingness to engage in the work.** Enthusiasm generates energy. Positive engagement communicates itself to everyone around you and allows you to work at a high level of effectiveness while also motivating your colleagues.

Bottom line: being an enthusiastic contributor makes people want to work with you. It's easy to fall into habits of boredom or disengagement or negativity, but consider the signals you're sending—is this really how you want to be known?

**An ability and willingness to continually reinvent ourselves.** This last point comes from information entrepreneur and coach Mary Ellen Bates, who identified it as among the key traits needed by newly graduated MLIS students.[4] Mary Ellen exemplifies the success that comes from this level of adaptability: her career includes being an information broker, columnist, book author, business consultant, seminar speaker, start-up coach, guest lecturer, and international keynoter. She has grown into these roles by continually reinventing herself, what she is capable of, and the value she is able to create for her clients and constituencies.

## Designing Your Career

Okay, you're in charge—where do you start? We'll explore each of these steps in greater depth in the following chapters, but essentially you'll explore questions, gather information, assess answers, establish agendas, and create strategies to execute your plans. This isn't necessarily a step-by-step plan of attack so much as an ongoing iterative journey whose direction is determined solely by you: by your immediate life circumstances, by your dreams for the future, and by your willingness to invest yourself in their realization.

As you work through your career design process, you'll:

**Do some information gathering.** For once, it really *is* all about you. Aside from a cursory Myers–Briggs assessment, few of us have taken time to really explore who we are—or want to be—in terms of all the aspects of our careers. Your first step will be to spend some serious time asking yourself lots of questions and then carefully noting your answers. This will provide a structure of self-knowledge on which to base career choices that support rather than sideline your goals.

**Explore the options.** The next step is to assess the many career paths open to information professionals, including traditional, nontraditional, and independent. There are dozens if not hundreds of variables here that can shape whether or not a given job or career path fits your needs, so it's helpful to consider the options from as many different angles as possible. This exploration of possibilities can also help you shape a flexible career that fits your life circumstances as they change throughout the decades of your working life.

Once you've developed your information base of self-knowledge and the universe of opportunities, you'll be ready to design your strategies. At this point, you'll want to:

**Consider your skill set.** You'll want to think about repackaging your skill set to most broadly define your capabilities and the arenas in which they can be deployed. This step is part brainstorming, part wordsmithing, and part research—how are jobs described, and how might your skills best be described to align with them?

**Consider how to position yourself for new opportunities.** Change can be your greatest ally when it comes to advancing your career, but only if you meet it head-on. One of the best ways to do that is to make sure your skill set matches the market opportunity. Once you've surveyed job postings, you'll have developed a good sense of skill gaps between jobs of interest to you and your existing skill set. This is where your learning process comes in—determining what you need to learn, when and where you'll learn it, and how you learn most effectively.

You'll also want to practice identifying opportunities that let you move in new career directions. There are systematic ways to ferret out circumstances that drive new opportunities, whether entrepreneurial or internal to your organization. And if the right opportunity isn't there? Then try out ways to create your own.

> **Focus on your professional equity.** In addition to building what you know (and can do with it), you'll want to determine how to grow your professional community and how to build a professional reputation that showcases the many ways you can add value to an organization.

Based on the work you've done asking questions, gathering information, and determining answers, you'll be ready to create your strategies for achieving the career you've envisioned. To get you from here to there, your next step will be to:

> **Lay out your career map.** After you've done your research and brainstorming, it's time to pull together your action plan. Think of goals, strategies, and tactics that will take you from where you are now to where you want to be and lay them out in a systematic, actionable plan.

Lastly, you'll want to think through how your career fits into the world, how it aligns with your life, and how you'll structure your decisions to drive the outcomes you seek. At this point, your goal will be to:

> **Figure out your frame.** How do you think about your career? Your world? Your life? What are your expectations of yourself and of your value in the workplace? How do you define success, and how will you know when you've achieved it? Thinking through your answers to these questions will allow you to use the information you've gathered and the strategies you've developed to shape a career path that fits who you are, where your life is at a particular moment, and what the world of information work looks like at any given time.

## Beginning Your Career Journal

As you work through the coming chapters, you'll be exploring all sorts of career options and opportunities. You'll be approaching things from two angles: the information itself, and your responses to it, in an effort to learn about various career paths as well as how appropriate they might be for you personally. In order to capture all that knowledge, I'm going to ask you to start a career journal.

What is a career journal? It's any sort of book, binder, portfolio, or folder that allows you to capture all of the elements of the journey you're about to set out on. A place where you can record ideas, identify questions and fill in answers, highlight key discoveries about yourself, draw connections, and engage in any other activities that document your findings.

This is where you'll keep your to-do lists, your descriptions of your perfect job, notes about your highest priorities. You can organize your career journal in whatever format best supports your process of reflection. You might want to use a notebook full of lined or blank pages; you might find that you'd rather draw pictures and relationships than outline ideas in order to represent your thinking. The goal is to create a resource that inspires you and motivates you, or in any other way keeps you moving forward toward your goals. It should become an organic document, one that continues to grow with you as your career grows.

Consider this, then, the first assignment for your upcoming career journey. Using a format that reflects your style and preferences, purchase a journal that will be solely dedicated to your career exploration. Write with colored pens and highlighters if you'd like, perhaps use sticky notes to record fleeting thoughts, or paste in pictures if they add meaning to your ideas. Populate your journal in whatever way best reflects how you interact with the world of information and ideas and inspiration.

Throughout this book, you'll use your career journal to write responses to chapter exercises, so that you can refer back to them and continue to build on them. But more importantly, you should use your journal to chart what's uniquely important to *you*.

When you're ready to start using your journal, try out some of the activities suggested in the section "Starting Your Exploration" and experiment with writing about the outcomes of your research. Remember, this journal is solely a reflection of you, so how you choose to chart the territory is up to you as well.

## Starting Your Exploration

As you work through this book, there will be many suggestions for things to think about and ideas to consider. But it's also important to be able to take concrete action, to move from internal reflection to external engagement.

With that goal in mind, consider one or all of the following activities to help you get started on your exploration:

- Read through the archived articles posted at LIScareer (liscareer. com). Note any articles that seem especially interesting to you, indicating *why* you find them interesting—is it the environment, the type of work, the service opportunity described?

- Go through the job posting sites listed under "Job Postings" (see Appendix B) and identify jobs that sound interesting to you. Check out the titles being used to describe them, the responsibilities each entails, and the skill sets required so you can get a sense of possible jobs of interest—both traditional and nontraditional—and their parameters. Both the current listings and archived postings are useful here.

- Read through the profiles and job descriptions provided in several of the career books listed at the end of this chapter. Do any of these descriptions resonate with you? For example, is the job of "records management" described in *The New Information Professional* something that sounds interesting to you? Why or why not?

If you're a student, also consider these actions:

- Use your time in your graduate program to get a sense of what different career choices offer in terms of flexibility, salary, challenge, self-direction, and opportunity. Use your course research assignments, ask questions of guest lecturers, explore options with your faculty, and peruse the professional journals in the library or through its LIS databases.

- When you have guest speakers in class, research what they will be speaking about and come prepared with questions. They'll appreciate your interest and engagement, and you'll establish a professional connection with someone who will probably be happy to counsel you regarding professional choices. Write thank-you notes to express your appreciation for their time and effort.

- Join appropriate professional organizations while you can still take advantage of the student rate and keep an eye out for any scholarships they have available to students for graduate school tuition, conference attendance, and so forth. Also, participate and get active and visible at the local chapter level; this gives you an opportunity to start building your professional community while still in school.

- As you enter the second half of your graduate program, develop and work on a strategy for transitioning from student to employed professional. Your job as a student should be as much about career exploration as about learning LIS skills; explore the profession as it exists, as it may become, and what paths you might like to pursue throughout your career. It's okay if you're not focused on a decision at this point, but you *can* focus on exploring.

Most importantly, for both students and professionals, get comfortable with the idea that you have a right to develop and/or pursue your own best career opportunities. Yes, we may be in a service profession, but that does not mean that we abandon our own well-being and best interests.

## Your Value Statement

As you explore your career options, you'll need to keep one key question always at the forefront of your thinking: what value do you, as a professional, bring? This will determine what paths your career may follow as well as what opportunities you may have. Your value will be built on your unique competencies, your expertise, and your ability to align these with the strategic goals of your potential employer or client.

Understanding your ability to add value is one of the key elements of career success emphasized in *The Start-Up of You*: it's not enough to love what you do and be great at it—your skills also need to be something *for which there is a market or employer need*. Today this market reality applies as much to libraries as it does to other organizations.

As Dr. James Matarazzo, dean emeritus of the Library and Information Studies program at Simmons College in Boston, presciently pointed out years ago, "The real question is not what you are called, but how do you add value?"[5]

Whether in the traditional library sectors of public, school, and academic, or in the nontraditional LIS career paths, it will increasingly be up to each of us to not just do a job, but to add value to the organization. If we create new programs, design new processes, conceptualize innovative services, or in myriad other ways contribute to the improvement of the enterprise, including our libraries, we are adding value—and building a career.

In *Flow: The Psychology of Optimal Experience* (Harper, 1991), psychologist Mihaly Csikszentmihalyi explains the optimal experience of *flow*, wherein one is completely immersed in a self-directed activity that is so emotionally and intellectually engaging that one loses track of time.

There are many opportunities to work at this level of personal engagement in the LIS profession, but, as with any profession, it will probably take some effort on your part to get there. You need information, strategies, and tactics as well as personal initiative and a willingness to take risks. You need the confidence to stand up for yourself and a commitment to your goals strong enough to help you over the rough spots.

You have the right to create the career of your dreams. But first, you'll need to get in touch with those dreams, the ones based on who you are at your most authentic, passionate core. That's what we'll explore next.

# Resources

## Books

*A Day in the Life: Career Options in Library and Information Science*. Priscilla K. Shontz and Richard Murray, eds. Libraries Unlimited, 2007. 464p. ISBN 1591583640.
Like having 90 LIS professionals sit down and tell you everything you ever wanted to know about what it's like to do their kind of work. Includes profiles from those practicing in school, public, and academic libraries as well as numerous nontraditional roles. Multiple voices, multiple career paths—a terrific resource.

Bridges, William. *JobShift: How to Prosper in a Workplace Without Jobs*. Da Capo Press, 1995. 272p. ISBN 0201489333.
Written over 20 years ago, *JobShift* focused on how individuals could prepare for emerging workplace changes by taking charge of – and creating – their own career/work opportunities.

Csikszentmihalyi, Mihaly. *Flow: The Psychology of Optimal Experience*. Harper Perennial Modern Classics, 2008. 336p. ISBN 0061339202.
Landmark work in the study of happiness, including its causes and conditions. Csikszentmihalyi's research suggested that happiness could be achieved through a state of immersive engagement, or "flow," activities.

de Stricker, Ulla and Jill Hurst-Wahl. *The Information and Knowledge Professional's Handbook: Define and Create Your Success*. Chandos, 2011. 294p. ISBN 1843346087.
These highly respected, experienced authors provide detailed, practical career advice that comes across as a cross between coaching, mentoring, and okay (in the nicest possible way), a bit of nagging. But it's clear their goal is to help readers avoid career potholes if possible. To that end, the tone and format is strongly prescriptive, letting readers know in no uncertain terms how certain situations should be handled in order to help ensure career success.

Dority, G. Kim. *LIS Career Sourcebook: Managing and Maximizing Every Step of Your Career*. Libraries Unlimited, 2012. 246p. ISBN 159884931X.
Overview of the key phases, stages, and transition points in LIS careers, including such topics as LIS job hunting, starting your career off right, managing, leading, and transition points (e.g., taking a career time-out

or relocating your career). Each chapter is split equally between information and recommended resources.

Hoffman, Reid and Ben Casnocha. *The Start-Up of You: Adapt to the Future, Invest in Yourself, and Transform Your Career.* Crown Business, 2012. 272p. ISBN 0307888908.
Cofounder of social networking juggernaut LinkedIn, Hoffman has coauthored a terrific book that mentions LinkedIn surprisingly few times. *The Start-Up of You* is an exceptionally practical guide to framing your career as an ongoing business start-up, that is, one in *permanent beta*. The authors are adamant about facing career market facts, with the triad of "aspirations, assets, and market realities" their informing model. See especially Chapter 3, "Plan to Adapt"; you'll probably want to have a highlighter on hand. (Key resource)

Hunt, Deborah and David Grossman. *The Librarian's Skillbook: 51 Essential Career Skills for Information Professionals.* Information Edge, 2013. 202p. ISBN 0989513319.
Deb Hunt (former SLA president) and David Grossman have collaborated on a guide that essentially lays out what LIS professionals should know in order to expand their career skill sets and adapt to new job opportunities. The book leads off with chapters on the importance of the skills identified, transferability of skills, and an introduction and overview of the 51 "hottest skills." Those skills are then grouped into chapters devoted to computer and technical skills, "beyond reference skills," and business and management skills, among others. A great resource for the profession.

Johnson, Marilyn. *This Book Is Overdue! How Librarians and Cybrarians Can Save Us All.* Harper Perennial, 2011. 304p. ISBN 0061431613.
In the midst of the profession's hand-wringing and anxiety attacks, Johnson has written a delightful, witty, and spot-on paean to the amazing work librarians do as educators, archivists, and community knowledge curators. For those considering the profession, this is an upbeat and positive take on the profession's future as well as its future opportunities.

Kane, Laura Townsend. *Working in the Virtual Stacks: The New Library & Information Science.* American Library Association, 2011. 167p. ISBN 9780838911.
Updating her previous work, *Straight from the Stacks* (ALA, 2003), Kane provides another valuable look at career paths for today's information professionals. The book's 34 profiles are grouped into librarians as (1) subject specialists, (2) technology gurus and social networkers, (3) teachers and community liaisons, (4) entrepreneurs, and (5) administrators. Each chapter leads off with an overview of the type of work, environments, responsibilities, skills, and relevant professional associations.

Lawson, Judy, Joanna Kroll, and Kelly Kowatch. *The New Information Professional: Your Guide to Careers in the Digital Age.* Neal-Schuman, 2010. 200p. ISBN 555706983.
An exceptionally detailed (and valuable) look at career options in the emerging digital information world, with extremely useful "career maps" of related career paths for specific fields, such as archives and preservation, records management, human–computer interaction, social computing, and information systems management, among others. (Key resource)

Markgren, Susanne and Tiffany Eatman Allen. *Career Q&A: A Librarian's Real-Life, Practical Guide to Managing a Successful Career.* CyberAge Books, 2013. 240p. ISBN 1573874793.

Many of us have been reading the authors' excellent Library Career People advice columns (http://librarycareerpeople.com) for years, and their book is both a compilation and expansion of their previous LIS career insights. Highly recommended for MLIS students, those new to the profession, and those who've been in their careers for a while but are encountering new career challenges. (Key resource)

Monson, Jane D. *Jump-Start Your Career as a Digital Librarian: A LITA Guide.* ALA Neal-Schuman, 2012. 248p. ISBN 1555708773.

A compendium of 12 essays contributed by 21 practitioners, this LITA guide first describes what a digital librarian is and does, how to prepare for this type of information role (MLIS coursework), and how to pursue a career as a digital librarian (as a new grad or career transitioner). The guide then covers technical aspects of digital librarianship, including coverage of digital imaging, metadata, and digital project management. Although as expected of any work that focuses on tech specifics, many of the details here will be superseded by ongoing tech changes and advances, the guide nevertheless provides a useful overview of this growing career opportunity.

*The Portable MLIS: Insights from the Experts.* Ken Haycock and Brooke E. Sheldon, eds. Libraries Unlimited, 2008. 316p. ISBN 1591585473.

If you're wondering whether a career as a librarian is for you, *The Portable MLIS* is a great place to start. With enthusiastic entries by some of the profession's best-known practitioners and leaders, this book will give you an insider's sense of what a career as a librarian might offer—both challenges and rewards.

## Online Resources

*Emerging Career Trends for Information Professionals*
http://bit.ly/1Izslkc

Subtitled "A Snapshot of Job Titles," this annual recap from the San Jose State University School of Information provides not only job titles but also job trends for the current information career universe. The report also identifies many of the requisite job skills for specific LIS roles and the skills hiring managers are currently emphasizing, based on an analysis of job posting sites (LIS and general). Especially valuable for those considering nontraditional career paths. (Key resource)

*Hack Library School (hls)*
http://hacklibschool.wordpress.com/

By, for, and about library school students, Hack Library School is a terrific window into the world of MLIS students and their challenges, issues, trends, and observations. Great reading for recent grads as well.

*"How to Become a 21st Century Librarian"*
http://lj.libraryjournal.com/2013/03/careers/how-to-become-a-21st-century-librarian/

This terrific article starts out with the wise advice that "if you want quiet and lots of time to read, think again." It's not only a great resource (and reality check) for those considering traditional librarianship, but also an equally great reminder of why library work can be so rewarding.

(Per *LJ,* "a version of this article by Rachel Singer Gordon was originally published June 1, 2005, under the title 'How to Become a Librarian.' It has been updated a number of times over the years with new information and resources, most recently [March 2013] by *LJ* News Editor Meredith Schwartz.")

*LibGig*
www.libgig.com/
Created and maintained by LAC Group, a leading recruiting, staffing, and placement company, LibGig "offers information professionals looking for work a place to connect with employers with a skills gap," while also hosting community and social networking opportunities. See also the professional development columns on the site for a broad range of LIS career information.

*Libraries of the Future*
http://librarysciencelist.com/libraries-of-the-future-visualization/
A very cool infographic, adapted from a 2012 keynote address for the State University of New York Librarians Association Annual Conference. See especially the "Roles of the Future Librarian."

*Library Career People*
http://librarycareerpeople.com/
A monthly career question-and-answer session with two exceptionally knowledgeable LIS professionals, Tiffany Allen (director of Library HR, University of North Carolina, Chapel Hill University Library) and Susanne Markgren (digital services librarian, Purchase College, State University of New York). Terrific, down-to-earth advice; see also the wealth of archived responses browsable by category (e.g., burnout, getting started, job seeking). (Key resource)

*Library Careers.org: Making a living making a difference*
http://librarycareers.drupalgardens.com/
An ALA initiative, this site provides information about careers in librarianship, including special librarianship. The information is fairly current, and to ALA's credit, under job outlook, it notes that although a large number of librarians may be retiring in the coming years, job growth is likely to be limited by budget constraints and a shift to both electronic, unmediated resources and library techs and assistants rather than MLIS-holding professionals.

*Library Journal.com: Movers & Shakers*
http://lj.libraryjournal.com/2014/03/people/movers-shakers-2014/
movers-shakers-2014/
*Library Journal* annually recognizes 50 librarians it deems to be "people shaping the future of libraries." The individual profiles are fascinating and provide an engaging way of considering what impact a passionate professional with an equally passionate community of colleagues can accomplish. (They're also a terrific source of potential informational interview subjects for course assignments or career information!)

*LibraryScienceList.com*
http://librarysciencelist.com/
"A new social community for librarians worldwide," LibraryScienceList describes itself as one run by data and editorial geeks with a community of diverse librarians. Its aim is to "showcase creative editorial around the field of librarianship." The site has a wealth of fascinating

articles, lists, and resources—a great place to explore the profession, its issues, and trends.

*LinkedIn LIS Career Options*
www.linkedin.com/groups?gid=3126663&trk=hb_side_g
　　A LinkedIn group focused on every possible aspect of LIS career options, whose members include students, practitioners, those considering librarianship, LIS recruiters, and vendors. The group's 11,000 members are from more than 60 countries. A subgroup of ALA's LinkedIn group (you don't have to be a member of ALA, only its LinkedIn group, to join). In order to find other LIS-related LinkedIn groups, search on Groups and enter terms such as "libraries," "librarians," "information management," "taxonomy," "taxonomists," and similar relevant words or phrases.

*LIScareer.com*
www.liscareer.com
　　LIScareer is now an archive of previous columns and contributions, but it remains a great resource for career exploration. The site archives articles, resources, and information on career planning, education, job hunting, experience, networking, mentoring, interpersonal skills, leadership, publishing, and work/life balance. Some materials have been created specifically for the site, while others are pulled in from a variety of resources both print and electronic. An extraordinarily content-rich tool for those contemplating a library/information-related career, wanting to advance their careers, or make a career change within the field.

*New Librarians' List (NEWLIB-L)*
http://walternelson.com/dr/newlib-l
　　Electronic discussion list for MLIS students and recent graduates that provides a forum for exchanging ideas, advice, concerns, and job information. Check the website for sign-up information.

*So You Want to Be a Librarian?*
http://bit.ly/1kO2v6e
　　From *Librarian by Day* blogger Bobbi L. Newman and subtitled "A Guide for Those Considering an MLS, Current Students & Job Seekers," this aggregation of articles related to LIS careers provides a great starting point for deciding whether a job as an LIS professional is for you. Articles are grouped within the categories of The Degree, The Job Search, General Professional Advice, and Skills. Very helpful decision support information if you're debating whether or not to pursue an MLIS.

# Notes

1. George R. Plosker, "The Information Industry Revolution: Implications for Librarians," *Online*, 27(6) (November/December 2003): 16–18.

2. Internet Live Stats, www.internetlivestats.com/google-search-statistics/

3. Edward B. Stear, "Predicting the Future Is Important, Navigating the Future Is Essential," *Online*, 22(1) (January/February 1998): 62.

4. Personal conversation with Mary Ellen Bates, March 2014.

5. Andrew Albanese, "Opportunity in the Air," *Library Journal*, 128(12) (July 15, 2003): 36–38.

# 2
# Self-Knowledge: Your Career Starting Point

*Be patient with all that is unsolved in your heart
and try to love the questions themselves.*
—Rainer Maria Rilke

Who are you, and what do you want to do when you grow up?

Although hopefully it's no longer parents asking these questions, most of us are still wrestling with them (the questions, not the parents) well into our careers. And—given the iffy state of many of our retirement funds—we're probably going to be asking them again and again as we change jobs, career paths, and even life goals over the coming decades.

Your career is likely to be knocked about by the disruptive technologies, demographic changes, and social/political issues emerging daily. But actually, that's good news—it means the number and breadth of opportunities that will open up, including ones not even on your horizon yet, will be dazzling.

Your challenge, as you position yourself to meet those opportunities, is to start getting a better handle on who you are and what you want to be *while* you grow up . . . over the next 10 or 30 or 50 years. And the best way to do that is to start asking yourself lots of questions.

As you go through this process, however, play close attention to who is driving your responses. Most of us are strongly influenced by the other "stakeholders" or interested parties in our lives—parents, spouses, faculty advisers, friends, coworkers, mentors, and others, many of whom have an understandably vested interest in the career choices we make. It's important to be able to distinguish between what you yourself want and what others have convinced you that you *should* want. It's important to be sure that *your* agenda is the one in place.

# Who Are You?

When Socrates first commanded his student to "know thyself," that guy probably had a lot fewer ways of looking at the issue. Today, knowing yourself can take many paths. What are your aptitudes, in other words, those talents that come to you naturally? What are your skills, your learned competencies? What are the specifics of your personality that you were born with *vs.* those that may have become ingrained after years of managing various job and life circumstances? What work processes, environments, activities, structures let you bring your best stuff into play?

What values have you developed, what commitments have you made as you moved through your adult life? Do you still like/dislike the things that drove you early in your career (or graduate program), or have you grown in different directions? Have changing life circumstances—perhaps the birth of a child or 18 years later that youngster's looming tuition payments—affected what you most need from your job right now?

And, as important as all of the rest of these questions, what would you simply *enjoy* doing?

For purposes of putting together careers that are personally rewarding, there are a number of ways to approach these questions. But as you explore these, keep two things in mind. First, few of us are "either/or"; rather, most of your answers will be on a continuum of response. Instead of "I *hate* working alone," your response is more likely to be in the "I'd *prefer* to work as part of a team" range. That's OK—it's still helping you understand your preferences.

Second, your needs, priorities, preferences, and sometimes even values are shaped by your life circumstances and stages. Who you are today is likely to be quite different from who you are 10 years from now. So keep in mind that your resilient career will be based to a great degree on your ability to remain fluid through not just the transitions of the workplace, but also those of your life.

# Finding Out about You

So what are some of the tools for self-assessment? Happily, there are many ways to explore, including a diverse collection of tools and approaches.

**Myers–Briggs**. Probably the best known is the Myers–Briggs personality-type indicator (MBTI). According to authors Tieger and Barron-Tieger in their *Do What You Are* (2014), the Myers–Briggs assessment considers four personality characteristics or dimensions:

- How you interact with the world and where you direct your energy—toward people and the "external world" of relationships, communities, and events (*extroversion*), or toward the "internal world" of information and ideas (*introversion*)?

- The kind of information you naturally notice—do you focus on facts and the clarity of evidence (*sensing*), or prefer to explore the often ambiguous intellectual unknown (*intuition*)?

- How you make decisions—are you the analytic type, relying on logic and objectivity (*thinking*), or are your decisions driven by personal beliefs, values, and feelings (*feeling*)?

- How you prefer to live your life—do you thrive on structure, stability, and plans (*judging*), or are you instead more of a free spirit who flourishes in a spontaneous flow of day-to-day events (*perception*)?

(And in case you were wondering—the two most common MBTI profiles for librarians are ISTJ and INTJ.)

If you're not familiar with the Myers–Briggs approach, *Do What You Are* provides an excellent and down-to-earth explanation of how to understand both your personality profile and its applications in your career choices. It's a great place to start exploring the inherent characteristics that drive how you relate to the world—and people—around you. Are you an ENFJ, one of those outgoing individuals who loves people? Or an INTP, an intellectual adept at solving problems? (The flip side of understanding your own profile, of course, is that it can help you understand how to work more effectively with others whose profiles are the polar opposite of your own.)

The Myers–Briggs conceptual scaffolding provides a great way to think about such questions as, for example, whether you, the extrovert, would really be happy with the somewhat solitary life of a cataloger. However, it's important to keep in mind that, as it states, the MBTI assessment simply provides *indicators* of your personality type, and personality type is not career destiny. For example, you may be an extroverted introvert, able to be highly engaged in social situations, but thriving in solitude. Or you may, like Susan Cain, author of the best-selling *Quiet: The Power of Introverts in a World That Can't Stop Talking* (Broadway Books, 2013) find a way to build your inherent personality characteristics, ones you might initially have perceived as weaknesses, into a platform for strength, accomplishment, and impact.

**Keirsey**. A second well-known personality test is the Keirsey temperaments assessment, which reframes the idea of personality types into four temperaments—traditionalists, experiencers, idealists, and conceptualizers. Like the Myers–Briggs test, the Keirsey approach is another way to understand how you process your environments and, by extension, how you can find a "right fit" in the work you pursue. (Keirsey presented not only his ideas but also their application in *Please Understand Me II: Temperament, Character, Intelligence* [Prometheus Nemesis, 1998], which provides the best starting place for understanding your temperament.)

Temperament becomes important as you consider not just the work that you do, but also the environment within which you do it, as we'll see later when we explore preference filters. For example, a conceptualizer, adept at ideas and innovation, would be less than effective in an administrative role but an excellent contributor in a strategy role. An idealist would be uninspired in most corporate bureaucracies, but bring passion and commitment if leading a nonprofit.

**Aptitudes**. Another part of who you are is what aptitudes or talents you're born with, as opposed to the skills you've acquired. Nearly every career book has some sort of aptitude checklist, but basically what you're looking for is the cross-point between those things you've always been good at and those you've always enjoyed doing. For example, someone may have an aptitude for math, or for many of us in the LIS profession, an aptitude for information. (Were you identified as an "information junkie" early on?)

As you explore your aptitudes, however, keep in mind that you're not identifying things that you've learned how to do (e.g., being an accountant or a cataloger), but rather exploring intellectual or creative activities for which you have an innate talent and that bring you joy.

## Information Aptitudes

One way to get a sense of your aptitudes is to do a sort of "archaeological dig" on your life work so far, including paid work, volunteer projects, grad school activities, and any other engagements where you brought your talents to bear in a way that was meaningful and enjoyable to you.

Consider the following beginning list of some possible information aptitudes for you in relation to the work you've found rewarding in the past. Which ones best reflect what you've been engaged in when you had the greatest sense of enjoyment and competence?

- Finding information
- Analyzing and synthesizing information
- Categorizing and classifying information
- Creating information systems
- Visualizing information
- Organizing information
- Sharing information
- Presenting information
- Creating information
- Doing something else with information, which was _____

How have these aptitudes played out throughout your career, or your graduate studies, or volunteer work you've engaged in? Have your career choices so far reflected these aptitudes? How might they form the core of your professional work going forward? Be sure to note your answers in your career journal, so that you can use them to begin to build your best-potential-careers profile as you move through the book.

Although you'll probably be able to unearth many other general aptitudes, identifying your information aptitudes will provide a starting point for building a career based on your natural gifts, the ones from which you derive the greatest joy.

In a broader career sense, you have other aptitudes that play across many professional environments in addition to the library/information marketplace. You may be a natural leader or have an innate ability to motivate and inspire people, strong powers of persuasion, or an ability to see opportunities before they're evident to anyone else. Although to some extent aptitudes can also be taught as skills to those who don't possess them naturally, for now your goal is to describe those areas of easy intersection between your inherent gifts and where your joy lies. Identifying those aptitudes will help you frame possible career opportunities.

**Innate strengths.** In an alternative spin on aptitudes, in their popular management book *Now Discover Your Strengths* (2001), authors Buckingham and Clifton identified 34 "themes" or strengths—such as achiever, analytical, deliberative, developer, futuristic, ideation, learner, relator, and strategic—that they believe to be among the most prevalent human strengths. The authors make an interesting point, arguing that our usual way of approaching aptitudes or natural strengths is backward.

According to Buckingham and Clifton, instead of supporting individuals' strengths, managers focus on trying to fix their staffers' weaknesses and consequently miss the opportunity to help people maximize the contributions they could otherwise make. In some ways, we as individuals often do the same thing. We tend to focus all our energy on our perceived failings, while simply taking for granted—or even dismissing—those collections of strengths or aptitudes uniquely our own.

Bottom line: what have you been doing when you've felt most alive? What activities give you energy? What gives you a deep sense of satisfaction and contribution? If you're not sure, you may want to take a look at Tom Rath's guide to these strengths, *StrengthsFinder 2.0* (Gallup Press, 2007).

**Information–people–systems–technology.** Most of us in the LIS profession find that we're inherently adept in one of these four areas; in other words, we're pretty good at it, we enjoy doing it, and we like to figure out how to get better at it. For example, I'm a born information junkie and thought I'd died and gone to heaven when the Internet showed up.

Colleagues of mine, on the other hand, have made wonderful contributions through their ability to connect with people, doing community outreach, establishing seniors' groups at the library, coaching college students through cool and engaging BI workshops, and organizing sixth-grade multimedia library projects. They bring an excitement and energy to these interactions that are amazing to watch. They've completely aligned their LIS skills with their passion for people connection.

Or you may find that you thrive on organizing the world's information, be it through indexing, cataloging, taxonomies, digitization structures, search engines, metadata schemas, information architectures, digital asset management, or enterprise knowledge management systems, among others. LIS professionals skilled at information organization are often also able to extrapolate patterns, relationships, and structures from a universe of details and data, using information technologies to create the infrastructures that enable all our work.

Those, however, with not only technology skills but also an understanding of how to use technology to create solutions, innovate, and expand the possibilities of information (and, often, libraries) are the information professionals most highly valued by organizations recruiting for high-impact contributors. If you have a high comfort level with the constant changes in information technology and the skill to make the most of them, you're likely to find many career doors open to you.

Whichever of these four areas most calls to you, they can be practiced in any LIS career path, including traditional, nontraditional, and independent. Additionally, keep in mind as you go through your career that you may accidentally discover a professional focus and passion in an area that previously held no interest for you.

**Generalist *vs.* specialist.** One of the questions most frequently asked by students is whether to specialize in a specific area such as cataloging or government information or graduate as a generalist, someone who has a broad range of skills but is not an expert in any. Ask five seasoned practitioners for their advice here, and you're likely to get five well-reasoned, passionate, and completely different answers.

The reason is that there are benefits and disadvantages to both approaches.

Being a generalist means you can easily transfer your skills from one environment to another, and you can pursue many avenues of intellectual curiosity that can be woven into your generalist knowledge base. You tend not to worry too much about your expertise becoming obsolete because its general nature means that it isn't tied to a specific process, technology, or market.

On the other hand, you never feel like you know enough. Since you tend to know a requisite amount about a lot of things, you never feel like you know anything in any depth. Keeping current in your field is a constant challenge, because often your "field" covers everything from LIS issues to research tools to business trends to international developments. When hanging out with LIS colleagues who have specialized in some area, you spend a lot of time feeling clueless, trying not to let on that you have *no idea* what all those acronyms they're throwing around really mean.

Being a specialist in any of the various LIS disciplines brings the opposite challenges and rewards. Your skills do not travel as easily, but there are fewer people who can do what you do, so less competition for available jobs. The more tied to a specific process, technology, or market your skills are, however, the greater the likelihood that they may become obsolete during your professional lifetime. You may find yourself going through a challenging learning curve at some point as you transition your core skill to a new technology platform or move into a related but new LIS discipline to stay professionally viable.

Depending on the professional area, specialists tend to be paid more (especially those in technology fields or at strategy levels). Also, you have the luxury of exploring in-depth a single topic, with all its ramifications, applications, and emerging issues. You get the ego boost of being an expert in something and have a built-in community of colleagues who share your passion (or understand your fixation).

**Key motivators.** Almost every job has its good points and bad, but what may influence how good or bad it is for you personally depends on understanding what motivates you. Interestingly, our understanding of what motivates people is now being studied by psychologists and scholars as a key element of well-being and/or happiness, and the one thing everyone seems to agree on is that what employers *thought* motivated staffers is pretty much not the case. For most people, it's generally not about the money. In fact, according to *Drive: The Surprising Truth about What Motivates Us* (Riverhead Books, 2011) by researcher and writer Daniel Pink, most of us are intrinsically motivated by three things: *autonomy* (the ability to direct our own lives), *mastery* (the engagement that comes from learning and creating new things), and *purpose* (working for a cause greater than ourselves). However, it's important to remember that what may motivate you *intrinsically* at any given point in your career may be outweighed by external factors, such as the need to prioritize a high salary, job flexibility, or a predictable routine because of personal commitments.

## Preference Filters: How Will You Work?

In addition to understanding your intrinsic aptitudes and strengths, it's useful to consider your personal *preferences* when it comes to working. There are many ways to think about these, many filters within which to consider your options. These include types of LIS work, types of organizations, your workplace environment, your individual working style, your preferred way of dealing with interpersonal relations, your professional and employment expectations, and job-specific considerations. These are starter filters; you may have several others that are unique to who you are—for example, value filters.

Also, keep in mind that some considerations may be more important to you than others. Consider the following preference filters to be simply examples to start you exploring the criteria that *are* most important to you. Remember that your responses will most likely fall on a continuum that will indicate a preference rather than an absolute, and that some items might be critically important to you while others are not at all. It's the critical ones that need to drive decisions for you.

To track your preferences among these choices, create a four-column page in your career journal that allows you to identify the choice in question, your preference, your reasons why you prefer one option over the other, and how important this criterion is to you. Or, simply photocopy the following pages with your responses to include in your journal.

**Organizational characteristics.** There are many ways to characterize organizations, having to do with their missions, their markets and constituencies, their size, and similar criteria. Consider the following choices regarding a potential employer and note which options seem more appealing to you:

- **Library *vs.* nonlibrary:** For many LIS professionals, working within the library community is central to who they are; for others, the work they do is more important than where they do it.

  Library _____  Nonlibrary _____  Importance _____

  Reason for preference _____

- **Nonprofit *vs.* for-profit:** Nonprofits may include political and religious groups and professional and trade associations as well as socially beneficial or community-based organizations, but they are usually mission—rather than profit—driven.

  Nonprofit _____  For-profit _____  Importance _____

  Reason for preference _____

- **Education focused *vs.* product/service focused:** Education organizations support and deliver knowledge, whereas product/service-focused organizations generally use information to sell something in a competitive marketplace.

  Education _____  Product/service _____  Importance _____

  Reason for preference _____

- **Technology focused *vs.* technology neutral:** Technology-focused organizations assume and demand a high level of tech expertise and necessitate an ongoing commitment to staying ahead of the technology curve.

Tech focused _____   Tech neutral _____   Importance _____

Reason for preference _____

- **Emerging industry/discipline *vs.* established industry/discipline:** Organizations based on emerging industries and disciplines tend to offer exciting and challenging opportunities, while those in established or maturing disciplines often provide saner workplaces.

  Emerging _____   Established _____   Importance _____

  Reason for preference _____

- **Large organization *vs.* small:** Large organizations generally bring the trade-off of stable job expectations *vs.* rigid management structure, while smaller organizations may tend to be more responsive to new ideas but offer less direction.

  Large _____   Small _____   Importance _____

  Reason for preference _____

- **Established organization *vs.* start-up:** Established companies can usually offer superior benefits, while start-ups may be more willing to negotiate other perks such as stock options and flextime in lieu of traditional benefits.

  Established _____   Start-up _____   Importance _____

  Reason for preference _____

- **Local or community-based *vs.* national:** Local or community-based groups often invest more in being good community citizens, but are prone to mirror the ups and downs of the local economy, whereas national organizations may have less of a commitment to your community but are also less likely to be damaged if it suffers economic woes.

  Local _____   National _____   Importance _____

  Reason for preference _____

- **Focused on patrons, students, customers, clients, or business colleagues:** The nature of the working relationship and the expectations of those we work for/with shift based on the organizations we work within; which most appeals to you?

  Patrons/students _____   Customers/clients _____
  Colleagues _____   Importance _____

  Reason for preference _____

Now go through the same exercise for the choices here:

**Workplace environment.** Working environments can bring out our best abilities to contribute or throw us into a black hole of bad morale. Some of the options include:

- **Structured *vs.* unstructured:** Do you do your best work in a structured environment or thrive in its absence? Most traditional libraries offer fairly structured environments, while nonprofit and for-profit start-ups can epitomize "freewheeling."

  Structured _____   Unstructured _____   Importance _____

  Reason for preference _____

- **Formal *vs.* casual:** Organizations vary immensely as to their tone and expectations of their employees. Do you feel more comfortable with established standards of dress and behavior or prefer a week of casual Fridays?

  Formal _____   Casual _____   Importance _____

  Reason for preference _____

- **Hierarchical *vs.* flat organization style:** This choice is about how decisions are made. Hierarchical enterprises are primarily top-down, flat ones are more likely to distribute decision-making responsibilities (which may impact quality and speed of decisions).

  Hierarchical _____   Flat _____   Importance _____

  Reason for preference _____

- **High accountability/reward *vs.* more moderate accountability/reward:** The former usually is found in the for-profit world; although it can be financially lucrative, it can also carry a substantial stress factor.

  High _____   Moderate _____   Importance _____

  Reason for preference _____

- **Project focused or consistent workflow:** Projects are typical of client work (e.g., information brokering), while a consistent workflow is usually found in more traditional, structured environments.

  Projects _____   Consistent workflow ____ Importance _____

  Reason for preference _____

- **Structured/lots of direction *vs.* minimal structure/direction:** Depending on a library's leadership, jobs in traditional libraries usually offer the most structure and direction, while the opposite end of the spectrum is being self-employed.

Lots of direction _____ Minimal direction _____
Importance _____

Reason for preference _____

- **Established hours *vs.* flexible or nontraditional schedule:** If you prefer a traditional eight-hour day, your best choices may be working as a school librarian or for a for-profit or nonprofit. Public and academic librarians are more likely to work evenings or weekends as part of their regular workweek.

  Established _____ Flexible/nontraditional _____
  Importance _____

  Reason for preference _____

- **Family friendly *vs.* family neutral:** Depending on your life circumstances and what personal responsibilities you are juggling, this may be *the* most important consideration for you.

  Friendly _____ Neutral _____ Importance _____

  Reason for preference _____

**Interpersonal dynamics.** Another facet of your approach to work is how you prefer to connect with people in your professional life. Do you thrive on the mix-it-up energy of dynamic groups, or seek out the uninterrupted focus of solitude? Do you enjoy managing staff, or dread dealing with "people issues?"

Note your responses in your career journal, so that you can refer to them when exploring possible job options and career strategies. As you answer, keep in mind that your responses may change with your life circumstances, but asking these questions is a way to help yourself be aware of where you are now.

Do you . . .

- **Prefer formal or informal relations with people at work?** Formal relations are usually more common in larger, more structured, or hierarchical organizations, whereas informal, peer-to-peer relations are generally the hallmark of small or start-up groups.

  Formal _____ Informal _____ Importance _____

  Reason for preference _____

- **Draw energy from people or from solitude?** If you derive energy from people, the often solitary life of an independent may not be for you.

  People _____ Solitude _____ Importance _____

  Reason for preference _____

- **Like meeting new people, or prefer to stay with people you know?** Meeting new people can be a major component of vendor sales and/or training jobs, many public library outreach positions, and independent information work.

  New people _____    Existing friends _____    Importance _____

  Reason for preference _____

- **Comfortable supervising others or uncomfortable being in a position of authority?** A critical question if you aspire to management or executive-level positions, where you will be responsible for holding others accountable for their work.

  Supervise others _____    No supervision _____
  Importance _____

  Reason for preference _____

- **Prefer working as part of a team (collaborator) or prefer working solo?** Although some independent work involves collaboration, more frequently you're working solo; also, some extremely hierarchical organizations are known for having departmental "silos" that preclude collaboration.

  Team work _____    Solo work _____    Importance _____

  Reason for preference _____

- **Enjoy contact with the public, or prefer to avoid contact with the public?** A _very_ important question if you are considering any sort or public service work, for example, becoming a reference librarian.

  Lots of contact _____    Minimal contact _____
  Importance _____

  Reason for preference _____

- **Thrive on intellectual exchange with colleagues, or prefer to focus on work-specific discussions?** If you thrive on intellectual exchange, consider academic librarianship, where this is an important and ongoing component of the profession.

  Intellectual _____    Work-focused _____    Importance _____

  Reason for preference _____

**Professional/employment expectations.** What job requirements are you willing to meet in order to land the job of your dreams? Again, these may change as your life circumstances do; for example, a willingness to travel or work weekends may shift as family obligations show up. But thinking about your responses to these questions will help you determine that some career paths definitely aren't for you, at least at this point in your life. For example, if you find you're not willing to write, publish, and/or volunteer for advancement, then you'll probably not want to target a job as an academic librarian.

As you consider these questions, remember to note your responses in your career journal. Are you . . .

- **Willing/not willing to work substantial extra hours?** Generally, established organizations offer fairly established and reasonable work hours, unless they've recently undergone a downsizing, whereas start-ups are often operating on the assumption of 12-hour days.

  Extra hours _____   No extra hours _____   Importance _____

  Reason for preference _____

- **Willing/not willing to work weekends?** Public and academic library jobs, as well as vendor sales, often entail weekend work.

  Weekends _____   No weekends _____   Importance _____

  Reason for preference _____

- **Willing/not willing to work a schedule that changes regularly?** As with the question of extra hours, established organizations may offer fairly established and reasonable work hours, whereas start-ups generally operate on a more chaotic schedule.

  Changing schedule _____   Standard schedule _____
  Importance _____

  Reason for preference _____

- **Willing/not willing to undertake more schooling to achieve professional goals?** Academic librarians may need a second master's degree, and corporate librarians may consider an MBA or a master's in some aspect of data or knowledge management critical for career advancement.

  More schooling _____   No more schooling _____
  Importance _____

  Reason for preference _____

- **Willing/not willing to write, publish, volunteer if necessary for advancement?** An ongoing requirement of academic librarianship if tenure is involved.

  Willing to write, etc. _____   Not willing to write, etc. _____
  Importance _____

  Reason for preference _____

- **Willing/not willing to relocate for job?** In all areas of the LIS profession, your willingness to relocate may substantially increase your odds of landing the job you want at the salary you seek.

Relocation OK _____   No relocation _____   Importance _____

Reason for preference _____

- **Willing/not willing to travel for business?** Any sort of vendor sales usually requires substantial travel.

  Travel OK _____   Minimal travel _____   Importance _____

  Reason for preference _____

- **Focused mostly on job or focused more on personal and family time?** A key consideration with start-ups, whether yours or someone else's, is the intense amount of time they demand; if personal time is important to you, you may want to focus on a more established and predictable work environment.

  Job focus _____   Personal focus _____   Importance _____

  Reason for preference _____

## Job-Specific Considerations

For some of us, having a flexible work schedule determines whether or not we'll even consider a job. For others, a solid benefits package is the critical factor. As you consider the following criteria in terms of your own preferences, keep in mind that most, if not all, of these items can be negotiated as part of an employment package for jobs not in the public sector (public sector jobs often have fairly established parameters that can't be negotiated).

Before you think about negotiating, however, you'll need to know what's most important to you, what's need-to-have *vs.* nice-to-have. As you consider the following aspects, rank them by priority and then note in your career journal your top three need-to-haves. That way, you'll be able to quickly identify whether a specific job opportunity offers you "goodness of fit" or can be negotiated in that direction.

| Job Structure | Very Important | Somewhat Important | Not Important |
|---|---|---|---|
| Full-time/part-time | | | |
| Allowed to work remotely | | | |
| Flexible hours | | | |
| Opportunities for growth (expand knowledge base) | | | |
| Opportunities for advancement (increased levels of responsibility) | | | |

| Salary Requirements | Very Important | Somewhat Important | Not Important |
|---|---|---|---|
| Salary competitive with industry benchmarks | | | |
| Base salary plus bonus (for sales) | | | |
| Performance bonuses (individual/team) | | | |
| Established process, expectations for raises | | | |
| Pay based on performance | | | |

| Non-Salary Requirements | Very Important | Somewhat Important | Not Important |
|---|---|---|---|
| Health benefits | | | |
| Number of vacation days | | | |
| Family medical leave support | | | |
| Tuition reimbursement | | | |
| Support for professional development | | | |

| Opportunity for Growth | Very Important | Somewhat Important | Not Important |
|---|---|---|---|
| Presence of formal or informal mentoring program | | | |
| Support for interdepartmental cross-training and collaboration | | | |
| Atmosphere of innovation and intellectual openness | | | |

# Exploring Your Career Preferences

To continue to gather information about what job characteristics might be a match for you, consider the following activities, noting your findings and reactions in your career journal as appropriate.

1. If you haven't done so already, take the MBTI test in *What Type Am I* and determine your personality profile. Talk to your

colleagues who seem to enjoy their jobs and ask them about their MBTI profiles to get a sense of how profiles match various types of LIS work.

2.  Think through all the jobs you've had so far and assess them against the filters we've identified. What can you learn from your job history? One of the challenges here is to distinguish among all the aspects of a given job that contributed to it being a good or bad experience for you (e.g., great work *vs.* great boss).

3.  Make a list in your journal of what you consider to be your innate strengths and weaknesses, and then solicit feedback from your friends, family, or colleagues to see whether they agree with your assessment—they may see a strength that you overlook simply because you assume everyone has the same strength. Also, consider when and/or how your strengths, taken to the extreme, may become a liability, or your weaknesses under the right circumstances become assets.

4.  Test your assumptions. Interview LIS professionals who are successful and happy in their jobs, with a focus on what they especially like in their work and how those aspects line up with their personalities to get a sense of how you might approach your own job choices. Ask them what aptitudes and personality characteristics they feel are necessary to perform effectively in their positions. Write up your findings; they'll provide another way to judge the jobs and career paths we'll look at in the next three chapters.

5.  If you're a student, pay close attention to what coursework you most enjoy and then speak with your instructor about possible career paths based on that type of work. Research those that appeal to you (and consider writing up your findings for the student newsletter).

6.  Use your time in grad school to explore the generalist *vs.* specialist question. Often, the choice will become evident for you as you move through your program. You may find yourself gravitating to a specific area of interest (e.g., UX, data analysis, public outreach, school librarianship, information architecture). Or you may enjoy sampling all of the different LIS courses and find that you enjoy the research component of each or the technology aspects. This process of discovery is one of the most important aspects of being a student, so whenever possible pay attention to where your interests are drawing you.

7.  Also if you're a student, whenever the opportunity arises, ask your class guest speakers about their career preferences, and in what ways these have shaped their career choices and paths. In what way might their preferences mirror yours?

8.  Finally, consider that, as Shakespeare wrote, the past is prologue. Wander back through your childhood and remember what activities used to delight you. Be as specific as possible. For example, not just "I loved pretending to be Nancy Drew," but "I loved pretending to be Nancy Drew when she would figure out clues and chase the baddies and help bring them to justice. Plus

then she got to ride off to a new adventure." Write those child-hood activities down in your career journal and then take it one step further. Why did you enjoy this? What aspects of a specific activity particularly engaged you, and what applicability might they have to your career? For example, channeling your inner Nancy Drew might mean you thrive on risk-taking, and/or enjoy project work (a new adventure) rather than a set routine.

# How Preferences Shape Career Paths

One of the first choices you have in terms of career and personal preferences is the path you choose to pursue your goals. Again, none of these paths is necessarily a lifelong commitment, but simply a choice that reflects your current interests or priorities. However, some options are more suited to certain personality types than others.

For example, someone who successfully works as an *independent* or *freelancer* usually enjoys working alone, has a strong ability to self-manage, is adept at managing multiple tasks and deadlines, and is strong on detail and "learning on the fly." Although many independents—classic introverts—don't necessarily enjoy the people/social demands of constant marketing, they've learned strategies for getting the job done.

An *entrepreneur* building up a small business, on the other hand, will need to rely on strong leadership skills to motivate his or her team, will need the ability to think strategically, must have no compunctions about working regular 80-hour workweeks, and will need to be extremely comfortable with risk-taking. Entrepreneurs need to possess strong egos, an enormous amount of self-confidence, and a high tolerance for uncertainty and unpredictability.

An *intrapreneur*, someone responsible for starting up new initiatives or even businesses within existing companies, must possess many of these same skills, although the risk-taking is not quite so extreme because of whose money is at stake (the company's rather than yours). Generally, an intrapreneur has a higher ability to accept corporate control and restriction than does an entrepreneur, but a similar eye for identifying business opportunities.

Someone targeting an *executive* or *leadership* role within an organization, whether library focused, for-profit, or nonprofit, will need to be strong on strategic thinking, possess excellent people and communication skills, be willing to commit long hours on an ongoing basis, and be willing to take responsibility for outcomes (which they may or may not have control over), whether successes or failures. As with entrepreneurs, strong egos and lots of self-confidence are must-haves.

A *management* role, on the other hand, demands the ability to multi-task, to manage people, projects, and priorities, to deal with difficult interpersonal issues, and to diplomatically and effectively manage up as well as down. Effective managers, those adept at balancing people needs *vs.* profit priorities, are able to blend the roles of teacher, coach, and team leader to bring out the best in their staff.

A *social entrepreneur* combines the opportunities of entrepreneurship with the social values that motivate many who go into librarianship. Social entrepreneurs are individuals who take a business approach to solving a social problem. Their enterprises may be established as nonprofits, but are run with an eye toward becoming financially self-sustaining so that they can contribute to the community on a long-term ongoing basis. Social entrepreneurs need to have the same business and strategy skills, leadership ability, and self-confidence necessary for any chief executive. But they also possess the creativity to envision innovative solutions, the management skills to execute them, and the ability to generate excitement and buy-in among others for their vision.

The point of all your explorations is to try many different pathways to connect what brings you—or has brought you—joy and a sense of engagement. By writing down your ideas and remembrances and questions and answers in your career journal, you'll have begun to build the base of self-knowledge against which you'll be able to evaluate the possible career paths we explore in the next chapters: traditional, nontraditional, and independent.

Again, as you work through this self-assessment process, keep in mind that as your life progresses, some of the responses you've given at this point will change—that's to be expected. One of the great things about information work is its flexibility. With a bit of advance planning, you should be able to sequence your career engagements, jobs, projects, and activities to support your life transitions. We'll discuss how to do that in the coming chapters, but your goal at this point should be to start becoming familiar with the process of "taking your own pulse" or increasing your self-awareness factor when it comes to your career.

# Resources

## Books

Beck, Martha. *Finding Your Way in a Wild New World: Reclaim Your True Nature to Create the Life You Want.* Atria Books, 2013. 320p. ISBN 1451624603.

Beck, the best-selling author of *Finding Your Own North Star: Claiming the Life You Were Meant to Live* (Three Rivers Press, 2002) and *Steering by Starlight: The Science and Magic of Finding Your Destiny* (Rodale Books, 2009), once again provides a pathway that is funny, practical, and compassionate through the challenges of identifying your way. A life coach with a doctorate in sociology from Harvard, Beck went through her own struggle to find her path, and her guidance is informed by the lessons she learned as well as the insights she has gained from her clients. A key resource for identifying, describing, and nurturing your dreams, whether personal or professional.

Bolles, Richard Nelson and Mark Emery Bolles. *What Color Is Your Parachute? 2015: A Practical Manual for Job-Hunters and Career-Changers.* Ten Speed Press, 2014. 368p. ISBN 1607745550.

Bolles focuses on practical, immediately actionable advice and tactics that are geared to quickly move you from identifying your career goals to successfully pursuing them. A familiar and reliable resource for job hunters and those considering career transitions.

Buckingham, Marcus and Donald O. Clifton. *Now, Discover Your Strengths.* Free Press, 2001. 272p. ISBN 0743201140.

Following on the success of Buckingham's first business best-seller, *First Break All the* Rules (Simon & Schuster, 1999), this work asserts that trying to help people correct/improve their weaknesses is a waste of time; it makes more sense to build on people's innate strengths. In combination with its website, the book helps readers identify their unique strengths. Another way to assess your personal characteristics, although as a career strategy, ignoring your weaknesses seems a bit questionable at best! (For more on identifying your individual strengths, see *StrengthsFinder 2.0* later.) (Key resource)

Cain, Susan. *Quiet: The Power of Introverts in a World That Can't Stop Talking.* Broadway Books, 2013. 368p. ISBN 0307352153.
How to create a thriving, resilient career while dealing with the challenges of being an introvert in what often seems like an extroverts' world. A terrific resource for those of us who *are* introverts as well as for those who work with them, are raising them, managing them, married to them, etc. One of the points Cain makes most impressively is that as you consider career options, you don't need to restrict yourself to those you feel would be comfortable for only introverts or extroverts; instead, you can discover or create ways to shape jobs to focus on your innate strengths.

Gostick, Adrian and Chester Elson. *What Motivates Me: Put Your Passions to Work.* Culture Works, 2014. 272p. ISBN 0996029702.
More and more employers are realizing the key to engaged, high-performing employees is figuring out what motivates them. (The good news is that any advances in motivation knowledge can benefit employees as well.) The authors identify 23 workplace motivators within five clusters of "identifiers"—achievers, builders, caregivers, reward-drivers, and thinkers. Understanding where you fit among these categories will help you identify what jobs and professional roles are likely to let you contribute your best stuff. (Key resource)

Hogshead, Sally. *How the World Sees You: Discover Your Highest Value through the Science of Fascination.* Harper Business, 2014. 448p. ISBN 0062230697.
Although Hogshead comes from the advertising world and her approach can occasionally feel a bit over the top, *How the World Sees You* is included here because of her approach to personality archetypes and how they may shape your "best-fit" career choices. Not scientifically based, but a useful read nevertheless.

Kaplan, Robert Steven. *What You're Really Meant to Do: A Road Map for Reaching Your Unique Potential.* Harvard Business Press, 2013. 256p. ISBN 1422189900.
Kaplan is a leadership expert with the Harvard Business School who works with students and executives to help them find "what they're really meant to do." Here he outlines and advocates a systematic and long-term approach to exploring your own answers, including assessing your strengths and weaknesses, finding your passions, understanding yourself, making the most of your opportunities, and more. A logical and practical approach to exploring your passions and preferences.

Keirsey, David. *Please Understand Me II: Temperament, Character, Intelligence.* Prometheus Nemesis Book Co., 1998. 350p. ISBN 1885705026.
A revision of the third edition of *Please Understand Me* (1978), *II* again focuses on the four temperaments: artisans, guardians, idealists, and rationals. Unusual is that Keirsey takes assessment a step further by

identifying not just a single temperament for each of us, but a layered "ranking" of the various temperament characteristics within given personalities. (Key resource)

Little, Brian R. *Me, Myself, and Us: The Science of Personality and the Art of Well-Being.* Public Affairs, 2014. 288p. ISBN 1586489670.
In order to assess what potential career paths may best align with who you are, it's important to understand, well, who you are. Research psychologist Little draws on recent studies of human personality to suggest that we all fall somewhere on the spectrum of five personality dimensions: degree of conscientiousness, agreeableness, neuroticism, openness, and extraversion. Although you may be able to change (or mitigate the strength of) some aspects of your personality, Little makes the point that although we can act/behave "out of character" when the need arises, we're most likely to thrive in environments and careers that align with our basic personalities.

Lore, Nicholas. *The Pathfinder: How to Choose or Change Your Career for a Lifetime of Satisfaction and Success, rev. ed.* Touchstone Books, 2012. 448p. ISBN 1451608322.
Lore does a great job of combining left-brain strategies, goal-setting, and checklists with right-brain Zen exploration. Worth reading not just for the great quotes, but also as a solid tool for career strategizing.

Pink, Daniel. *Drive: The Surprising Truth about What Motivates Us.* Riverhead Books, 2011. 288p. ISBN 1594484805.
One of the seminal works in workplace motivation, *Drive* presents an alternative to the "money as motivator" thinking and instead asserts that autonomy, mastery, and purpose are the keys to unlocking our best efforts.

Rath, Tom. *StrengthsFinder 2.0.* Gallup Press, 2007. 183p. ISBN 9781595 620156.
Once you've read *Now Discover Your Strengths* (Buckingham, earlier), then turn to Rath's guide to get the clearest assessment of your particular strengths. If you purchase the book (rather than check it out of the library), it comes with an access code for taking the online strengths-finder assessment for free.

Tieger, Paul D., Barbara Barron, and Kelly Tieger. *Do What You Are: Discover the Perfect Career for You through the Secrets of Personality Type.* Little Brown, 2014. 432p. ISBN 031623673X.
*Do What You Are* is widely used by individuals not only to identify and understand their Myers–Briggs profile but also to then bridge that understanding to optimum work choices. In other words, if you're an INTJ, what types of work and work environments are most likely to provide you an opportunity to thrive? (Key resource)

## Online Resources

*Note: Keep in mind that good assessments can give you a useful snapshot of who you are and what may be important to you at any given time, but it's important to remember that they can reflect the breadth and depth of neither who you are nor who you become as you continue to grow in your career and life.*

*The Best Jobs for Every Personality Type*

http://bit.ly/1Cvwqam

From *Business Insider*, this infographic shows each of the four personality characteristics, their combinations, and then the jobs recommended in *Do What You Are* (Tieger, Barron, and Tieger) for each of the 16 Myers–Briggs personality types. One of the most interesting aspects of this easily scanned visual layout is that although "librarian" is noted under ISFJ ("modest and determined workers who enjoy others"), you can quickly see how easily other personality types could succeed in other information-related roles, for example, project manager (ESTJ), web development engineer (ISTJ), sales representative (ESFJ), detective (ESTP), and executive and market research analyst (both ENTJ). The infographic serves to reemphasize the point that information professionals not only come in all sizes, shapes, and personality types, but also can create or step into roles across the widest spectrum of careers.

*Career Assessment Tools & Tests*

www.quintcareers.com/career_assessment.html

From career development and job-hunting site Quintessential Careers, this page provides a good starting point for finding a multitude of personal and career assessments.

*Keirsey.com*

www.keirsey.com

An extensive collection of information resources related to the Keirsey temperaments (artisans, guardians, idealists, and rationals) plus role variants within temperaments, such as composer, crafter, performer, or promoter within "artisan." A fascinating, content-rich site.

*Motivational Appraisal of Personal Potential (MAPP)*

www.assessment.com/

The MAPP assessment comprises "71 triads of three statements" for which you select the statement you *most* agree with and the statement you *least* agree with (one remains blank). The goal is to measure your "potential and motivation" for various types of work, while also profiling your temperament, aptitude, and possible career matches. There are a number of MAPP variations, several of which could be valuable to career exploration, but the assessment evaluation is fee based—you'll want to check out the cost before determining its value for you.

*Myers–Briggs Test*

www.myersbriggs.org

A comprehensive collection of information about the Myers–Briggs personality type test, including the assessment tools, results interpretations, and information on how to use your results (e.g., personality and careers, type and learning, and type in personal growth). An outstanding resource.

*Personality Lingo*

http://personalitylingo.com/

A site that provides information about the multitude of personality assessments and types, describing the "lingo" used by the most popular assessments to help you understand both your own outcomes and those of your colleagues, friends, and family. See especially the materials listed under the Resources tab.

*"Personality Types and Librarians (Part 1)"*
http://libraryworksuccess.wordpress.com/2012/10/14/personality-types-and-librarians/
A terrific overview by Jennifer A. Keach of librarians' MBTI statistics and the impact of those stats on potential career choices. See also her follow-up piece at http://bit.ly/1Tpd64E. (Key resource)

*Workplace Relationships Quiz: What Kind of Co-Worker Are You?*
www.quintcareers.com/co-worker_assessment.html
This assessment relates more to how you behave in and feel about your current workplace environment than to your overall personality type. Once you've completed the answers, you can mail them to Dr. Randall S. Hanson, the Quintessential Careers cofounder, for scoring and an analysis of what your answers indicate about your personality style in your workplace. This can add another element to your collection of self-knowledge data points.

# 3
# Traditional LIS Career Paths

*To the extent that your work takes into account the needs of the world, it will be meaningful; to the extent that through it you express your unique talents, it will be joyful.*

—Laurence G. Boldt

Now that you've explored your aptitudes, interests, and preferences, the next step in designing a career that aligns with them is to consider what options are available. Those generally fall into the categories of traditional, nontraditional, and independent.

Although it's debatable whether *any* of today's libraries can be described as "traditional," for purposes of this chapter, we'll use that term to describe the three major types of facilities-based libraries: public, school, and academic. They represent the paths the majority of librarians have set out on when graduating from a master's degree program.

There are two ways to think about careers in traditional libraries—by the type of library you might work in, and by the type of work you might do within that library. Generally, regardless of what type of library you worked in, the work had fallen into one of three categories: user or public services, technical services, or administrative services, including management. Today a fourth category is coming on strong, that is, working with data.

*User services* (also known as *public services*) generally includes all of the ways librarians "reach out and touch someone"—that is, reference; research assistance; community outreach; Internet and/or bibliographic instruction (BI); readers' advisory; programs for children, seniors, immigrants, and other special populations; and similar types of activities. Sometimes the circulation (book checkout, reserves, holds, interlibrary loan [ILL]) function is considered part of user services, sometimes part of technical services.

*Technical services* includes acquisitions (ordering/purchasing/receiving resources), collection development (deciding which resources to purchase), serials management (subscribing to, checking in, shelving, and binding journals and magazines), processing (including cataloging) materials, shelving, and managing the library's computers and system technologies. Although the library's website is always a collaborative effort, generally its management has been considered a tech services function. In addition, systems librarians (sometimes also called automation librarians) usually fall within the purview of technical services.

*Administrative services* includes process organization, personnel management, budget setting, staff development, external liaison and communication (with mayors, school principals, chancellors, friends groups, donors, advisory boards, and assorted other stakeholders), organizational management, and leadership, among other functions. As per the U.S. Department of Labor's *Occupational Outlook Handbook*, librarians in this role "oversee the management and planning of libraries: negotiate contracts for services, materials, and equipment; supervise library employees; perform public-relations and fundraising duties; prepare budgets; and direct activities to ensure that everything functions properly."[1]

Crossing between and among each of these areas is, however, an increasingly important discipline for librarians and information professionals, that is, *working with data*. More and more decisions in every type of organization—including libraries—are data driven. Consequently, data gathering, management, and analysis are skills much in demand. For example, sophisticated data analysis may be used to support grant funding and budget allocations for large public libraries, library-supported data management may assist academic researchers and the teams responsible for campus-wide outcomes assessment, and large-scale data analytics may inform predictive forecasting models for all types of organizations.

As Amy Affelt notes in her excellent *The Accidental Data Scientist: Big Data Applications and Opportunities for Librarians and Information Professionals* (Information Today, 2015), "The promise—and the peril—of Big Data is foremost in the minds of directors and CEOs. They are wondering how to find the golden needles in the haystacks of information that will affect their relevancy and revenue, and ultimately, their ability to fulfill the mission of their organizations and strategic plans for the future."[2]

Data science work may underlie or be a part of each if not all of the other three focus areas, and it can be found in many types of organizations, including libraries.

Each of these job areas differs somewhat—or even substantially—based on which type of library they're performed in. Also, depending on library size, one person might end up covering several bases in public, administrative, or tech services. In addition, based on size and system organization, some multibranch public libraries may centralize tech or administrative services in one location, while school libraries that are part of larger school districts may have their tech and administrative services handled at the district level.

What are some of the specifics of these three types of libraries?

# Public Libraries

There are roughly 9,000 public libraries in the United States[3] employing about 46,800 MLIS-holding librarians, according to ALA's count.[4]

Public libraries are where many of us first fell in love with the *idea* of libraries. The quiet, calm, nurturing environment, the helpful librarian, the world of ideas—and all those books, just waiting to be devoured.

However, today's public libraries are as much about ebooks and maker spaces, Internet and social media instruction, 3-D printers, small business resources, English-as-a-second-language tutoring, and exam proctoring for local online students as they are about books. Electronic resources—including ebooks and databases—consume an increasing portion of library budgets, and entire categories of new jobs are now tied to dealing with automated systems, regional collaborative networks, and web-based patron interactions.

Public libraries—and the librarians staffing them—are on the front lines of community changes and challenges. A career in *public services* in a public library brings you into contact with a patron base as diverse as your community (with, of course, the same proportion of delightful *vs.* crazy-making people). The opportunity to have an impact on people's lives is substantial, as often you are helping them find and use information to improve their lives.

*Tech services* roles in public libraries vary based on a number of circumstances, including:

- The size of the library and whether or not it's part of a larger system (e.g., a branch library, with most cataloging done at the main library)

- The level of technological sophistication of the library (are internal systems automated and integrated with regional networks, or stand-alone?)

- The library's funding (which determines, for example, whether or not the library has a state-of-the-art community meeting space)

- The library leadership (does the director resist new ideas or constantly press the tech services group for innovative, cool pilot projects using the latest technologies?)

*Administrative services* in today's public libraries often focus on constantly doing a bit more with a lot less, as libraries have taken increasingly severe budget hits over the past years. This affects the library's processes, its staffing and staff development resources, its collection development priorities, and its ability to meet the community's expectations of what a library should be.

The original "people's universities," public libraries in many communities may also face skeptical city administrators who fail to understand the library's strategic value in an online world. Because of this, more and more library directors are taking an active, highly visible communications and marketing role as well.

*Data work* within a public library may encompass a wide range of activities, including gathering, organizing, managing, mining, and extrapolating meaning and context from the relevant data. That may involve working with census data, usage numbers, economic development information, circulation return-on-investment figures, or other types of large-set numbers. The goal with data analysis is always, in one form or another, decision support. Those decisions might relate to budget allocations, the launch of new programs or initiatives, support for grant funds, just-in-time staffing, or even providing the information to argue persuasively for a new branch library building.

Public library LIS professionals who choose to work with data may end up performing all, one, or several of the main components of this type of work, that is, gathering, organizing, managing, mining, and "sense-making" or providing context and conclusions from identified patterns of data for those making decisions based on this information. (They may often also be called on to create understandable presentations, or data visualizations, that portray data findings in accessible, actionable ways.)

## Salaries and Education

According to the *2012 ALA-APA Salary Survey*, salaries earned in 2012 varied substantially based on geographic region (North Atlantic is generally highest, Southeast and Great Lakes/Plains areas are generally but not always in the lower range), size of library (the largest public libraries tend to pay substantially higher salaries), and of course, level of responsibility. In terms of size of the library, ALA considers five categories:

- Very small public libraries (serving a population of less than 10,000; amazingly, nearly 60 percent of U.S. public library systems fall within this category)
- Small public libraries (population ranging from 10,000 to 24,999)
- Medium-sized public libraries (population ranging from 25,000 to 99,999)
- Large public libraries (population ranging from 100,000 to 499,999)
- Very large public libraries (population of 500,000 or more)

With exceptions (check the full report to determine specifics), median national salary ranges (in thousands of dollars) generally broke out as approximately:

- Low 30s to mid-40s for beginning full-time librarians with an MLS but no professional experience.
- Low 40s to high 60s for librarians with no supervisory responsibilities.
- High 40s to high 50s for library managers and those who supervised support staff.
- Mid-50s to mid-60s for department heads/coordinators/senior managers.
- Low 70s to mid-80s for deputy/associate and assistant library directors (with the exception of very large public libraries, where the regional salary means and medians range from about $100,000 to more than $125,000).
- Low 80s to just more than 100 for public library directors (again, with the exception of very large public libraries, where the regional salary means and medians range between $140,000 and $188,000).[5]

These salary ranges are very strongly influenced by the size of the library from which data were gathered as well as by the state of the local or regional economy; some states and municipalities have been strong public library supporters, others less so. Also, the salary survey is based on information submitted for full-time employees and consequently doesn't reflect an increasing rise in part-time hiring driven by budget cuts, a situation faced by a substantial number of MLIS graduates just entering the profession.

These part-time jobs often have no benefits and a much lower pay rate than do full-time positions, so these employees may find themselves cobbling together a collection of part-time jobs simply to pay rent in the early stages of their careers. The bottom line? There *are* great library jobs that pay decent salaries, but you may need to be flexible about relocation and/or your early career work schedule.

An MLIS degree (or some variation of this title) is usually required for professional, rather than support or paraprofessional, jobs in public libraries. Additional skills of value might be subject expertise in an area such as consumer health information or small business resources, second-language proficiency if that language is prevalent in the community, or teaching ability. Strong technology skills are always an asset and are increasingly expected of MLIS graduates now coming into the profession.

## Exploring Public Library Careers

To learn more about public library jobs and how they might align with your skills, aptitudes, and preference filters, consider the following activities:

1. Shadow several different public librarians (if possible, in different libraries) for a day each to get a sense of the different types of activities that make up their jobs. Note the following in your career journal:

   - Do these work activities appeal to me? Why or why not?

   - What can I tell about the culture of the organization? Do I think I would thrive in this culture? Why or why not?

   - Does this position focus on people, collections, systems, data, or administrative processes? Whichever it is, does it seem like an area of expertise I would enjoy learning more about and growing in professionally?

   - Does the person I am shadowing seem to be happy in his or her job? If not, does it seem to be a mismatch between the individual personality and the requirements of the job? Would this be the same or different for me?

2. Read through the public librarian profiles in the LIS career resource books included in the "Resources" section of this chapter. In your career journal, note answers to these questions:

   - What career paths seem most interesting to me, based on the profiles I've read? Why? What questions do the profiles, interviews, and articles raise that I should pursue further, possibly by contacting the individual profiled?

   - Imagine that five years from now I'm being interviewed or asked to write an article. What would I want to be writing about? What aspects of public librarianship would I want to be known for, be considered an expert in?

   - Do the profiles include discussion of recurring, ongoing problems or issues generic to public librarianship that might be especially problematic for me personally, given what I now know about who I am and what I need? (Needless to say, this is keeping in mind that no job or career is without challenges!)

- What career options have I discovered that I'd like to explore further, for example, public library marketing or community information systems?

3. Read six recent issues of *Public Library* magazine to get a good sense of the state of the profession today. As you peruse the articles, note in your career journal the following information:

- What articles seem most interesting to me? Am I most engaged by stories about creating a community website, developing new outreach programs, policy issues, management challenges, or some other aspect of public librarianship?

- What specifically engages me about the articles? Creating new solutions? Helping others? Contributing to the betterment of a community? Employing technology in innovative ways? Developing team leadership skills?

- Are there practitioners who have written articles that caught my eye who I could contact to learn more from?

- Do there seem to be areas where I believe my unique skills, aptitudes, and insights could contribute? Where and how?

4. After reviewing your responses to the information you've noted in your career journal, answer these questions:

- Based on what I discovered through my previous self-assessment process and what I now know about my preferences and priorities, does public librarianship seem like a career path that could offer me the levels of growth, challenge, security, and engagement that I need to thrive?

- If I still am unsure about this question, what other information will I need to make this assessment?

- How will I gather that information?

---

**Why You Might Love Being a Public Librarian**

Sue Considine, executive director of the Fayetteville Free Library (NY) and a 2013 *Library Journal* Mover & Shaker, notes the joy of working with newly minted LIS professionals who share a commitment to the values of public librarianship:

*EVERYTHING we do is about relationships and people, isn't it? It is my absolute pleasure to work with all of the incredibly talented professionals and support staff members on my team. I especially enjoy working with new professionals. My staffing model is unique. The Syracuse University iSchool is in our backyard, so my entire front line staff are current MLIS students. Each day our team and community benefits from the enthusiasm, creativity, knowledge and risky thinking that these talented individuals bring to the team and the community.*

*I have been staffing this way since 2003. To date, all but one of the professional librarians on my team was once a student support staff member. The most important element of any successful relationship is trust; I have worked with these students, sometimes for up to three years, before I bring them on board with the professional team. Reciprocal trust has already been established before that professional interview. I know their interests, talents and what motivates them. This model of team building has created an "incubator" type environment at the FFL; innovation happens every day when staff at all levels are encouraged to think and take risks together.*

*People give and do their best when they understand that their unique talents are a key contributing factor to the teams' collaborative success.*

*Also, helping support the students who graduate and move through their job search is tremendously gratifying to me. I am grateful to have regular opportunities to leverage my network to help open doors for these bright new professionals and to contribute further to the development of our next industry leaders by helping to position them to be and do their best. It's all about people!*

In addition, working with the public on a daily basis usually involves a high degree of variety, an excellent environment for those who thrive on diverse human interaction and intellectual challenge.

There is also the sense of purpose and camaraderie that comes from belonging to a respected professional community with a long tradition of dedicated, selfless commitment to values such as intellectual freedom, First Amendment rights, and equality of access. In communities where the role of the public library is respected and supported, this career path can offer the enjoyment of an ever-changing environment, the opportunity to contribute professionally, and a sense of personal reward from helping others.

Rochelle Logan, now-retired Douglas County Libraries (Colorado) associate director of Support Services, confirmed this aspect of public librarianship, noting that "every day I see how the presence of this library contributes to the community. Feeling that my work helps improve the lives of the people in the county where I live is very fulfilling." Logan, who was present during the design and building of her town's new public library, said participating in the process meant that she can now "look at this library and say to myself, 'I helped build that.'" And in many ways, this sense of contributing to the building of not just a library, but a community, is one of the greatest rewards of public librarianship.

Public libraries take on multiple roles for those they serve: among other missions, they function as community information centers, as resources for change in their patrons' lives, and as advocates for and maintainers of our shared culture, whether locally, nationally, or globally. If this public service mission aligns with your goals and values, few choices could be more rewarding.

## School Library Media Centers

There are nearly 98,500 school libraries in the United States[6] employing about 92,660 full- and part-time professionals plus about 47,400 other paid staff. Of those school libraries, approximately 14,100 are in private schools.[7] Although most states used to mandate a certified school library media specialist at the high school level, many are now exploring legal alternatives that will enable them to avoid this requirement. There are fewer and fewer states that continue to have librarians for elementary or middle schools. (This trend is especially discouraging since school librarians are often the first librarians to touch the lives of our children. Because of this, they have a unique potential to shape students' lifelong attitudes and assumptions about libraries and those who work in them.)

Are you considering a school librarian career path? If so, regardless of what other professional attributes you may have, certainly the most important one will be the ability to take delight in working with kids and teenagers. If that describes you, then school librarianship can be a truly rewarding option.

Unlike most public or academic libraries, where individuals tend to specialize in a given functional area such as serials management or readers' advisory, school library media centers generally offer the opportunity to engage in a diverse range of activities. Your day might include any combination of these roles:

- *Teacher*, as you demonstrate the use of reference materials and key topic resources to students

- *Instructional partner*, as you collaborate with a 10th-grade history teacher to develop class assignments interweaving information literacy skills and scout for cool online resources that can be incorporated into a lesson plan

- *Coach*, as you work one-on-one with students to help them identify, evaluate, and use appropriate information resources for a specific assignment

- *Technologist*, as you demonstrate the use of new communications, research, and online tools to both students and teachers

- *Collection development and acquisitions specialist*, as you draw on your professional resources and faculty input to identify and acquire appropriate materials to support student learning

- *Manager*, as you set priorities, manage projects, supervise clerical help, and interact with school teachers, library volunteers, and administrators

- *Circulation clerk, shelver, and chief bottle-washer*, as you pick up the assorted tasks that remain when aides leave for the day

This multitasking approach is especially prevalent in private schools, which often encompass grades one through eight in one location. In this case, if there is a school librarian in place, he or she may provide story times for the youngest students; teach basic information literacy skills to fourth graders; tutor the sixth graders on Internet navigation, research, and evaluation skills; coach the seventh graders through their initial efforts in organizing a research paper; and support the eighth graders who are now in the throes of actually *writing* those research papers.

A career in public school librarianship, on the other hand, is more likely to also offer paths into management and administrative technologies. Depending on the size of the school system, for example, you might become a library automation specialist at the district level or a media cataloger at a centralized technical services facility.

Whether in a public or private school media center, however, school librarians have experienced the same impacts from electronic resources as have their public library colleagues. Students are growing up in a digital information surround at home and in their communities, and they expect the same in their libraries. Consequently, more and more of a school librarian's job focuses on evaluating, aggregating, and teaching the appropriate, effective use of nonprint resources.

## Salaries and Education

Generally, the salaries of school library media specialists, like those of teachers, increase with years of experience and additional levels of education. Like those of public librarians, school librarians' salaries vary depending on location (e.g., large city vs. small town), size of school, and often the affluence of the school district. The National Education Association produces an annual report, "Average Starting Teacher Salaries by State," that can provide a good sense of current salaries. For example, the national average starting teacher salary for the 2012–2013 school year (most recent statistics available) was $36,141.[8]

The education requirements for becoming a school library media specialist are unusual in that you can take one of two paths to become certified. The first is to obtain a master's degree in library and/or information science from a school that includes the school library media curriculum and certification among its program offerings. (In addition to the certification, you'll need a teaching degree for the state in which you plan to work.) The second option, intended primarily for teachers who have decided to transition into the school library profession, is to complete a one-year "school library media certification" program that builds on students' existing teaching credentials.

Each state sets certification standards for its school librarians, so that a school librarian certified in Nebraska would need to be certified again in the specific states to work in, for example, California or Maine.

## Exploring School Library Media Specialist Careers

To learn more about school library media specialist jobs and how they might align with your skills, aptitudes, and preference filters, consider the following activities:

1. Volunteer several days each at two or three local school libraries, preferably at different levels (e.g., elementary and high school). If possible, arrange your volunteer hours when the librarians are engaged in different activities so you can get a sense of the broad range of tasks involved. After each visit, note your answers to the following questions in your career journal:

   • What about these activities might engage or bore me? Would I do them the same way, or would I do them differently? How? Why?

- What can I tell about the relationships among the school library media specialist, the teachers, the administration (e.g., the principal), and the students? Do I think I would thrive in this environment? Why or why not?

- Does the multitasking, multiple-role nature of this work appeal to me? Would I enjoy organizing everything and thrive on the challenge of staying on top of things, or would I find it too stressful?

- Does the level of people interaction suit my personality? Would I be comfortable with the increasing focus on electronic and online resources in school libraries?

2. Sign up for one or two of the school library media specialist LinkedIn groups (such as "School Librarians" or "Secondary School Teacher Librarians") and monitor the online postings for a month or two. Your goal is to get a sense of the questions asked and issues discussed, and then note in your career journal answers to the following:

- Do these questions and issues engage me? Why or why not?

- What changes to the profession are being discussed? How might these changes impact a potential career I might have as a school library media specialist?

- Do school librarians seem to focus their energy and passions in areas that resonate with my skills and aptitudes? Does it seem that the majority of questions are devoted to administration, teaching, new resources, managing relationships, student coaching, or a balance of these? Whatever the ratio looks like, does this balance reflect my interests?

- Does there seem to be a general attitude toward change (positive, negative, or neutral), and would I be comfortable with this? Are postings solutions oriented, and can I see myself contributing to those solutions?

3. After reviewing the responses you recorded to the self-assessment questions of Chapter 2, put together a hit list of questions that help you understand how school librarianship might align with your professional goals. Based on these, contact at least five school library media specialists and ask them if you can interview them via e-mail, phone, or in person. Some starter questions might include the following:

- In general, what percentage of your time do the following activities occupy: library administration, student programs and instruction, working with teachers, working with school administration, resource review and evaluation, other?

- Which activities do you enjoy the most, and why? The least, and why?

- What do you consider to be the most important skills for an effective, successful school library media specialist?

- What do you see as the biggest threats or opportunities to the continued viability of school librarianship as a good career path?

- Would you choose this career again? Why or why not?

  Include their responses in your career journal, noting any recurring themes. Consider how their comments do or don't align with what you know about your own strengths and preferences.

4. After reviewing your responses to the information you've noted in your career journal, answer these questions:

   - Based on what I discovered through my previous self-assessment process and what I now know about my preferences and priorities, does school librarianship seem like a career path that could offer me the levels of growth, challenge, security, and engagement I need to thrive?

   - If I'm still unsure about this question, what other information will I need to make this assessment?

   - How will I gather that information?

### Why You Might Love Being A School Librarian

Summers off—need we say more?

Seriously though, school librarianship can be a great career choice for those who love working with children who are entering the world of learning, preteens just emerging from childhood, or adolescents whose lives are fraught with all the emotional upheaval of life's toughest transition. It's a profession where your successes can change lives; a good school librarian can help a student find his inner scholar, can connect a high school athlete with her college aspirations, can help kids become savvy, successful navigators of our digital knowledge universe.

It can also be a good career fit if you like to take on multiple roles. The job often includes a bit of everything—although heavy on public services (i.e., student and teacher contact), there's often also a substantial amount of tech services (serials management, collection development, special-item cataloging) and plenty of administrative work. In addition, you may be increasingly involved in supporting the Common Core initiative with both teachers and students. You get to collaborate with teachers, contribute to the learning process, and stay current with emerging information technologies and resources.

Betty Bankhead, project director for Colorado Power Libraries, specifically highlighted the excitement inherent in the leadership aspects of school librarianship, noting that "leadership is no longer positional in good schools, and successful school librarians must influence and motivate their colleagues to partner with them to create the next generation of proficient library users." Said Bankhead:

*I think being a professional school librarian encompasses the best of three worlds: libraries, education and entrepreneurship. People who are successful in our field are those who enjoy and excel at the management aspects of library work by being organized, efficient and cost effective. But, along with that management expertise, they must have the ability and enthusiasm to teach by making information literacy and technology skills understandable and achievable for the school community, which includes both students and adults.*

*And finally, most successful school librarians must be entrepreneurs in that they have to provide the leadership to "create" a strong information management and technology presence within a complex content curriculum.*

Emily Woodward, lower school librarian at the Baldwin School, an all-girls private school in Bryn Mawr, Pennsylvania, loves the impact her work has both inside and outside of the library's walls:

*Being a school librarian you get to impact so many people! As an elementary school librarian I feel like I am there for the formative time when they discover what they love. I not only get to build relationships with the students, but I also get to teach them valuable research and library use skills that they will utilize for the rest of their life. Getting summers and weekends off is a great benefit too!*

*It's hard work not having a large staff to rely on, you're a one person show, but you also can make important decisions that impact your users. I also love collaborating with teachers and seeing the benefit of the library move beyond its walls.*

Clearly, a career as a school librarian can represent an excellent choice for someone who thrives on a day that includes a highly diverse set of tasks, a lot of people interaction, and a high level of self-direction.

Ladawna Harrington, librarian at Millburn High School in New Jersey (one of the highest-performing schools in the state), has been a school librarian for 18 years and is clearly passionately engaged in her work, about which she states:

*Why do I love my job? It's the people, the students and the teachers I get to work with. I love being the intermediary that meets kids at their point of need. I love the collaborative partnerships I have with content teachers....*

Regarding working with students, Ladawna reflects further:

*The voices of the students are why I love my job: "Learning more about organization." "I learned a lot of helpful and valuable things that will definitely help me throughout my life...like how to search for things/topics I don't know anything about...research would be impossible if it weren't for a library." "I am a better note taker. I can scan information better." "I've learned to have patience. I learned to be more organized. I learned to put things together step by step. I've learned to investigate." "This research will help me in other classes because I have learned how to look for stuff."*

When describing her work as a school librarian, Ladawna can chart a trajectory from the days of little-to-no technology to today's digital resources surround, but in many ways, the intrinsic rewards remain unchanged. In particular:

*This past summer I had a wonderful email arrive in my inbox. It was from one of my former middle school students who is now studying robotic engineering at Princeton University. He graduated valedictorian from his high school. He wanted to meet me for lunch, give me a tour of his "office," and fill me in on his passion for his studies. I met this guy in my little middle school library. He was in my tech club. You have to understand that the middle school I taught in was in the middle of a large working class school district and in particular my middle school's population was mostly from a transient population.*

*This student has kept in touch with me through his high school experience, applying the web design knowledge he learned in my tech club to building the website for his high school. He reminds me in his periodic emails of the things he learned in the library, about how to think about problems in a way that has helped him succeed along the way. Having an impact on learning in such an individualized way is the greatest feeling in the world. This is why I love my job.*

## Academic Libraries

The *Online Dictionary for Library and Information Science (ODLIS)* defines an academic library as:

*A library that is an integral part of a college, university, or other institution of postsecondary education, administered to meet the information and research needs of its students, faculty, and staff.*[9]

The term "academic library," however, encompasses a number of distinct types of higher education libraries differentiated by the mission of the institution, the nature of its student body, and the size of its collection. One way to categorize academic libraries is by whether they support two-year or four-year degree programs, masters-level and/or doctoral degree programs. Another way is whether the library is an *undergraduate* or *graduate library* (i.e., supports undergraduate or graduate students and curricula), or a *departmental library* (e.g., a library devoted solely to supporting a business school program and its students). A *college library* may be one of several specialized libraries supporting separate "colleges" within a large university. The role of these libraries is primarily to support the curriculum- and course-related research needs of their specific constituencies, including both students and faculty.

An academic library that is considered a *research library*, on the other hand, has a somewhat different mission. A research library is expected to maintain a broad and very deep collection of primary and secondary sources of value to serious scholarly research in a specific topic area or discipline. Such a collection often includes archives of original manuscripts, rare books, personal letters, and similar types of scholarly resources.

A further distinction among academic libraries is whether they are part of a *research university*, that is, one of the major research institutions such as Johns Hopkins University, UCLA, the University of Wisconsin, the University of Michigan, Massachusetts Institute of Technology, Stanford, or the University of Pennsylvania. This distinction is generally based on the amount of federal and/or private-sector research funds flowing into a given institution on an annual basis and thus the volume of faculty research, among other criteria.

The official classification system used to categorize types of American colleges and universities is the Carnegie Classification of Institutions of Higher Education, developed by the Carnegie Foundation for the Advancement of Teaching. Although the classification system is currently under revision, you can see a summary of the existing classification and distribution of institutions at the Carnegie Classification website (http://carnegieclassifications.iu.edu/).

According to ALA, there are 3,793 academic libraries in the United States, of which 2,489 are associated with four-year-and-above institutions and 1,304 with less-than-four-year colleges (think community colleges, vocational colleges, and similar types of schools).[10] Academic libraries employ approximately 26,600 professional librarians. In addition, many of the proprietary schools (also known as vocational or technical schools or career colleges) and for-profit colleges (e.g., University of Phoenix) provide library resources and services to their students.[11]

The states with the highest number of academic libraries (and therefore, theoretically, the greatest number of job openings) are California (341), New York (260), Pennsylvania (211), Texas (183), Illinois (153), Ohio (143), Florida (120), North Carolina (118), Massachusetts (114), and Michigan (99).[12]

Regardless of the types and sizes of academic libraries, user or public services, tech services, and administrative services generally follow the same outlines of activity. The goals of the library are to select, acquire, and maintain a resource collection that supports the curriculum as well as the research needs of students and faculty; teach students how to effectively use not only that collection but also the myriad other online information resources that exist; work with faculty to integrate relevant information resources as well as advanced information and communications technologies into the learning dynamic; and create and support technology infrastructures that enable each of these goals.

Academic librarians working within the *public* or *user services* arena will find themselves in a strong teaching and coaching role with students (and occasionally faculty). *BI* has traditionally been a core responsibility on the reference desk, but today BI is moving into the broader embrace of *information literacy*—teaching students not only how to use the information resources offered by the library, but also how to be effective, informed users of *all* information resources.

In addition, the entire reference interaction is moving increasingly into a virtual or digital exchange, requiring new skills of academic reference librarians, including a strong ability to communicate effectively in an online environment. Also, the advent of online courses has seen an increase in the embedding of information literacy assignments into the courses themselves ("at the point of need," rather than in a separate BI session).

This trend has resulted in many reference librarians developing a new set of collaborative skills around theories of learning styles, lesson plan development, and instructional design. In response to this increasingly common circumstance, the term "embedded librarian" is now regularly used to identify academic librarians who are "embedded" in the teaching team. (Note: embedded librarianship also describes a type of special librarianship, as we'll see in the next chapter.)

In the *tech services* arena, serials management plays a much greater role in the workings of an academic library than in public or school libraries because serials are such a large part of academic holdings. In addition, ebooks and electronic journals are changing how collections are developed, licensed, and managed. Helping to create, manage, and support databases has also grown as a tech services function. ILL continues to be an important part of academic library services, although online (and immediately available) resources are somewhat lessening the demand for ILL. And depending on the nature of an institution's holdings, "original cataloging," that is, cataloging unusual items from scratch rather than relying on OCLC's cataloging services, may be a large part of the catalogers' jobs.

*Administrative services* in academic libraries are similar to those in public libraries, although the external communications are more likely to be with chancellors, donor groups, deans, and department heads than with the broader public community. In many academic libraries, the librarians are also part of the larger academic community and its expectations (e.g., tenure-track activities), which changes to some extent how personnel management issues and staff development initiatives are approached.

## Salaries and Education

Academic librarians' salaries, like those of school and public librarians, are based on a wide variety of circumstances. Size, financial well-being, prestige, and geographic location of the institution are all factors, as is whether an institution is publicly or privately funded. But academic librarians often have other job benefits that augment their salaries. For example, they usually have free tuition at their employing institution, often have the opportunity to seek the job security of tenure-track faculty, and frequently have substantial vacation, healthcare, and retirement benefits packages. Also, for those contemplating upcoming kids' tuition payments, a job in an academic library may offer the delightful perk of free college tuition for family members.

According to the *2012 ALA-APA Salary Survey*, with exceptions (check the full report to determine specifics), salaries (in thousands of dollars) generally fall into the following ranges:

- High 30s to low 50s for beginning full-time librarians with an MLS but no professional experience at both colleges and universities.

- Low 40s to high 50s for librarians with no supervisory responsibilities at two-year and four-year colleges, and mid-50s to low 60s for those at universities.

- Mid-40s to high 60s for library managers and those who supervise support staff at two-year and four-year colleges, and mid-50s to mid-60s for those at universities.

- Low 30s to low 70s for department heads/coordinators/senior managers at two-year and four-year colleges, and low 60s to low 70s for those at universities.

- Mid-40s to mid-70s for deputy/associate and assistant directors at two-year and four-year colleges; mid-80s to just more than $100,000 for those at universities.

- Low 60s to mid-80s for directors and deans at two-year and four-year colleges, and $116,000 to approximately $145,000 for those at universities.[13]

Education requirements for professional jobs in academic libraries vary by institution, although almost all have required the MLS. The debate is whether or not you need also to complete an additional master's degree in a subject area such as life sciences, American literature, or social sciences. (Also, a trend to note is that a number of academic libraries are beginning to experiment with hiring PhD subject specialists rather than hiring an MLIS professional with subject knowledge. It's unclear at this point how successful or prevalent this practice will prove, but it's something for academic library job-seekers to be aware of.)

The argument *against* an additional degree is that the salaries paid to academic librarians are simply too low to expect this level of education, financial, and time investment. The argument *for* the second masters is that it gives you an edge over other job applicants, may convince faculty to respect (and treat) you more as a peer, helps support tenure efforts, and may be an important asset when applying for administrative and/or management positions. Like so many career considerations, at the very least, a second subject-oriented master's degree may simply open up more and better options for you long term. However, if you don't already have an additional master's, this is a choice you'd want to weigh very carefully.

## Exploring Academic Library Careers

To learn more about how being an academic librarian might suit your career interests and goals, consider the following activities:

1. Shadow several academic librarians in different departments (e.g., reference, collection development, circulation) for a day each to get a sense of the different types of activities that make up their jobs. Note the following in your career journal:

   - Which of their daily activities seems most interesting and enjoyable to me? Does one position seem to align with my skills and aptitudes more than the others, or are there aspects of each that appeal? If so, what are they?

   - How do colleagues interact with each other? Is it a strong collaborative environment or are departments "information silos?" Do I think I would thrive in this culture? Why or why not?

   - What does the person I'm shadowing most enjoy about his or her job? Most dislike? If the person is willing to discuss his or her personality type, do the "dislikes" seem to be a mismatch between job requirements and personality (e.g., an introvert staffing the reference desk)? Would this be the same or different for me?

   - Would I be comfortable working with students, scholars, and faculty, and their broad range of attitudes about and expectations of the library and librarians?

2. Sign up for one or two of the position-specific academic library groups on LinkedIn (e.g., Digital Libraries, Instruction in Academic Libraries, New Academic Librarians: Networking to Success) and monitor the online postings for a month or two. Your goal is to get a sense of the questions asked and issues discussed, and then note in your career journal answers to the following:

- Do I think I would enjoy learning more about the issues discussed and contributing my knowledge and solutions?

- What seems to be the general level of community morale in the group discussions? Are people excited about their jobs, and the work they do? Is there a sense of mutual support, and are newcomers welcomed?

- What role does technology seem to play in the disciplines in question, and does this level of technology engagement align with my skills? If my skills are lower, would I be comfortable learning more? If higher, would I enjoy becoming the technology "guru?"

3.  Read six recent issues of *The Journal of Academic Librarianship (JAL)* (either in your local academic library or online at its website). Consider the articles' high level of research and scholarship. As you peruse the issues, note in your career journal the following information:

    - Would I enjoy this level of professional scholarship and find it a rewarding aspect of my career, or would I find it intimidating or too much pressure?

    - Do I find the article topics engaging? Which ones most so/least so? Does there seem to be a spirit of openness to new ideas among the contributors, so that new theories and solutions would be welcomed?

    - Do there seem to be areas where I believe my unique skills, aptitudes, and insights could contribute? Where and how?

4.  After reviewing your responses to the information you've noted in your career journal, answer these questions:

    - Based on what I discovered through my previous self-assessment process and what I now know about my preferences and priorities, does academic librarianship seem like a career path that could offer me the levels of growth, challenge, security, and engagement that I need to thrive?

    - If I still am unsure about this question, what other information will I need to make this assessment?

    - How will I gather that information?

---

### Why You Might Love Being an Academic Librarian

If you love ideas, the learning process, and teaching students from 18 to 80 how to become effective users of information resources, academic librarianship may offer you a career of ongoing intellectual and professional engagement. An academic library is a dynamic environment, and in a well-funded one, you'll be on the cutting edge of advances in information and communications technology, working with faculty to design interactive multimedia assignments that engage and teach students. You'll be exposed to a wide variety of scholarly disciplines and be challenged to stay abreast not only of the institution's resources but also those of the information universe at large.

Plus, many institutions offer a great work schedule: 10-month contracts, multiple holidays, two weeks off at Christmas and another at spring break, and free tuition for your employing institution's courses and degree programs. The work hours are flexible, and the rich mixture of on-campus political, arts, and cultural events is inexpensive and easy to attend. And if you're one of those whose idea of heaven is being a perpetual student, it's hard to imagine a more enjoyable career choice than academic librarianship.

When asked what she loved about her job, Allison Cowgill, public services librarian at California State University, Fresno, talked about the rewards of "connecting users with the resources that best meet their research needs and instructing them on how to access those materials." She also noted the personal reward of "working with students at all levels, from freshmen to doctoral candidates," coaching them on how to do research for their classes "that really helps them succeed academically."

David Cappoli, web services librarian for the UCLA School of Law, previously served nearly 13 years as digital resources librarian for the UCLA School of Information Studies. Reflecting on his career trajectory thus far, David commented that

> *Being at UCLA, and in an earlier position with Glasgow Polytechnic, I have been provided with opportunities to interact with librarians, students, and other academics throughout the many disciplines on campus. It has exposed me to the variety of research, activities, and new ways of approaching challenges that, in many ways, are only present within the university environment. I have worked with and learned from librarians who teach, investigate, manage people and technology, catalog, preserve, archive, and lead. And they do so in a diverse array of libraries, from science, engineering, and biomedical, to art and music, to management and law.*

David has also enjoyed the collegial aspects of association work that are part of the "service" component of an academic librarianship career:

> *The requisite professional work that comes with being an academic librarian has led me to present at conferences and workshops while also taking on progressively more demanding leadership positions within associations. And it is this work and the connections that I have made while undertaking it that have enriched me and made me more professionally marketable. In fact, I credit my involvement with SLA as having given me the self-confidence and relevant experience to successfully interview for my current position within UCLA Law.*

Lindsay Roberts, reference and outreach librarian, Library and Learning Commons at Arapahoe (Colorado) Community College, is passionate about the challenges and rewards of working with her student community:

> *What I love most about being a community college librarian is that I get to do a bit of everything. This keeps me constantly learning and engaged in my job. In the past year, I helped the library migrate to a new ILS, created video tutorials, helped renovate our website,*

*cataloged a special collection of 200 art books, started a library out-reach program at our branch campuses, and taught over 100 research classes. While my job title is Reference and Outreach Librarian, with a staff of five, we all wear many hats! Working with community college students is especially rewarding.*

*We serve concurrent enrollment high school students, aged 14–18, through lifelong learners in their 80's and beyond. Community college students may be juggling many responsibilities and identities, including working full-time, parenting, overcoming substance abuse or past trauma, returning to school after many years, returning veterans, or learning English as a second language. We have the opportunity to help students feel empowered to find information, learn new technologies, and succeed in their educational and personal goals. We often develop close relationships with students and get to cheer them on throughout their academic career. I really feel that my work makes a difference for our students, faculty, and staff.*

Each of these academic librarians cited the variety of their jobs (in terms of activities, technologies, intellectual challenges, and types of people served) and noted how enjoyable it was to work with service-oriented colleagues who supported the college and/or university goals of research and scholarship.

## Types of Jobs within Traditional Libraries

As suggested previously, there are two ways to consider traditional library career paths. One is to categorize by type of library—that is, school, public, or academic. The other is to approach by type of role or activity, including those found among public, technical, and administrative services. As noted, a library's size often determines how specialized these roles and activities become.

For example, a small public library may have only a library director, a couple of reference librarians who double on the circulation desk, and one hardy soul handling all technical services. A large academic library, on the other hand, is likely to have individual reference librarians dedicated to specific academic disciplines such as humanities, sciences, and business, with a similar breadth and depth of coverage across all of the functional departments.

Also, technology advances and electronic resources continue to blur the lines between and among functional areas, so that the roles of, for example, adult services, user education, and web development will regularly overlap in an ongoing collaboration. However, as a starting point, brief descriptions of many of the positions found in traditional libraries are provided. (Given the breakneck pace of change in our profession, all of the job titles, descriptions, and comments noted here should be considered at best a snapshot in time.)

### Public Services Roles and Activities

**Access services librarian.** Oversees all the ways in which the library provides access to its collections, including circulation, reserves, ILL, and document delivery. Involves management of people and processes, plus strong attention to detail.

**Adult services librarian**. Creates and/or manages programs and resource collections that meet the needs of the library's adult users (as distinct from those of children or young adults). A creative, service-oriented job that involves working with the public and responsiveness to patron input.

**Business librarian.** In a public library, works with the local business community (or with individuals considering starting a business) by developing and maintaining a collection that supports business information needs and training users on how to most effectively use the appropriate resources. In an academic library, has the same responsibilities, but focused on students and faculty in the school's business program or courses. Entails lots of people interaction, broad and deep knowledge of existing business information resources and their uses, as well as constant monitoring/mastering of emerging resources.

**Children's librarian.** Creates and/or manages programs and resource collections that meet the needs of the library's youngest users (as distinct from those of young adults or adults). Especially rewarding for those who love working with children and parents and bring a high level of creativity to their work.

**Instructional services librarian.** Responsible for BI in academic libraries or teaching individuals how to locate, evaluate, and use the resources offered in the public library. With the advent of the Internet, this position now focuses on the broader "information literacy" mandate, that is, teaching students how to use and evaluate *all* information resources effectively, including those of the institution's collection. In a large public library, a similar focus is often called "user education." A great path for those who would enjoy combining a teaching role with their information skills; often involves substantial use of technology-based instructional tools.

**Outreach librarian.** Designs and delivers programs to meet the needs of underserved populations and special constituencies, for example, the visually impaired, non-English-speaking groups, the homebound, or local small business development centers. Usually found in larger public libraries. A great career choice for individuals with strong people skills, a high level of comfort addressing groups, and high comfort level with taking initiative.

**Reference librarian**. The job that many fall in love with when first considering librarianship. Answers patron or student questions in person, by phone, e-mail or text, or via interactive "chat" using one of the new virtual reference software programs. Frequently, the reference librarian may also be called on to help provide user instruction, explain the use of the library's technology, and collaborate on collection development. In larger academic institutions, the reference librarians may have areas of specialization, such as the humanities, sciences, or social sciences. A good option for those who enjoy a lot of people contact, who thrive on the research process, and who can patiently coach users through the intricacies of various reference tools.

**Readers' advisory services**. A service often provided by an adult services librarian where specific books or authors are recommended to a patron based on his or her reading interests. Readers' advisory services may also include helping to organize and support book clubs and may also be crafted for children and young adults. For those who know and love genre reading (fiction and nonfiction) and enjoy connecting readers with the books they'll love.

**Young adult/youth services librarian**. Creates and/or manages programs and resource collections that meet the needs of the library's young adult patrons (i.e., adolescents in the 9th through 12th grades). Usually involves collection development work, program design and implementation, and readers' advisory services. Similar to adult services, a great choice for those who love working with teenagers and have a strong sense of creativity.

Keep in mind that all of these roles and activities are increasingly playing out in a digital surround, resulting in job descriptions like digital collections specialist, online business librarian, and e-reference or virtual reference librarian. In fact, no matter what area of public services you might be in, it's a good idea to assume at least part of your job will involve online delivery (and virtual communication skills).

## Technical Services Roles and Activities

**Acquisitions**. Manages the *ordering and purchase* of all materials (as opposed to collection development, which involves *selecting* the materials to be purchased). Deals with vendors, licenses, contract negotiation, and budgets, and often collaborates with regional buying consortia to secure the best prices for the organization. Smaller public and academic libraries may combine the acquisitions and collection development functions. Involves strong work organization skills and attention to detail, as well as ability to effectively negotiate and monitor vendor contracts and performance.

**Bibliographer**. Creates subject-focused, usually annotated, lists of resources to be used for teaching, collection development, and scholarly research. Primarily in larger academic libraries. Best for those with strong research, analysis, and writing skills, a passion for a specific discipline or topic, and an interest in continuing to grow topic expertise.

**Cataloger**. Creates the bibliographic records that allow us to find and retrieve specific items among the library's holdings. A bibliographic record will include a physical description of the item as well as its subject headings, classification number, and—depending on the nature of the collection—other information that will assist the user. Catalogers are in the forefront of the work being done with digitization and metadata issues, and are taking the lead on many virtual library access and retrieval issues. *Original* cataloging entails creating the entire record from scratch, while *copy* cataloging relies on cataloging that has already been created by national cataloging entity OCLC. Takes an extremely high level of attention to detail, an in-depth understanding of cataloging and classification structures, and an ability to apply them precisely. Often entails minimal people contact.

**Circulation**. Manages all processes related to checking materials in and out of the library and compiles statistics related to circulation data (e.g., what resources are most popular based on their circulation numbers). Requires strong process orientation and attention to detail, high level of comfort with technology-based systems.

**Collection development**. Relying on a wide range of reviewing and evaluation tools, identifies materials to purchase based on the nature of the collection and the library's constituency. For example, a public library collection would reflect a stronger consumer-interest focus, while a two-year college collection would have a less scholarly emphasis than would a research-level university supporting numerous doctoral programs. In academic libraries, collection development librarians may have a second master's degree in their subject area. Involves substantial interaction with peers and colleagues, ongoing monitoring of multiple and diverse review sources, and ability to manage decision processes.

**Document delivery and interlibrary loan (ILL)**. Obtains materials such as books, articles, reports, and multimedia that have been requested by patrons, students, or faculty, and are unavailable in the library's existing collection. Most ILL and document delivery requests are processed through a collaborative online system, either regional or national, that transfers requests among participating libraries. The emergence of ebooks, resource digitization, and full-text articles available online will have a substantial impact on how—and how much—document delivery and ILL is required in the future. Requires strong focus on following consistent (often technology-based) processes and attention to administrative detail; may involve some public contact, but minimal.

**Preservation and conservation**. Maintains rare and archival materials through the management of environmental conditions (e.g., light, temperature, humidity), by controlling access to the materials, and by undertaking appropriate actions to repair damage and deterioration. Digitization is an increasingly important method for preserving delicate or deteriorating resources. Although some large public libraries with archival special collections are involved in preservation and conservation, this function is more usually found in special collections archives of universities and cultural institutions. Although this is an increasingly technology-based function, it still often requires extreme patience and extraordinary attention to process details, as well as the ability to be painstakingly careful with physical objects.

**Reserves**. In academic libraries, maintains a separate collection of materials (including books, reports, and articles) as stipulated by faculty to provide supplementary course materials for their students. *E-reserves*, or digitized full-text documents, are an increasingly popular solution for providing these resources online, with access through the library's website or portal. Online courses sometimes offer the option of embedding e-reserves directly into the online course delivery. Similar to document delivery/ILL work, the reserves function requires strong focus on following consistent (often technology-based) processes and attention to administrative detail. Generally involves interaction with both faculty and students.

**Serials librarian**. Manages the subscriptions, receipt, check-in, shelving, binding, and sometimes contract negotiation for all of the library's periodicals (an especially important role for academic libraries), including digital subscriptions. Some shared activities with acquisitions and cataloging departments. Best for those with strong process orientation, with an ability to establish and/or manage administrative processes, and who collaborate easily (for instance, with other departments). Also requires ability to effectively negotiate and monitor vendor contracts and performance.

**Systems librarian**. Responsible for the development and maintenance of the library's hardware, software, and networking capabilities. In most academic and many public libraries, integrated automation systems now coordinate the efforts of cataloging, circulation, serials management, acquisitions, e-reserves for academics, ILL, and the online catalog, so this is an increasingly critical role. Takes a strong combination of advanced technology skills, substantial cross-departmental collaboration, an ability to prioritize among many competing demands, and solid communication skills. Patience and an ability to remain calm are major pluses!

**User experience librarian.** Potentially part of the webmaster role (see later), responsible for usability, user experience (UX), and user interface design and implementation. Think of the UX librarian as the voice of the patron (or employee or customer)—that is, the users of a given website. On a broader basis, a UX librarian may also be asked to consider the user experience for the library as a whole, rather than just its digital presence.

**Visual resources librarian.** Depending on the type of library and its specific collections, organizes and maintains collections of digital images, film and/or video, photographs and slides, and similar types of visual resources. Position is found primarily in large academic, public, or special libraries with visual resource collections. May also be called "video" or "moving image" librarian. Job entails knowledge of video resources, their review sources, and their organizing and cataloging methodologies.

**Webmaster.** Also known as the web manager, responsible for designing, developing, and maintaining the library's website. This position is an increasingly collaborative one and requires strong interpersonal communications and team leadership skills to complement technology expertise. A critical role in public and academic libraries, and a component of many school librarians' jobs. In public and academic libraries, this job may require skills similar to those needed by a systems librarian: that is, a strong combination of advanced technology skills, substantial cross-departmental collaboration, an ability to prioritize among many competing demands, and solid communication skills.

## Administrative Services Roles and Activities

As noted earlier, administrative services include process organization, personnel management, budget setting, staff development, external liaison and communication, and leadership.

These are standard functional areas within any organization. For example, the human resources department (or person) generally manages hiring and firing, personnel policies, legal issues of HR, staff development, and benefits and compensation issues. The library dean or director puts together a budget, perhaps with the assistance of a business manager or finance director. These types of roles are rarely covered in depth in an MLIS program, although they may be touched upon in the occasional management class. Instead, these skill sets are more likely to be picked up on the job or by taking some outside classes on topics such as marketing or public speaking.

## Data Collection, Management, and Analysis

As noted, this role might land within the tech services category or might just as easily be identified as an administrative or management function to support high-level decision making. In general, however, data collection, management, and analysis are likely to become embedded roles throughout the organization in order to best support both departmental and enterprise strategic goals. For the immediate future, it's likely that data librarian roles will be most prevalent in large libraries or institutions that can afford the costs associated with gathering and mining "big data."

All four of these areas—public, technical, administrative, and data services—offer opportunities to move into management positions, if that's a direction you'd like to go. Although each organization has a different hierarchy of terms, generally these positions include, in order of increasing responsibility (and salary), *supervisor, manager, director* (at the department level), *head,* and *dean* or *director* of the library. Larger organizations may also have *assistant, associate,* and *deputy* positions to further subdivide responsibilities. On the other hand, some job descriptions may say "public services librarian" and indicate a position that is essentially a department head supervising six professionals. Consequently, if you're doing a job search, keep in mind that every library has its own unique terminology for management positions.

## Multifunctional or Cross-Departmental Positions

There are a number of roles within librarianship that are based on the ability to integrate several of the functions described earlier into a single position. Some of these are as follows:

**Archivist/curator.** Responsible for managing the resources of a specialized collection of historical significance. The collection may include books, documents, letters, photographs, memorabilia, multimedia, and other materials. The archivist may be responsible for processing the items or may oversee the work of others (e.g., catalogers or a digitization team). Archival collections may be found in public or academic libraries, as well as many special libraries. Archivists often combine a history degree with their LIS skills and also need to be adept at managing donor relations, that is, have strong people skills when needed.

**Data analyst.** As noted, use data and data analysis tools to analyze, interpret, and deploy analytics to inform the development of user services and community outreach, among other programs. Such data can also be used to justify budget requests, to make collection development decisions and to provide support for innovative new programs.

**Digital asset manager.** An emerging role that, like data analyst, is being defined on a daily basis as more and more organizations determine new strategic uses for their knowledge assets.

**Government documents librarian.** Oversees the library's collection of government documents, including hearing transcripts, reports, periodicals, and statistical data. Govdocs librarians have mastered both the unique Superintendent of Documents (SuDocs) classification system and an understanding of the legislative, judicial, and executive branch processes that produce the documents in question. With the mandated migration of government documents to the Internet, this job increasingly involves aggregating and organizing online resources. Primarily found in larger academic libraries and those libraries (public and academic) designated as depository libraries. Entails strong organizational skills, plus the patience and/or passion necessary to stay current with the extraordinarily complex government information environment.

**Map librarian**. Responsible for preserving and maintaining a collection made up primarily of maps and related cartographic materials. This type of collection can be found in academic institutions, some public libraries, and some special library collections. Maps included in such a collection are often thematic, that is, historic, scientific, demographic, and so on. A good career choice for those with an innate love of maps who have also mastered the organizing principles of map cataloging and classification. Focus is generally on managing a specialized collection rather than on interacting with people, although in some situations (e.g., working geology collections), this job involves substantial patron interaction.

**Photo-archivist**. Responsible for preserving and maintaining an archive of thematically related photographs, for example, a history collection or a design-awards collection. Can be found in public or academic libraries with special collections, as well as in special libraries, wherever a collection of thematic photographs may be maintained. This job requires skills similar to those of a map librarian, substituting a passion for photography for that of cartography.

**Rare books librarian**. Similar to archivists, curators, and photo-archivists, rare books librarians are responsible for maintaining a specialized collection of materials—in this case, rare books. Usually found in special libraries, or in major academic institutions, whose rare book collections are often contributed by donors. Many of these books are now being digitized for preservation purposes and to make their contents available to a wider community of scholars. Combines a love and knowledge of rare books with knowledge of publishing, printing, and book preservation. Similar to an archivist position, this role also occasionally demands strong people skills, as when managing donor relations.

**Special collections librarian**. A librarian who manages a specialized collection, which might include rare books, photographs, and original manuscripts. Often special collections are housed within a larger library, such as a major public or academic library, and they rarely circulate. A *special collection* differs from a *special library* in that the latter is an entire library established by its host organization (e.g., a business or professional association) to meet the needs of that organization. As noted for map librarians and photo-archivists, special collections librarians generally must have solid knowledge of their collection's topic or focus area, as well as an understanding of how to organize and maintain it. The amount of people interaction is unique to each collection.

## Is a Traditional LIS Career Path for You?

Is it important to you to be associated with a public service or education mission? If so, then working in a public, school, or academic library might be a great option for you. Do you thrive in a structured workplace? Do you look forward to sharing professional camaraderie with other LIS professionals in your workplace? Would you feel "out of place" working in a nonlibrary setting? Then you may want to seriously explore one of the career paths open through public, school, or academic librarianship.

# Resources

## Multidisciplinary Coverage of Traditional Librarianship

*Periodicals*
*Note: There are many periodicals in the LIS world that focus on specific aspects of information and library work. However, there are also many whose coverage spans the entire range of LIS environments. The following publications are representative of some of the best-known and most highly respected cross-disciplinary periodicals.*

*Against the Grain.* Against the Grain, 1989–. 6/yr. ISSN 1043–2094.
www.against-the-grain.com
With the stated goal of "linking publishers, vendors & librarians," *Against the Grain* is the brainchild of Katina Strauch, assistant dean for Technical Services and Collection Development at Addletsone Library, College of Charleston. *ATG* is a terrific source of information about trends among libraries, publishers, and vendors. Since the dynamics among these three groups are increasingly complex (but also offer many potential job opportunities), *ATG* can be a good starting point for exploring alternative LIS careers. *ATG* also sponsors the annual Charleston Conference (www.katina.info/conference).

*American Libraries.* American Library Association, 1907–. 11/yr. ISSN 0002–9769.
www.ala.org/alonline
Sent to all ALA members, *American Libraries* provides an excellent overview of the current state of affairs for traditional libraries throughout the country. As the official organ of the organization, the magazine's content reflects a combination of ALA news and information and other contributed articles on topics of interest to librarians.

*D-Lib Magazine: The Magazine of Digital Library Research,* 1995–. Bimonthly. ISSN 1082–9873.
www.dlib.org
Focuses on "digital library research and development, including but not limited to new technologies, applications, and contextual social and economic issues." A place for thought leaders among the digital library community to share knowledge. Free archives at the website.

*First Monday: Peer-Reviewed Journal on the Internet.* University of Illinois at Chicago, 1996–. Monthly. ISSN 1396–0466.
www.firstmonday.org
Hosted by the University of Illinois at Chicago's library staff for nearly 20 years, *First Monday* is an open-access, peer-reviewed journal devoted to the study of the Internet and its related issues and impacts. Its advisory board—and contributors—represent the thought leaders in this area. A challenging, and important, publication on an important topic for all LIS professionals.

*Library Journal.* Reed Business Information, 1876–. 20/yr. ISSN 0363–0277.
www.libraryjournal.com
The most important resource for broad-based coverage of libraries, the library profession, and the industries that support it. *LJ* issues include news items, an events calendar, industry analyses, vendor overviews, features, profiles, and several special issues per year. Its book reviews are relied on by librarians for their objectivity and usefulness.

The website is an extraordinarily content-rich resource with archived articles, salary surveys, a career resource center, and job postings all available for free. (Key resource)

*Library Leadership & Management.* Library Leadership and Management Association, American Library Association, 1985–. Quarterly. ISSN 1945–8851.

Official journal of the Library Leadership and Management Association (an ALA division), *LL&M* focuses its peer-reviewed articles on "assisting library administrators and managers at all levels as they deal with day-to-day challenges." An important resource for those in library management or professional leadership roles.

## Associations

AMERICAN LIBRARY ASSOCIATION (ALA)

www.ala.org

The most important player in the traditional library profession. ALA's mission is to provide "leadership for the development, promotion, and improvement of library and information services and the profession of librarianship in order to enhance learning and ensure access to information for all." Representing public, academic, and school libraries, ALA is the only library organization that seeks to promote strong libraries of all types throughout society. The annual conference in June is huge, diverse, and often overwhelming for newcomers, but well worth attending at least once every several years for those who can afford to do so. Membership includes a subscription to the monthly *American Libraries* magazine. Discounted memberships for students. (For an excellent overview of the challenges facing ALA, see "ALA and Reunifying Librarianship" by Daniel O'Connor and Phil Mulvaney, *Library Journal,* March 1, 2014; http://lj.libraryjournal.com/2014/01/opinion/backtalk/ala-and-the-re-unification-of-librarianship/.)

AMERICAN SOCIETY FOR INFORMATION SCIENCE AND TECHNOLOGY (ASIST)

www.asis.org

With a primary mission of "leading the search for new and better theories, techniques, and technologies to improve access to information," ASIST draws its membership from the computer science, linguistics, management, librarianship, engineering, law, medicine, chemistry, and education disciplines. Its website includes information about the society, its goals and programs; memberships; and many special-interest groups and chapters, including multiple student chapters. ASIST holds an annual conference (proceedings available) plus several special-topic gatherings. Substantially discounted student memberships.

CANADIAN LIBRARY ASSOCIATION

www.cla.ca//AM/Template.cfm?Section=Home

CLA represents 57,000 library workers, vendors, public library board members, and LIS students in graduate or community college programs throughout Canada. The organization includes 22 special interest groups (e.g., action for literacy, entrepreneurship in librarianship, library and information services for older people) and numerous student chapters. Check the website for library career resources. CLA offers substantially discounted memberships for students.

NEW MEMBERS ROUND TABLE (NMRT)

www.ala.org/nmrt/new-members-round-table

The focus of NMRT is to help those new to the profession find ways to engage and participate in association professional activities. Its goals include structuring "formal opportunities for involvement and/or training for professional association committee experiences on the national, state, and local levels" and developing "ongoing programs for library school students that encourage professional involvement and networking." The NMRT electronic discussion list provides a way to connect with peers across the country.

*Online Resources*
ALA ELECTRONIC DISCUSSION LISTS
> http://lists.ala.org/sympa
> Explore and sign up for one or more of ALA's approximately 350 electronic discussion lists, hosted by ALA's many divisions and special interest groups.

## Public Librarianship

*Books*
De La Pena McCook, Kathleen. *Introduction to Public Librarianship, 2d ed.* Neal-Schuman, 2011. 524p. ISBN 1555706975.
> Public libraries exist in a complex world of service mission, community expectations, government oversight, demographic diversity, and technological upheaval. McCook does an excellent job of helping students understand that complexity, but effectively makes the case that public libraries can nevertheless be well-managed resources of leadership and community impact.

Prentice, Ann E. *Public Libraries in the 21st Century.* Libraries Unlimited, 2010. 222p. ISBN 1591588537.
> Prentice, former dean of the University of Maryland MLIS program, charts the reemerging role of public libraries as the centers of their communities. An inspiring read for those committed to the traditional role of public libraries (the people's universities) as well as their future ability to improve the lives of the individuals and various constituencies within their communities.

*Periodicals*
*Public Libraries.* Public Library Association, 1961–. Bimonthly. ISSN 0163–5506.
> www.ala.org/ala/pla/plapubs/publiclibraries/publiclibraries.htm
> The official publication of PLA, *Public Libraries* covers industry news, association updates, and articles, columns, and feature stories of value to those managing the country's more than 9,000 public libraries. Recent articles (accessible to the public at the magazine's website) have included "Opposing the USA Patriot Act," "Branch Management," and "Increasing Technical Services Efficiency to Eliminate Cataloging Backlogs." (Key resource)

*Associations*
ASSOCIATION FOR RURAL & SMALL LIBRARIES (ARSL)
> http://arsl.info/
> "A network of people dedicated to the positive growth of rural and small libraries and a collection of resources relevant to member needs," ARSL is an active, engaged group of individuals (including librarians, students, retirees, friends, volunteers, and library staff) dedicated to sustaining their libraries in small communities and rural areas throughout the United States.

PUBLIC LIBRARY ASSOCIATION (PLA)

www.pla.org

Founded in 1944, PLA supports its more than 9,000 members through "a diverse program of communication, publication, advocacy, continuing education, and programming." Membership includes a subscription to the bimonthly *Public Libraries* magazine. PLA also publishes books and reports, offers educational symposiums as well as a biannual national conference, and supports various advocacy programs. Check out the PLA website for information about PLA committees and advocacy groups, publications, and information resources about public librarianship. Student memberships available through primary ALA membership.

URBAN LIBRARIES COUNCIL (ULC)

www.urbanlibraries.org

ULC membership comprises approximately 150 public libraries that are located in major U.S. metropolitan areas and the vendors who support them. The organization's focus is on challenges and opportunities unique to urban libraries serving large and diverse populations and on serving "as a forum for sharing best practices resulting from targeted research, education and forecasting." Membership is at the organization level only.

*Online Resources*

LIBRARY FACT SHEETS

www.ala.org/tools/libfactsheets

A wide-ranging collection of key statistics about all of America's libraries, including numbers of libraries by type, types of services provided, numbers of staff by type of library, information technology stats, total library expenditures with breakdowns by categories of spending and by type of library, and funding sources.

PUBLIB LISTSERV

https://bestofpublib.wordpress.com/2012/01/15/subscribe-to-the-publib-listserve-part-deux/

Founded in 1992, PubLib covers (among other topics): collection development, acquisitions, management and weeding, including traditional and new media; reference services; issues related to library facilities— security, new buildings, renovations; policy and guidance; trustee relationships; Internet access for staff and public; intellectual freedom; library administration; sundry library "how-tos" and queries for equipment; personnel issues; public library jobs and related conferences. Check the website for instructions on how to subscribe. See also *The Best of PubLib,* a collection of previous discussions at https://bestofpublib.wordpress.com/.

RISING TO THE CHALLENGE: RE-ENVISIONING PUBLIC LIBRARIES

http://csreports.aspeninstitute.org/Dialogue-on-Public-Libraries/2014/report

Published in 2014 by the Aspen Institute Dialogue on Public Libraries, and described as "a multi-stakeholder forum to explore and champion new thinking on U.S. public libraries, with the goal of fostering concrete actions to support and transform public libraries for a more diverse, mobile and connected society...focuses on the impact of the digital revolution on access to information, knowledge and the conduct of daily life." The report explores what the forum identified as the three key assets of public libraries: people, place, and platform.

## School Librarianship

*Books*

Weisburg, Hilda K. *School Librarian's Career Planner.* ALA Editions, 2013. 136p. ISBN 978–0838911785.

A terrific resource for soon-to-be or current school librarians who are taking a proactive stance regarding building a sustainable career in school librarianship. Given the multitude of changes going on in schools today, Weisburg's book is a timely guide to topics such as landing your first job, acing the interview, polishing your skills, and more.

*Whole School Library Handbook 2.* Blanche Woolls and David V. Loertscher, eds. ALA Editions, 2013. 176p. ISBN 9780838911273.

Building on the successful model of ALA's *Whole Library Handbook* (ALA Editions, 2013), Woolls and Loertscher have produced a work that's basically "everything you wanted to know about school libraries but couldn't figure out who to ask." Articles, resources, tools, checklists, and more—an eclectic, engaging, and highly useful reference for anyone interested in school libraries.

Woolls, Blanche. *The School Library Media Manager, 3d ed.* Libraries Unlimited, 2004. 352p. ISBN 1591581826.

It may well be that Blanche Woolls knows more about school librarianship than anyone else in the country. This guide, written primarily for SLMC students but also of use to practitioners, covers all aspects of school library media centers: history, management, facilities, personnel, budget, services, and issues such as filtering, federal mandates, and eliciting faculty and administrative engagement. A key resource, due for an update. (Key resource)

*Periodicals*

*Knowledge Quest.* American Association of School Librarians, 1997–. 5/yr. ISSN 1094–9046.

The official journal of AASL, *Knowledge Quest* focuses on issues of interest to building-level media specialists, supervisors, library educators, and others involved in managing school library media centers. Check the website for excellent archived articles; students considering this career path should especially see Carol A. Brown's article, "Trends and Issues: What's Important for the 21st Century School Librarian?" *Knowledge Quest* continues the previous AASL publication, *School Library Media Quarterly.*

*Library Media Connection.* Linworth Books/ABC-CLIO, 1982–. Bimonthly. ISSN 1542–4715.

www.librarymediaconnection.com/lmc/

For and by librarians, *LMC* focuses on "the issues most important and relevant to school librarians and educators today." Topics covered may include technology, literacy, advocacy, and student engagement, among others.

*School Library Journal.* Reed Business Information, 1961–. Monthly. ISSN 0362–8930.

www.schoollibraryjournal.com

Provides information, resources, and insights for librarians who work with kids and young adults, whether in schools or public libraries. Focus is on integrating "libraries into the school curriculum," while also helping school librarians "become leaders in the areas of technology, reading, and information literacy, and create high-quality collections for children and young adults." The website offers archives and a career center for subscribers only.

*School Library Monthly*. Libraries Unlimited, 2009–. 8/school year. ISSN 2166–160X.
www.schoollibrarymonthly.com/
Formerly *School Library Media Activities* (1984–), *School Library Monthly* provides insights and information designed to support K–12 librarians as they collaborate on instruction and information literacy initiatives with teachers. Written by practitioners who share best practices, success stories, and lessons learned.

*Teacher Librarian: The Journal for School Library Professionals*. Rockland Press, 1998–. Bimonthly. ISSN 1481–1782.
www.teacherlibrarian.com/about_us/magazine.html
Previously known as *Emergency Librarian*, this publication explores topics of interest to school librarians who focus strongly on a teaching mission. Articles address such areas as collaboration, leadership, technology, and management. A useful collection of annotated links, articles, guides, and white papers may be accessed for free via the website.

*Associations*

AMERICAN ASSOCIATION OF SCHOOL LIBRARIANS (AASL)
www.ala.org/aasl/
The stated mission of the American Association of School Librarians is to "advocate excellence, facilitate change, and develop leaders in the school library media field." To further that mission, AASL promotes and supports collaboration among school librarians, advocates for leadership roles, encourages members to participate as "active partners in the teaching/learning process," and generally supports such initiatives as information literacy and life-long learning.

Student memberships available through primary ALA membership.

CANADIAN ASSOCIATION FOR SCHOOL LIBRARIES (CASL)
www.caslibraries.ca
A division of the Canadian Library Association, CASL's mission is to provide a national voice for and promote excellence in school libraries, to provide members with professional growth opportunities, and to promote all forms of reading and information literacy. Publishes *School Libraries in Canada Online* (www.schoollibraries.ca).

*Online Resources*

AASL RECRUITMENT TO SCHOOL LIBRARIANSHIP
www.ala.org/aasl/education/recruitment
Information about careers as school library media specialists, including job outlook, state licensing, information about the job itself, and education requirements. (Key resource)

Traska, Maria R, "District Library Supervisors Under Duress," *American Libraries*, 45(11/12) (November/December 2014), 34–38.
www.americanlibrariesmagazine.org/article/district-library-supervisors-under-duress
Summarizes and provides context for the results of the Lilead Project, which surveyed 25,000 supervisors nationwide in districts with 25,000 or more students. The findings are discouraging, but provide important

data points and benchmarks for those currently in or contemplating a school library career.

## Academic Librarianship

*Books*

Alire, Camile A. and G. Edward Edwards. *Academic Librarianship.* Neal-Schuman, 2010. 383p. ISBN 1555707025.
From two well-known library leaders, *Academic Librarianship* provides an overview of not only the work of academic librarianship but also what it takes to succeed in a career as an academic librarian given the rapidly evolving nature of the profession.

Budd, John M. *The Changing Academic Library: Operations, Culture, Environments, 2d ed.* American Library Association, 2012. 412p. ISBN 0838986129. (Key resource)
Budd, widely respected for his thought leadership within the profession, delivers an excellent overview of the challenges and opportunities facing academic librarians today. The second edition both expands on the topics introduced in the first (2005) edition and brings in the myriad changes that have been disrupting higher education since then. This book works equally well as a thorough introduction to the profession for students or as a good environmental scan for practitioners. (Key resource)

Crumpton, Michael A. and Nora J. Bird. *Handbook for Community College Librarians.* Libraries Unlimited, 2013. 172p. ISBN 9781610693462.
Community college librarianship is a career option not often discussed in MLIS programs, yet it can be an incredibly rewarding and fun type of academic librarianship. Crumpton and Bird provide a great overview of this role and how to best support the diverse students you're likely to work with.

*Embedded Librarianship: What Every Academic Librarian Should Know.* Alice L. Daugherty and Michael F. Russo, eds. Libraries Unlimited, 2013. 201p. ISBN 1610694139.
A collection of 12 articles on academic embedded librarianship that addresses various aspects of this collaborative integrated approach to information literacy coaching.

*How to Stay Afloat in the Academic Library Job Pool.* Teresa Y. Neely, ed. ALA Publishing, 2011. 152p. ISBN 0838910801.
Those who've negotiated the academic library job process know that it can often be complex, confusing, and opaque—why *is* that search committee waiting for six months before making a hiring decision??? Neely and her contributors, academic librarians at the University of New Mexico and experienced search committee members, explain how the academic library search process works, what to expect, and how to best position yourself to succeed in your quest for a library job in academe.

*Periodicals*

*The Chronicle of Higher Education.* Editorial Project for Education, 1966–. Weekly. ISSN 0009–5982.
http:// chronicle.com
The leading publication for news, in-depth features, analysis, and job information for higher education, including academic librarianship.

The Chronicle provides a useful overview of all aspects of higher education—as an industry, a public good, and a profession. The website offers some content for free (including a very extensive listing of posted jobs—search on "librarians/library administration"), but you must be a subscriber to access its large online archive of articles and career information. An extremely valuable resource for those interested in academic librarianship.

*College & Research Libraries.* Association of College and Research Libraries, 1939–. Bimonthly. ISSN 0010–0870.
http://crl.acrl.org/
Articles of interest to those working in and/or managing college and research libraries. Topics covered include research studies, case studies, new projects and initiatives (how undertaken, what results), and issues discussions. Articles are archived at the website, but are available to ACRL members only. A refereed journal. See also ACRL's *College & Research Libraries News,* which provides articles on the current trends and issues affecting academic and research libraries. Regular columns focus on scholarly communication, Internet resources and reviews, grants and acquisitions, and technology, among other topics. (Key resource)

*Journal of Academic Librarianship.* Pergamon, 1975–. Bimonthly. ISSN 0099–1333.
www.journals.elsevier.com/the-journal-of-academic-librarianship
A highly regarded, refereed journal, *JAL* provides academic librarians a forum through which to share ideas, challenges, scenarios for the future, and solutions for today. Much of the content is research based, which provides authority for the ideas discussed. An excellent and useful, if expensive, professional resource.

*Associations*

ASSOCIATION OF COLLEGE & RESEARCH LIBRARIES (ACRL)
www.ala.org/acrl/
ACRL describes itself as "a professional association of academic librarians and other interested individuals" dedicated to "enhancing the ability of academic library and information professionals to serve the information needs of the higher education community and to improve learning, teaching, and research." Its membership is primarily individuals, rather than institutions, and among them, those individuals represent many diverse communities (see Appendix A for an overview of ACRL's committees, task forces, and discussion groups). ACRL publishes *College & Research Libraries, College & Research Libraries News, Choice,* and a number of highly regarded monographs.

ASSOCIATION OF RESEARCH LIBRARIES (ARL)
www.arl.org
The ARL mandate is to influence "the changing environment of scholarly communication and the public policies that affect research libraries and the communities they serve." The membership is made up of academic institutions; there are no individual memberships. Its website, however, has a rich collection of resources for everyone. See especially the sections on Diversity (www.arl.org/diversity), Career Resources (www.arl.org/careers/index.html), and the Leadership and Career Development Program (www.arl.org/diversity/lcdp/index.html),

all resources and programs geared toward expanding the number of librarians from underrepresented racial and ethnic groups in academic librarianship.

CANADIAN ASSOCIATION OF COLLEGE AND UNIVERSITY LIBRARIES (CACUL)

www.abqla.qc.ca/tags/canadian-association-college-and-university-libraries

CACUL "promotes professional development opportunities to its membership of almost 700 academic librarians," while also offering members "the opportunity to build community" through its electronic discussion list, and professional development workshops and conference programming. Check the website for professional development resources, CACUL publications, and the association's online discussion list.

LIBRARIANSHIP IN FOR-PROFIT EDUCATIONAL INSTITUTIONS INTEREST GROUP

www.ala.org/acrl/aboutacrl/directoryofleadership/interestgroups/acr-iglfpei

This special interest group within ACRL is intended as "a forum for librarians in for-profit educational institutions to network, share knowledge, and collaborate on tasks, direction, and issues specific to their roles within the for-profit education industry." Because academic librarians within for-profit institutions often receive much less support than those in not-for-profit colleges and universities, this group can be an especially valuable source of information and support for them.

*Online Resources*

ACRLOG

http://acrlog.org/

ACRLog provides "blogging by and for academic research librarians," to quote its tagline. The nine bloggers hail from nine different academic institutions across the United States, so represent a broad spectrum of insights and commentary. A terrific resource for current and would-be academic librarians.

KEEPING UP WITH...

www.ala.org/acrl/publications/keeping_up_with

Monthly current awareness/trends resource from ACRL. All online editions focus on a single topic, such as "critical librarianship," "competency-based education," and "patron-driven acquisitions."

# Notes

1. "Occupational Outlook Handbook: Librarians," accessed at www.bls.gov/ooh/education-training-and-library/librarians.htm.

2. Amy Affelt. *The Accidental Data Scientist*, Information Today, 2015, p. 4.

3. ALA Library Fact Sheet 1—Number of Libraries in the United States, accessed at www.ala.org/tools/libfactsheets/alalibraryfactsheet01.

4. ALA Library Fact Sheet 2—Number of Paid Staff in the United States, accessed at www.ala.org/tools/libfactsheets/alalibraryfactsheet02.

5. *2012 ALA-APA Salary Survey*, Lorelle Swader, Project Director, American Library Association-Allied Professional Association: The Organization for the Advancement of Library Employees and American Library Association, Office for Research and Statistics, 2012, pp. 22–36.

6. ALA Library Fact Sheet 1.

7. ALA Library Fact Sheet 2.

8. "2012–2013 Average Starting Teacher Salaries by State," National Education Association, accessed at www.nea.org/home/2012–2013-average-starting-teacher-salary.html.

9. *Online Dictionary for Library and Information Science (ODLIS)*, ABC-CLIO/Libraries Unlimited, accessed at www.abc-clio.com/ODLIS/odlis_A.aspx.

10. ALA Library Fact Sheet 1.

11. ALA Library Fact Sheet 2.

12. ALA Library Fact Sheet 2.

13. *2012 ALA-APA Salary Survey*, pp. 37–55.

# 4
# Nontraditional LIS Career Paths

*While there is no magic bullet to guarantee success...
the general direction is clear: the greatest chance of
success will come from affiliating the library with
the unique goals of its parent organization and the
needs of the people working to hit those targets. This
goes beyond parroting a mission statement or tweak-
ing position names and titles; it demands practitioners who are strategic thinkers. Librarians must
become the catalysts for increasing the productivity
and effectiveness of their customers, whether they be
bench scientists or management consultants.*
—Dr. James M. Matarazzo and Dr. Toby Pearlstein,
*Special Libraries: A Survival Guide*

As we've seen, traditional career paths can offer substantial rewards for
those who pursue them. So, too, can nontraditional ones. However, because
there are so many different ways to approach nontraditional work, it can
sometimes be challenging to figure out where to start. And because nontraditional opportunities are limited only by imagination, the following should
be considered a sampling of possible paths.

For starters, there are a number of ways LIS professionals can choose
to reframe their skills in nontraditional ways. These include:

- Doing nontraditional things within a traditional library setting
  ("traditional," for purposes of this overview, being public, school, and
  academic).

- Performing traditional library roles but within an organization whose mission is not librarianship or education (usually a special library).
- Taking on nontraditional roles within traditional special libraries.
- Doing these nontraditional activities embedded in operational units.
- Performing library-focused activities outside of—but for—libraries and librarians.
- Building on skills honed in a library-based job by bridging those skills into a new, nonlibrary role.
- Creating your own job, either within a library or for a nonlibrary organization.

**Performing nontraditional activities within a traditional library setting.** The most innovative public, school, and academic libraries offer excellent opportunities to create nontraditional career paths within their structures. This approach is based on taking an entrepreneurial approach to your career and looking for places to create unique contributions. For example, you might combine a subject expertise with a functional expertise to create your own professional niche.

Say, for instance, in your job as a public librarian, you've developed a knack for creating highly effective outreach programs for specific underserved populations. Based on that ability, you might, in addition to creating those programs, decide to put your ideas into a best-practices idea bank that can be made accessible to public librarians throughout the region or perhaps nationally. You might eventually write articles or a book about unique outreach programs and ways to conceive, plan, and execute them, and then perhaps give workshops to other public librarians on how to do this. You will have created a new role based on your specialized skills, one that adds unique value to your public library employer while also establishing your expertise among other potential employers, clients, or constituencies.

**Performing traditional library roles but within an organization whose mission is not librarianship or education.** This reflects the traditional definition of special librarianship, where an individual or a team of librarians acquires or licenses, organizes, distributes, and maintains information resources that support the strategic goals of the organization. Special librarians' responsibilities have generally fallen within the categories of:

1. Identifying, aggregating, and managing internal information.
2. Gathering, analyzing, synthesizing, and presenting external information.
3. Creating content, systems, and/or services and products for internal and/or external use.

Depending on the size of the organization or its library, your specific job responsibilities might include one or all of these. Naturally, the characteristics of your job would also be influenced by what sort of special library you were in—generally, categorized by subject area or discipline covered (aerospace engineering, horticulture, pro rodeo), type of material in the collection (e.g., industry standards, original manuscripts, photographs), or type of institution (perhaps a corporation, trade association, cultural institution, or government agency, among other possibilities).

Although the centralized *corporate* resource—alternatively called the corporate library, the business or corporate information center, the knowledge center, and/or some other variation thereof—is losing popularity to a distributed or functional-team-based model, there are still many highly successful special libraries. (How many? According to numbers cited by ALA on its "Number of Libraries in the United States" web page, there are more than 7,616, not counting those found within the armed forces (265) or government agencies (1,006).[1] Also, as part of those libraries' statistics, many organizations such as trade associations, nonprofits, and cultural institutions continue to employ librarians to support staff and membership inquiries as well as the information-gathering and distribution mandate of the organization.

Needless to say, special libraries might be located in almost any organization. Some of the most likely candidates are:

- Advertising agencies
- Architecture firms
- Art museums, institutes, and centers
- Consulting firms
- Corporations, medium to large, in all industries
- Correctional institutions (e.g., prison libraries)
- Cultural institutions—museums, zoos, historical societies, presidential libraries
- Engineering firms
- Financial services, investment, market analyst, and venture capital firms
- Genealogy organizations
- Government agencies—federal, state, local
- Law firms
- Marketing and public relations (PR) agencies
- Medical libraries of all types including those in
  - Hospitals, university health centers, veterinary centers, and medical research facilities
  - Health/medical/life sciences companies such as those specializing in pharmaceuticals, bioengineering, or biomechanical devices
  - Professional associations supporting the medical and health sciences fields
  - Academic institutions focused on training health professionals such as doctors and nurses
- Military—on a base, as part of an operational unit, or with military academies
- Music libraries, including those for orchestras
- News organizations—print, broadcast (although this is a contracting area)
- Nonprofits

- Print media groups—magazine and book publishers
- Private libraries (often owned by individuals, families, clubs, corporations, or foundations)
- Professional and trade associations
- Recruiting (employment) firms
- Religious institutions (e.g., churches and synagogues)
- Research institutes and think tanks
- Science and technology firms
- Corporate universities and/or enterprise training and development departments
- Theater and performing arts organizations
- Visual and art resources/film organizations

As noted, the roles and opportunities opening up within the special librarianship space are different from those of previous years, but they can certainly be no less interesting or rewarding. However, it's also important to consider that in the first edition of this book (2006), the ALA source cited identified more than 9,500 special libraries, not counting armed forces or government libraries. With the current count at roughly 7,600, that's a decrease of just about 20 percent over the past seven years.

**Taking on nontraditional roles within traditional special libraries.** Many special librarians find their opportunities to align with organizational strategy have increased as they've been asked to help build learning portals, take on records management, and set up centralized competitive intelligence monitoring systems through the library, among other activities. The focus here is increasingly on collaboration with key functional units within the organization, based on an ability to understand and support the group's strategic mission.

This sort of opportunity depends, however, on your willingness and ability to connect outside the library and get your broad range of strategically valuable skills "on people's radar." Department heads and key decision makers won't know what you can do unless you take the initiative to show them your stuff.

The range of LIS activities and responsibilities possible within organizations is continually expanding. Some of the common roles today, however, may include:

- Organizing and maintaining a digital corporate archive.
- Designing and developing the user interface and user experience (UX) elements for the consumer-facing website of an e-commerce start-up.
- Leading or supporting creation of an enterprise-wide information architecture for organizing and providing access to an organization's information assets.
- Creating and/or managing internal information resources enterprise wide (may include materials such as knowledge databases, internal company communications, databases of employee expertise, customer presentations, client proposals, lab notes and/or engineering

drawings, a best-practices/lessons-learned database, and technical reports).

• Leading or assisting in process design to ensure that enterprise information resources are available at the point of need, that is, at key decision points; includes helping other departments use enterprise information strategically.

• Collaborating as the information specialist on other departments' projects and/or initiatives (such as new product development or market research).

• Developing and managing the organization's social media and content marketing strategy in alignment with key strategic goals.

• Conducting primary and secondary research on individuals, companies, industries, competitive threats, potential opportunities, legislative and regulatory impacts, demographic trends, market share, and similar business drivers.

• Creating customized content and/or information products such as executive information updates, internal and/or external newsletters, trend reports, ghost-written presentations/speeches/articles, meeting-prep briefings, executive-level current awareness alerts, issues backgrounders, and company blogs.

• Providing synthesis and/or analysis of research findings to use in decision support, for example, trends analysis, scenario forecasting, SWOT (strengths, weaknesses, opportunities, threats) analyses, data mining, and market opportunity assessment.

Another area of opportunity for LIS professionals is based on compliance issues related to the Sarbanes-Oxley Act of 2002, which mandates financial reporting requirements for U.S.-based, publicly held businesses. Known variously as SOX, Sarbox, or just Sarbanes–Oxley, this law vaulted the normally low-key world of records management and retention into the front lines of corporate financial and legal procedures. Often, many millions of dollars and possible prison terms ride on compliance with government regulations regarding documentation. Not surprisingly, substantial effort is now going into designing foolproof records management systems for storage and retrieval of critical financial and operations documents.

**Doing these nontraditional activities embedded in operational units.** Although an increasing number of special libraries are falling prey to budget cuts, many smart companies are nevertheless holding on to their intellectual assets by embedding their information experts (the librarians) into functional departments.

These may include marketing (market research skills), business development (competitive intelligence and industry analysis skills), research and development departments (primary and secondary research), product development (patent searching, usability studies), information systems (web portal development, knowledge management systems, information architecture), training and development (online tutorials, best-practices research, best-in-class topic resources), communications/PR (speech-writing, white papers, statistics, quotes), and executive decision support (executive information services, environmental scanning, futures forecasting). More recently, the emerging role of data analyst is playing across the strategic goals of numerous operational departments within large organizations.

David Shumaker's *The Embedded Librarian: Innovative Strategies for Taking Knowledge Where It's Needed* (InfoToday, 2012) identified the ways this role is being deployed throughout not only organizations but also academic institutions, schools, and public libraries. Shumaker's model of embedded librarianship within a special library setting assumed the existence of a central information center or corporate library, with some of its librarians working outside the library department, "embedded" into operational units as described earlier. However, in conversations with the author and fellow information professionals, it's becoming clear that in addition to understanding the role of embedded librarians, we need to consider an alternative possibility, which could be called "integrated" librarians, a term coined by information entrepreneur, author, and coach Mary Ellen Bates.

Integrated librarians perform work very similar to that identified by Shumaker for embedded librarians, with the difference being that the organization has no designated central library to which they report; there exists no dotted-line relationship between a corporate information center and the librarian because there no longer exists a corporate information center. Instead, integrated (special) librarians are incorporated as value-contributing members of whatever operations department they work within. Information professionals in these positions are rarely, if ever, called librarians; instead they go by any number of non-LIS business titles, many of which are identified further on in this chapter.

In addition to describing the emerging environment for embedded librarianship, Shumaker identified five key ways in which embedded librarians differ from traditional librarians, differences that apply equally well to integrated librarians:

- They anticipate rather than respond.
- They work with an entire community of users rather than a single client or patron.
- Service is tailored to the strategic needs of the group, rather than standardized.
- Success metrics are based on value added to the group's goal, rather than on number and outcome of individual transactions.
- The librarian is a collaborative partner rather than a service provider.

These key points vastly simplify the depth and sophistication of Shumaker's concepts, but make clear how effectively he's charted the differences between the old and new roles of many special librarians. (His book is a must-read for anyone contemplating a career as a special librarian, as is Matarazzo and Pearlstein's *Special Libraries: A Survival Guide* [Libraries Unlimited, 2013].)

**Performing library-focused activities outside of—but for—the library community.** Anyone who's worked in a school, public, or academic library for any length of time knows how these organizations work, which makes that individual an invaluable asset to organizations that market products or services to libraries. A quick check with the online *Librarian's Yellow Pages* (www.librariansyellowpages.com) identifies thousands of publications, products, and services under the headings of accessible products; audio producers/distributors/wholesalers; automation/software; book publishers/distributors/wholesalers; equipment/supplies; furniture & furnishings; government, IGO/NGO documents; online resources; periodicals/

serials; services; shelving/storage/display; and video producers/distributors/ wholesalers. All of these products and services are produced by vendors that employ individuals in product development, marketing, sales, product training, customer relations, tech support, and management—preferably professionals with a working knowledge of the library market.

In addition, a number of consulting, outsourcing, and temporary employment organizations that work with libraries offer yet another career alternative, one that often provides a high level of scheduling flexibility.

A representative list of types of jobs that are library focused but outside of libraries includes:

- Account rep/sales for library vendor
- Acquisitions editor for library/info science publisher
- Education director for library-related association
- Manager for library network or bibliographic utility, regional or national (e.g., Lyrasis)
- Industry analyst for company tracking LIS/education market
- Consultant (marketing, systems, organizational development, among other specializations)
- Recruiter for library employment, placement firm
- Faculty for MLIS degree program
- Vendor trainer

**Building on skills honed in a library-based job by bridging those skills into a new, nonlibrary functional role.** Have you developed an expertise in project management, team building, innovative marketing programs, content development, web design and implementation, community relations, or training? These are all skills that are readily portable into new organizations not necessarily associated with librarianship. A library director has the same skills necessary to run a nonprofit; a public library webmaster can be equally valuable to a start-up company; an instructional services librarian in an academic library can port these skills into another organization's training department.

This "leaving the profession" career option presents an interesting dilemma for a lot of LIS professionals. Many of us feel so much a part of the LIS community and its values that working in a field where we're no longer connected to it would feel, well, weird (at best). On the other hand, others might be ready for just such a change.

**Creating your own.** The tagline of Careerealism, a popular career site, is "because every job is temporary." Okay, not *every* job, but enough of them are potential budget-cut targets that being able to conceptualize and implement a new way to apply your skill set pretty much on the fly can be an extremely useful career edge. How to do this? Identify a need on the part of a potential client or employer and apply your skill set to creating a solution, resulting in a paying project or job.

In their book *The Start-Up of You*, authors Hoffman and Casnocha make the point that in order to adapt to and thrive within the unpredictability of today's employment environment, "we need to rediscover our entrepreneurial instincts and use them to forge new sorts of careers." Essentially, assert the authors, regardless of what profession you're in, "you need to also think of yourself as an entrepreneur at the helm of at least one living, growing start-up venture: *your career.*" In terms of creating your own job, this means that rather than thinking of your job as a fixed set of responsibilities, it might be wise to instead explore your organization for opportunities to deploy your skills in new ways.

How do you go about creating your own work? Once you become familiar with an organization and its goals, processes, markets, issues, and potential threats and opportunities, start looking for unmet needs. (This assumes, of course, that you've already done such a great job in your current position that you're seen as a reliable, responsible, and capable professional.) Think creative, think strategic, and see whether there's a role you can design that allows you to contribute in a new way. Write up your ideas in a proposal that focuses on benefits to the organization, ways your new responsibilities will align with strategic goals, and key aspects of the job you envision. Assume you'll be hit with questions about salary, title, handling current job or project responsibilities, and other "whatabouts," and be prepared to answer them thoughtfully and with confidence.

Creating your own job is one of the most rewarding ways to grow your career. It lets you define work parameters that reflect your unique skills and abilities. Since the job you're describing hasn't been previously codified into anyone's HR manual, you often have much greater flexibility in terms of title and salary. And you get the challenge of taking on new work and making it your own, instead of following the path that countless others before you have laid down.

## Building a Nontraditional Path

The number of these types of alternative career paths open to LIS professionals is, in fact, limited only by your imagination. You might be a library director for a professional medical association, a children's librarian in a natural history museum, researcher for an alternative magazine, director of a corporate business information center, librarian for an industry research center, manager of a hospital consumer health information center, digital archivist for a regional newspaper, information architect for a design firm, director of library services for a botanic gardens, or an information resources specialist for a Native American rights foundation. Or you might be performing an entirely new role whose title we haven't yet seen but that signals a cool new career path.

Here's an example of how some of these options might work for someone who not only works in a public library doing reference and patron Internet training but also has a background in the medical field. Some of these activities could be done full-time, some part-time, or as a sideline to your regular job.

- Become a corporate librarian or information specialist for bioengineering, veterinary medicine, pharmaceutical company.

- Become a consumer health specialist for a public library system, developing patron programs, online research guides, and a collection development alerting service for all of the system's libraries, and/or create a service based on these components that can be offered to all public libraries.

- Develop a research-oriented service for veterinarians, doctors, or other healthcare providers, creating information guides for their patients describing illnesses, treatments, and recommended resources (print and online), and/or create an alerting service for the vets and doctors on topics specific to their practices.

- Become a librarian or information specialist for a medical/healthcare-oriented trade or professional association, and/or establish an "on-demand" research capability for the organization's membership.

- Do research and analysis for a market research or investment firm specializing in the medical, healthcare, and/or consumer health industries.

- Create and teach an online course on medical research for one or more of the online nursing or LIS programs.

Obviously, not all of these ideas would be appropriate for every individual, but they illustrate ways to think more broadly about possibilities. Also, keep in mind that none of these necessarily requires a lifelong commitment or a permanent change away from a traditional library career. Instead, they may simply be steps in developing a dynamic, diverse, and resilient career as an information professional. Being an information strategist today does not mean you can't choose to become certified as a school librarian five years from now. The goal is to design a career flexible enough that it can grow *with* you, rather than *keep* you from growing.

# Workplace Environment

Nontraditional LIS work can be fun, challenging, and offer opportunities to engage in activities well beyond your comfort zone. Because you're surrounded by colleagues who rarely understand what information professionals do or know, you may be either underestimated or highly valued, depending on how good you are at positioning your skills strategically (more on that later).

Compared to jobs in many traditional library environments, a career in a nontraditional setting may allow you more flexibility in terms of job definition and structure, hours scheduling, and career growth. With less rigidly structured job categories, nontraditional positions may allow you to take on new opportunities and higher-level responsibilities more quickly than if you were in a public, academic, or school library.

You may be with a nonprofit, you may be working for a commercial entity, but whether you're engaged in primary research, competitive intelligence, market analysis, knowledge management, digital rights management, or data analysis, your goal will be to in some manner help the organization meet its strategic goals. Unless you're working for a nonprofit, the emphasis of all of your work will be on driving bottom-line revenues and profits plus future opportunities for your employer. For a nonprofit, your contribution may help expand membership, expand the visibility or impact of the organization, increase donations (or the number of donors), or directly support the mission of the organization with its constituency.

Although a nontraditional career path can offer stimulation and challenge, it can also be fraught with anxiety, for any number of reasons. First, special librarians are expected to have a very high level of professional knowledge about their topic area, because high-risk decisions (e.g., life-changing medical decisions, million-dollar corporate investments) may on occasion rest to a degree on their expertise. You'll need to not only know core LIS skills but also have a working knowledge of business basics, as well as the ability to stay on top of existing and emerging knowledge and information resources in your organization's core discipline and industry. Staying ahead of the knowledge curve can be exhilarating, exhausting, or both—often depending on how the week is going!

As described previously, corporate librarians face an additional challenge, as their libraries and information centers are being downsized or dismantled at an alarming rate. Job security simply doesn't exist, no matter how highly regarded the corporate library—or its library director. However, offsetting the decline of corporate libraries is, as noted, the emerging trend of embedded/integrated information professionals who become part of departmental teams such as marketing or product development or engineering. As part of such a team, your focus will be on accountability, speed, and active contribution. You'll be delivering just-in-time information, rather than collecting just-in-case resources. And you'll be evaluated on measurable outcomes and results, rather than on transactions and credentials.

# Types of Work

The types of work (and job titles) involved in a nontraditional career are diverse and constantly growing, as creative information professionals come up with new, innovative ways to use their skill sets. But a selective list of some real-life positions and activities culled from job listings, colleagues, discussion list postings, and recruiting agencies includes the following items, grouped by major types of work:

**Research Skills, Information Resources Roles**

- Business analyst
- Business development analyst
- Business information coordinator/officer/analyst/specialist
- Business intelligence analyst
- Competitive intelligence (CI) analyst
- Data analyst
- Donor/prospect research
- Executive information services
- Industry analyst
- Information associate
- Information resources specialist
- Information scientist
- Information services specialist
- Information specialist
- Knowledge analyst
- Knowledge resources specialist
- Legislative analyst
- Librarian
- Market analyst
- Market research
- Mergers and acquisitions (M&A) research
- Patent searcher
- Policy analyst
- Product analyst
- Product research
- Research associate
- Research librarian
- Research services team leader

- Risk management researcher
- Senior information analyst
- Social media researcher

## Information Organization Roles, Materials-Level

- Archival processor
- Authority control
- Cataloging/cataloging and metadata services librarian
- Document analyst
- Electronic document manager
- Electronic resources cataloger
- Indexer/abstracter
- Metadata specialist/librarian

## Information Organization/ Technology Roles, Systems-Level

- Archivist
- Corporate archivist
- Compliance information resources
- Data analyst
- Data curation
- Data manager
- Data mining
- Data scientist
- Data services librarian
- Database design analyst
- Database editor
- Database manager
- Digital archivist
- Digital assets/rights manager
- Digital collections coordinator
- Digital image control specialist

- Digital initiative librarian
- Digital library production services
- Digital preservation specialist
- Digital product manager
- Digital services librarian
- Director, archives and records
- Document controller, manager
- Document services coordinator
- Electronic documents librarian
- Electronic resources officer
- Electronic text and imaging center management
- Emerging technology specialist
- Enterprise content manager
- Health or science informatics administrator/analyst
- Imaging coordinator
- Information architect
- Information manager
- Information resource manager
- Information systems engineer
- Intranet manager
- Knowledge engineer
- Knowledge management/ manager
- Knowledge network specialist
- Learning resource center manager/coordinator
- Management information systems (MIS)
- Network designer
- Ontology conceptualization
- Photo-archivist

- Preservation coordinator
- Records conversion specialist
- Records manager/records management specialist
- RIM (records and information management) analyst
- Strategic information manager
- Systems architect
- Taxonomy building/taxonomist
- Technical information specialist
- Technology development librarian
- UX designer/specialist
- Video archivist
- Web content manager
- Web development librarian
- Web services librarian
- Website manager

## Content Roles

- Acquisitions editor (publishing)
- Chief content officer
- Content developer
- Content manager
- Content/information/resource aggregator
- Content/information/resource curator
- Content/information/resource developer
- Content/information/resource evaluator
- Content/information/resource licenser
- Content/information/resource marketer
- Corporate blogger

- Digital acquisitions coordinator
- Digital content manager
- Editor
- Electronic content manager
- Intellectual property analyst
- Manager, external content
- Social media specialist
- Web content producer

## Information Services/Resources Management Roles

- Business resource manager
- Chief information officer
- Chief knowledge officer
- Compliance manager
- Coordinator, information services
- Corporate librarian
- Curator
- Digital assets manager
- Digital resources librarian
- Director of research
- Director, archives
- Director, information services
- Director, information technology services
- Head curator
- Information center director
- Information officer
- Information resources officer
- Knowledge integrator
- Knowledge leader/manager/director
- Knowledge management services administrator
- Library director
- Manager of information services

- Manager, electronic text and imaging center
- Preservationist
- Research director
- Special collections librarian

**Additional Roles**

- Account manager/representative (sales or account management)
- Copyright specialist
- Embedded/integrated librarian
- Grants writer, manager
- Head, document delivery services

- Information project manager
- Information strategist
- Instructional designer
- Library consultant
- Marketing/copy writer
- Online community manager
- Product manager
- Project manager
- Social media strategist
- Training/teaching (internal, customer, or client)
- Vendor management

No doubt some of the roles I've identified could easily fall into one if not several of the other categories. In addition, what each of these jobs entails varies from employer to employer (and often project to project). However, you can get a good sense of the breadth of each by running the specific titles through job posting sites, including those specific to the LIS profession as well as the general and nonprofit sites (the LinkedIn Jobs feature can be especially helpful here). The individual listings should provide descriptions that indicate the job's scope, responsibilities, and requisite skills for a given employer or industry. Many will also indicate where these roles are located within the various organizations' departmental structure.

Keep in mind that the titles and roles listed earlier are simply a snapshot in time and only a selection of the opportunities LIS professionals are moving into. A year from now, there will undoubtedly be other titles and roles currently just below our professional radar.

## Salary and Education

One of the advantages of a nontraditional career path is that just as job descriptions may be more flexible, so may be the salaries. *In general,* positions for information professionals within nonlibrary organizations come with salaries that are higher—and more negotiable—than you would find at similar levels of responsibility within traditional libraries. In addition, there is often more room to negotiate nonsalary benefits, such as vacation time, flexible hours, professional development support, and tuition reimbursement.

According to the most recent SLA salary survey (2012), salaries for U.S.-based special librarians ranged from roughly $43,000 to $115,000, with a median salary of just over $70,000. For Canadian respondents, the salary range was $48,500 to $98,900, with a median salary of $70,000 Canadian.[2]

Although there will obviously be positions whose salaries are much lower—or higher—than the ranges indicated in the SLA survey, these numbers are a good indicator of what you might expect from nontraditional work.

In terms of education? Welcome to the world of lifelong learning. One of the greatest challenges—and delights—of a nontraditional career path is the ongoing need to expand and enrich your knowledge base. As noted, you'll need to have strong mastery of the basic LIS skills: depending on your position, this may include information research, organization, analysis, and presentation; content development and/or management; and/or system design and implementation.

You'll need to be familiar with basic business concepts, operations, and strategy in order to most effectively contribute to the goals of your organization, even if it's a nonprofit. And you'll need to understand the industry (or nonprofit space) in which your organization exists, as well as that industry's wealth of information resources. In addition, you'll want to understand your organization's competition, including any threats and/or opportunities they pose. Needless to say, all of these are moving targets, so you'll want to have a strategy in place that enables you to keep up with the dynamic knowledge environment that defines information work.

Wondering in which direction to expand your expertise? Here are some of the skill areas that may prove useful should you want to pursue a nontraditional LIS career (it should be noted that many of these would also be relevant to traditional LIS opportunities):

- Big data management
- Contract/vendor negotiation; purchasing and licensing
- Data analytics
- Digital rights management
- Document digitization and management
- External content integration
- Knowledge management
- Online content development
- Regulatory compliance
- Security/privacy
- Visualization tools (information, processes, and data)
- Web design/creation (especially UX)

For those following nontraditional LIS career paths, some of the major professional associations are Special Libraries Association (SLA), American Association of Law Libraries (AALL), Medical Library Association (MLA), Information Association for the Information Age (ASIS&T, formerly the Association for Information Science and Technology), and ARMA International (for records management). These and the many other associations listed at the end of this chapter often have core competency statements that indicate baseline skill levels for their members' professional roles, which is a great way to identify skills gaps or areas of potential growth for you.

For example, although SLA is currently revising its core competencies, its previous statement identified key abilities in four areas: managing information organizations, managing information resources, managing information services, and applying information tools and technologies. Other associations' core competency/professional benchmark statements cover similar ground and provide a solid starting point for identifying skills gaps you may have relative to the career path you seek.

# Exploring Nontraditional LIS Careers

As noted, nontraditional careers are basically limited only by your imagination, so when exploring the possible paths, you can be equally creative. As before, you'll want to combine two actions: gathering information and assessing your reaction to that information. Then be sure to record your responses in your career journal.

- To get a sense of job requirements for specific jobs that might interest you, go to several of the library employment sites and run specific job titles (e.g., any of those listed under "Types of Work" in this chapter). What skills and education do they require? Do the activities they describe appeal to you? What types of organizations offer these sorts of nontraditional jobs? Which ones do your current career skills align with? Which ones do your passions and interests align with? Can you imagine yourself doing this type of work?
  Also try running these job titles through some of the non-LIS job sites such as Monster.com and LinkedIn Jobs. Note your findings in your career journal and start building "job profiles" or descriptions for specific job types that interest you.

- Join SLA or any of the other relevant professional associations (if you're a student, use your student discount!) so you can network with LIS professionals in nontraditional roles in your geographic region and learn more about the work they do. Set up information interviews and ask questions that help define both the specifics of the jobs and their possible "goodness of fit" for you. (To get started, refer back to the interview questions suggested in Chapter 3.)

- Once you've joined a professional association, begin exploring any professional development resources on its website. With many associations providing multiple communities of interest, career guides, and topic resources, this is often an easy and effective way to check out paths that may engage you. Note any areas of particular interest and consider joining the appropriate communities of interest to learn more.

- To learn more about emerging nontraditional paths, monitor the key LIS job sites to see (1) what new job titles people are using to describe nontraditional positions, (2) what skills they call for, and (3) what departments these jobs fall within.

- If you're a student, organize a "special librarians' day" workshop and have local special librarians and nontraditional LIS professionals come and talk about their work and careers. Be prepared with questions that elicit information of value to your career exploration and record responses in your career journal. Be sure to send each speaker a thank-you note and consider following up with those whose career choices and paths most interest you. (Credit for this idea goes to former University of Denver student [now alum] Marcy Rodney, who landed her dream practicum after coming up with and organizing this program and inviting the special librarian she was hoping to meet.)

- Also if you're a student, interview several local nontraditional LIS professionals about their jobs and careers, with a focus on such questions as how they got their jobs, what skills they most rely on, what they wish they'd learned in grad school, what opportunities they see for LIS professionals, and perhaps other ways in which their organizations might use LIS skill sets. Then write up your findings for your student newsletter or online discussion group, as well as noting key points in your career journal.

- Now that you've gathered information, take some time to exercise your imagination. If a nontraditional path might be of interest, consider your "dream job" and all of its characteristics. Using the preference filters you worked through in Chapter 2, describe the specifics of both the work that you do and the environment in which you do it. Do you work with a small team or a large organization? Do you travel a lot? Is your work solitary or highly collaborative and engaged with others? Are you in a facilities-based library or working for a community organization or a corporate enterprise? What contributions are you making? Be as detailed and concrete as possible, so you can begin to build a profile of what your optimal nontraditional situation would be. Why? Because if you are considering this option, one of your biggest challenges will be to narrow down the choices to the ones that best fit you—so the more you know, the easier that will be.

### Why You Might Love a Nontraditional Career Path

A nontraditional career path can be exciting, financially rewarding, full of exhilarating challenges, and ripe with opportunities to create, innovate, and chart new territory. To a much greater extent than with a traditional career path, you'll be in charge of your own agenda. You'll often be able to negotiate your salary, benefits, and work schedule, and you may end up expanding the borders of your existing position if not creating an entirely new job description. The opportunities are potentially huge and are based to a large degree on your smarts, creativity, and ability to create solutions with your skills.

On the other hand, a nontraditional career can also be chaotic, unpredictable, unreliable, and crazy-making. Impossible deadlines and last-minute crises can be a regular feature of some of these jobs. There is often the professional isolation of being the only LIS professional in the organization, there is essentially *no* job security and often no visible path for professional advancement, and there are frequently no seasoned info pros to mentor you up through the ranks. In order to have a successful nontraditional career, you'll need to take charge of your career agenda, create your own opportunities, set your own priorities, and get used to continually demonstrating the value you deliver. You'll be out of your comfort zone on a regular basis.

For many, however, the benefits far outweigh the drawbacks. Remember the highly diverse career of Christine Hamilton-Pennell from Chapter 1? When asked about her work with her new employer, global enterprise Terumo BCT, she pointed out that ironically she had returned to the place where she started—as a librarian. "However, the twist is that I have never worked for a corporation before, much less a publicly-held corporation with dozens of offices in many countries; a medical device company in a very complicated space that spans manufacturing and innovation of medical devices, scientific and clinical indications, engineering, international regulatory concerns, and IT." One of the coolest things for Christine, however, is that at this point in her career, she's "learning tons each day" and working with a generationally diverse team of colleagues. Like many nontraditional information professionals, she thrives on new opportunities, especially ones that enable her to master new information and find new ways to contribute value.

When asked about the rewards of his very nontraditional LIS career path, Scott Brown, currently Cybrarian at Oracle, adjunct faculty in the San Jose State University iSchool, past president of the Association of Independent Information Professionals (AIIP) and SLA Fellow, had this to say:

> *I think we need to stop thinking in terms of "traditional" and "nontraditional" LIS careers. While there are still "traditional" positions in the LIS world, I think nontraditional career paths are now more the norm than the exception. And I think they are necessary and vital for LIS professionals, because nontraditional career paths allow us to gain breadth of experience and, just as importantly, needed skill sets that we can combine in powerful ways to drive our careers forward.*
>
> *For example, as part of my recent career path, I served as Content Development Editor for a publication and research house focused on corporate and special libraries. The experience and intangible gains from that position have served me extremely well going forward. The experience of writing regularly honed my ability to create content, write reports, and ultimately, bag my next job. By networking with and recruiting writers for the publication, I grew my professional network in ways that I simply could not have through other means. And, more importantly to me, I had a great time. The work was interesting, challenging, and very powerful in getting my career to the next level.*
>
> *That editing position is a great encapsulation of why I love my LIS career: There is* **so much cool stuff to do out there** *with information. . . . When I was graduating from my MLIS program, many of my colleagues were worried about finding a job. I had the same concerns, of course, but at the same time, I held this somewhat elusive sense that there was so much work out there that was interesting and cool, and I was willing to dive into it and learn to do it. I still feel that way. And I never want to lose that sense that there's more cool stuff to do, because I truly believe that. Look at some of what we're facing now in the information world: big data, analytics, the sheer flood of information, to name a few. What's not to get excited about?*
>
> *I never quite know where my interest might go next, but I do know, from this vantage point in my career, that almost every experience I've had—volunteering, work, projects, professional work, speaking—has contributed to building my career. What's important is to start to understand how you can combine your experiences and skills, to pay attention to what really interests you, and to be willing to dive in see what you can do.*

Yet another example of a nontraditional LIS career is my own. My most recent position was chief content officer for an online start-up, WebPsychology.com, where I was responsible for the overall content strategy and content development of the site. The job drew on my LIS skills of research, content curation, information evaluation, relationship building, and information creation, among others. It's a job I loved and found endlessly fascinating, but I find I'm drawn to use my LIS skills in other ways as well. Consequently, I now do content development for various clients via Dority & Associates, teach a course at the University of Denver in Alternative LIS Careers, present workshops and webinars on this topic, and am on the advisory board for Libraries Unlimited's Professional Learning Connection.

In addition, I've done both client and pro bono projects through my consulting company, Dority & Associates, Inc., have led a team of subject specialists in creating the first virtual academic library, been an executive information advisor to a telecommunications CEO, led the content creation team for a website focused on helping people with disabilities live their most independent lives, and completed a myriad of client projects related to information creation and dissemination. I've called on my LIS skills in every role and look forward to discovering the next cool way I can apply them. Currently I'm working on two interrelated projects, that is, creating a career website devoted to LIS career information and resources and offering LIS career-development courses online.

Not all nontraditional LIS jobs have a high level of diversity of opportunity and collaboration, of course, but many of them come close. Might nontraditional LIS work be a path for you? Possibly—if you thrive on change and challenge, are comfortable being in charge of your own outcomes, don't mind working outside of the library community, like to learn new things, and are okay moving *very fast* when circumstances demand. It can be a great option for individuals who do better with projects than with routine work, or those who feel constrained by the more structured career paths of traditional librarianship.

# Resources

## Books

Affelt, Amy. *The Accidental Data Scientist: Big Data Applications and Opportunities for Librarians and Information Professionals.* Information Today, 2015. 240p. ISBN 1573875110.
Director of Database Research for Compass Lexecon, Affelt is uniquely qualified to help LIS professionals understand big-data career opportunities and the knowledge necessary to pursue them. This is one of the emerging areas of professional opportunity for LIS grads and practitioners.

Law, Jonathan. *Business: The Ultimate Resource, 3d ed.* A&C Black, 2011. 1760p. ISBN 140812811X.
Like an MBA in a box, the third edition of *Business* follows the format of previous editions: hundreds of articles by topic thought leaders under the broad heading of "Best Practices"; a "Management Library" comprising overviews of important business books; a section devoted to profiles of 50 key business thinkers and "management giants" (both historical and contemporary) and the ideas for which they are known; a dictionary of key business and management terms; and over 200 pages of business

information sources, organized by topic (e.g., accounting, intellectual property, learning organization). Extensively cross-referenced, this reference book is a key resource for LIS professionals who need to become familiar with the business world and its vocabulary.

Lawson, Judy, Joanna Kroll, and Kelly Kowatch. *The New Information Professional: Your Guide to Careers in the Digital Age*. Neal-Schuman, 2010. 200p. ISBN 555706983.

Although this book was recommended as a resource in Chapter 1, it's also appropriate to note here for its wealth of job titles and descriptions that fall into the nontraditional category. This should be considered your starting point for exploring nontraditional LIS careers that entail working with/within organizations. (Key resource)

Matarazzo, James M. and Toby Pearlstein, with the assistance of Sylvia James. *Special Libraries: A Survival Guide*. Libraries Unlimited, 2013. 167p. ISBN1610692670.

Described as an advocacy book aimed at special/corporate librarians "who wish to retain their positions," this excellent compilation of savvy strategies and tactics pulls no punches when describing the fragile position of many special libraries today. However, the authors are both highly respected for their always-perceptive analysis of the special library environment, and theirs is the advice that's most likely to help you retain and strengthen that position. (Key resource)

Palmer, Kimberly. *The Economy of You: Discover Your Inner Entrepreneur and Recession-Proof Your Life*. Amacom, 2014. 239p. ISBN 0814432735.

Side-gig, side-hustle, microbusiness . . . whatever you call it, having a sideline or some regular freelance work can be a great way to not only create additional income but also test out potential full-time career paths and/or build a launch platform for a Plan-B option should your current full-time job disappear.

Shumaker, David. *The Embedded Librarian: Innovative Strategies for Taking Knowledge Where It's Needed*. Information Today, 2012. 240p. ISBN 1573874526.

The most current and comprehensive examination of the increasing trend for special librarians to become embedded in their organizations' operational units. A must-read for those considering special librarianship as a career. (Key resource)

## Articles

Abram, Stephen. "Curation: Buzzword or What?" *Information Outlook* 18, no. 5 (September/October 2014): 25–27. Accessed at http://www.highbeam.com/doc/1G1-391310219.html.

Terrific overview of what the term "curation" means—or could mean—for information professionals. A must-read for anyone considering, or needing to explain, digital curation work.

Gonzales, Brighid Mooney. "Preparing LIS Students for a Career in Metadata Librarianship." *SLIS Student Research Journal* 4, no. 1 (2014). Accessed at http://scholarworks.sjsu.edu/cgi/viewcontent.cgi?article=1 163&context=slissrj.

An excellent overview of how metadata work relates to traditional cataloging roles and knowledge sets, and how graduate programs can integrate metadata coursework into existing programs.

Sherman, Chris. "What's the Big Deal about Big Data?" *Online Searcher* 38, no. 2 (March/April 2014): 10–15. Accessed at http://bit.ly/1GCFMVP.
An overview of what constitutes Big Data, the nature of its two types (structured and unstructured, the latter of which refers to the Internet), and how these massive amounts of information can be mined for value across a wide spectrum of circumstances and organizational challenges.

Stuart, David. "Library and Information Professionals: Builders of the Ontological Universe." *Online Searcher* 38, no. 1 (January/February 2014): 11–15. Accessed at http://bit.ly/1NeRlUg.
Who better to assuage information overload anxiety than library and information professionals able to understand the importance of, as well as design and create, the ontologies that will bring order (and access) out of digital information chaos? A terrific explanation of this emerging field and the opportunities it provides information professionals.

"There's an App for That." *The Economist* 414, no. 8919 (January 3, 2015): 29–32. Accessed at http://econ.st/1y4UrmY.
A fascinating, scary overview of the coming workplace, shaped by freelance or contingent workers. Like so many changes, this may either be a terrific or terrifying disruptive change for information professionals. The tagline: "Freelance workers available at a moment's notice will reshape the nature of companies and the structure of careers."

## Periodicals

*Note: Periodicals likely to be useful to you in a nontraditional LIS position depend on what type of role you're in and the activities and responsibilities of that role. For example, you'd probably want to monitor your organization's key industry publications, plus the publications of any professional associations to which you belong. In addition, depending on your career focus, you'd want to monitor those periodicals that chart trends and information in your area of specialization. Examples of these types of publications:*

*EContent.* Information Today, 2004–. 10/yr. ISSN 1525–2531.
www.econtentmag.com
*EContent* states that it's intended for "decision-makers in the media, publishing, technology, and mobile sectors." It's also a great resource for anyone who works with econtent in any of its various iterations—for example, purchasers of ebooks, licensers of databases, and information professionals who use digital content in their jobs. Although this would be considered a publication to keep your professional skills current, another terrific aspect of *EContent* is its website coverage of nontraditional information disciplines—check out the "Topics" listed at the bottom of the page for a quick overview of 20 content-related topics and links to the related articles.

*Information Outlook.* Special Libraries Association, 1997–. Bimonthly. ISSN 1091–0808.
www.sla.org/access-membership/io/
Formerly titled *Special Libraries* (1910–1996), SLA's now-online official publication provides a forum for showcasing best practices, discussing emerging issues, and supporting information professionals across the diverse range of job responsibilities reflected in the SLA membership. An example of a relevant professional association publication.

*Modern Healthcare.* Crain Communications, 1974–. Weekly. ISSN 0160–7480.
www.modernhealthcare.com/
An example of an industry-specific magazine, *Modern Healthcare* is a
leading publication in the healthcare industry; its audience is healthcare business executives and decision makers, and those who support
them (including information professionals).

*Online Searcher: Information Discovery, Technology, Strategies.* Information
Today, 1993–. 6/yr. ISSN 1070–4795.
www.infotoday.com/onlinesearcher/
The result of combining *Online* and *Searcher* magazines in 2013, *Online
Searcher* content is geared toward those in "academic, corporate, government, law, medical, public library, knowledge management, web
development, and freelance environments." The publication is written
by and for information professionals, edited by well-known industry
observers Marydee Ojala and Barbara Quint, and covers such topics
as managing online research projects, client/employer research, new
research technologies and tools, industry trends, and strategizing new
information services. The website provides title access to past issues,
some of which are available for free, others for a fee. A must-read for
business researchers.

## Associations

*American Association of Law Libraries (AALL)*
www.aallnet.org
AALL represents more than 5,000 professionals working in "law firms;
law schools; corporate legal departments; courts; and local, state and
federal government agencies." Check the website for information about
the association, including its caucuses, chapters, and special interest
sections and AALL online professional development offerings. The
AALL "Competencies of Law Librarianship" statement, also found on
the website, will be especially valuable for students considering this
career path. Steeply discounted student memberships available.

*American Medical Informatics Association (AMIA)*
www.amia.org
Medical informatics is an area of potential opportunity for those with
technology-focused LIS skills and an interest in medicine/healthcare.
AMIA is included here as an example of a non-LIS association that,
although not specifically targeted to those with "library" skills, may
offer connections into these types of emerging alternative career paths.

*American Society for Indexing (ASI)*
www.asindexing.org
Founded in 1968, ASI promotes excellence in indexing, abstracting,
and database-building. The ASI website offers a directory listing of
indexers, links to resources of interest to indexers, articles and position papers about indexing, and information about ASI's special interest groups, which encompass an interesting range of specializations
(business, culinary, gardening/environmental, genealogy/transcription,
history/archaeology, legal, and sports/fitness, among others). No student membership discount, although a slight discount is offered to new
members.

*American Theological Library Association (ATLA)*
www.atla.com
ATLA's more than 1,000 members—individual, institutional, and
affiliate—draw from all avenues of theological and religious study,
regardless of denomination. It supports an extremely active publishing mandate, which includes the highly regarded ATLA Religion
database and related products. Hosts an annual conference and supports professional development seminars. Steeply discounted student
memberships.

*ARMA International*
www.arma.org
Billing itself as "the authority on governing information as a strategic
asset" and formerly known as the Association of Records Management,
ARMA is the oldest organization focusing on records and information management, a field that has undergone substantial challenges
since its inception more than 50 years ago. (Due to legal/compliance
requirements, records management is now central to the compliance
operations of almost every major corporation.) ARMA Canada (www.
armacanada.org) is a regional arm of ARMA International, comprising
14 chapters representing Canada "from coast-to-coast."

*Art Libraries Society of North America (ARLIS / NA)*
www.arlisna.org
ARLIS/NA describes itself as "a dynamic organization of over 1,000
individuals devoted to fostering excellence in art and design librarianship and image management." It hosts an annual conference,
supports an electronic forum that includes job postings (ARLIS-L),
and publishes a semiannual print publication (*Art Documentation*),
among other activities. Divisions (academic, art and design school,
museum, visual resources), sections (architecture, cataloging, reference and information services, art library students and new ARLIS
professionals), and 22 special interest groups let members share their
unique challenges and viewpoints. Substantial student membership
discount.

*Association for Information and Image Management (AIIM)*
www.aiim.org
AIIM positions itself in the enterprise content management space,
which it has defined as the "technologies used to capture, manage,
store, preserve, and deliver content and documents related to organization processes." The association publishes a number of resources
and offers topic-focused electronic discussion groups and professional
development resources. An indication of how much this discipline has
changed is that AIIM was originally founded in 1943 as the National
Microfilm Association. No student membership discount.

*Association of Canadian Archivists (ACA)*
http://archivists.ca
A 600-member organization whose goals include the preservation and
accessibility of Canada's "information resources and its documentary
heritage." In addition, ACA promotes appreciation of those resources
and that heritage by the general public and supports the role of the
Canadian archival community's efforts toward their preservation and
accessibility. Includes student chapters and several special interest
sections. Formerly the Archives Section of the Canadian Historical
Association (CHA).

*Association of Moving Image Archivists (AMIA)*
   www.amianet.org
   A fairly young organization (established 1991), AMIA represents
   more than 750 members "concerned with the acquisition, preservation, description, exhibition and use of moving image materials." The
   organization supports education and publication initiatives, hosts an
   annual conference, establishes and disseminates standards, and fos-
   ters collaboration throughout the world. Check the website for a wealth
   of publicly available information about best practices as well as an
   overview of the state of education for moving image archivists. Steeply
   discounted student memberships.

*Association of Prospect Researchers for Advancement (APRA)*
   www.aprahome.org
   Per APRA, "Prospect Development professionals are the individuals
   most able to meet the growing information needs of the fundraising
   community. Using the Internet and other technologies, they collect,
   evaluate, analyze, organize, package and disseminate publicly available information in a way that maximizes its usefulness and enables
   accurate and educated decision-making." APRA's more than 2,100
   members can take advantage of its educational programs, networking
   opportunities, publications, and career resources. For the latter, see the
   Career Center section of the APRA website, which offers a job postings
   directory as well as access to peer/member mentors and a description
   of the APRA skill sets. No student membership discount.

*Business Reference and Services Section (BRASS)*
   www.ala.org/rusa/sections/brass
   One of the largest, most active, and most influential special interest
   groups, BRASS membership includes "reference librarians, business
   information specialists, and others engaged in providing business reference and information services." Check the content-rich website for
   the section's topical business guides, collection of guides to business
   reference, and a wealth of other equally valuable resources and tools.
   You can elect to join BRASS as part of your ALA membership.

*Canadian Association for Information Science (CAIS)*
   www.cais-acsi.ca
   CAIS has as its mission the following goal: to "promote the advancement of information science in Canada, and encourage and facilitate
   the exchange of information relating to the use, access, retrieval, organization, management, and dissemination of information." Membership
   includes information scientists and archivists, librarians, computer scientists, and documentalists as well as those in information-intensive
   fields (e.g., economists, educators, journalists, and psychologists) who
   support its objectives.

*Canadian Association of Law Libraries (CALL)*
   www.callacbd.ca
   Focuses on "developing and supporting legal information specialists."
   Check the website for publications, professional development initiatives, special interest groups, a listing of legal research links, and other
   valuable resources.

*Canadian Association of Special Libraries and Information Services
(CASLIS)*
   www.cla.ca/caslis/index.htm

The diverse membership of CASLIS includes special libraries personnel, information specialists, documentalists, vendors, and others involved in delivering special library services throughout the country. A division of the Canadian Library Association.

*Canadian Health Libraries Association (CHLA)*
www.chla-absc.ca/
Focuses on professional development, networking, and advocacy for Canada's health sciences librarians and libraries. Check the website for blog posts and full-text articles from the association's journal.

*Church and Synagogue Library Association (CSLA)*
http://cslainfo.org/
CSLA has an exceptionally strong mission of information dissemination in service of its members' needs. To this end, it offers members-only training sessions, publications, a peer community, an annual conference focused on continuing professional education and networking, a monthly publication, and a series of topical guides in areas such as selecting and cataloging materials, reference services, and handling archival materials.

*Council on Botanical and Horticultural Libraries*
www.cbhl.net
Established to collect, preserve, and share plant knowledge both for its roughly 100 members and for the future of botany and horticulture studies. The site lists its member libraries with URLs; most are botanical gardens or universities that house separate research libraries.

*Indexing Society of Canada (ISC)*
www.indexers.ca/
Although the majority of its members specialize in indexing, ISC members also do "cataloguing, fact checking, glossary writing, HTML encoding, project management, teaching, thesaurus construction—and of course abstracting." See the Resources section for a list of books, periodicals, discussion groups, LinkedIn groups, related special interest groups, online resources, education programs, and indexing software.

*The Information Association for the Information Age (ASIST)*
www.asist.org
With a primary mission of "leading the search for new and better theories, techniques, and technologies to improve access to information," the ASIST organization draws its membership from the computer science, linguistics, management, librarianship, engineering, law, medicine, chemistry, and education disciplines. Website includes information about the society, its goals and programs; memberships (discounted for students); and many special interest groups and chapters, including multiple student chapters. Formerly known as the American Society for Information Science & Technology. (A key resource)

*Major Orchestra Librarians' Association (MOLA)*
www.mola-inc.org
Established in 1873, MOLA has as its primary focus improving communication among orchestra librarians, with a secondary focus of "assisting librarians in providing better service to their orchestras, presenting a unified voice in publisher relations, and providing support and information to the administrations of performing arts organizations." Its annual conference offers education and networking opportunities, a quarterly newsletter highlights issues of common interest,

and an electronic discussion list keeps members in touch. If this is a potential career choice for you, be sure to read "The Orchestra Librarian: A Career Introduction" (http://mola-inc.org/page/Career). Member dues are based on the budget size and type of orchestra, but apprentice memberships for students who are accepted into the organization are quite reasonable.

*Medical Library Association (MLA)*
www.mlanet.org
Over 100 years old, MLA has approximately 3,500 individual and institutional members based in the health sciences information field. Focus areas include education of health information professionals, health information research, and promoting universal access to health sciences information, national and international. The MLA website includes information about the organization, a solid collection of career resources, resources, and descriptions of and links to the association's two dozen sections (e.g., cancer librarians, dental section, hospital libraries, and medical informatics). Steeply discounted student memberships.

*Music Library Association*
www.musiclibraryassoc.org
Music librarians can be found in "large research libraries such as the Library of Congress or the New York Public Library; in the music section or branch library in universities, colleges, and conservatories; in public libraries; in radio and television station libraries; with music publishers and dealers; with musical societies and foundations; and with bands and orchestras." The Music Library Association represents librarians from all of these arenas, with a focus on music librarianship, its materials, and its careers. For those interested in music librarianship as a possible career path, check out the excellent career overview on the website (see at Our Profession > About Music Librarianship). Steeply discounted student memberships.

*National Association of Government Archives and Records Administrators (NAGARA)*
www.nagara.org
The association is dedicated to the improvement of federal, state, and local government records and information management. NAGARA supports this mission through an annual conference; quarterly publications that address trends and issues at the national, state, and local levels; numerous govdocs initiatives; and various continuing education opportunities. The website primarily describes NAGARA and its activities, but also includes job postings. No discounted memberships for students.

*National Association of Media and Technology Centers (NAMTC)*
www.namtc.org
NAMTC members include regional, K–12, and higher education media/tech centers, plus the vendors who work with them. The organization's focus is to promote leadership through "networking, advocacy, and support activities that will enhance the equitable access to media, technology, and information services to educational communities." Check out the website for information and resources related to motion/digital media and copyright, media reviews, archived newsletters, and related resources.

*Patent Information Users Group (PIUG)*

www.piug.org

Provides a forum and resource/information collection for individuals who do professional patent research, including 700-plus members from 27 countries including the United States. Part of the International Society for Patent Information, PIUG's website notes that it has "... nearly 300 patent information professionals who do patent searching for corporations, over 100 patent information consultants, over 80 patent information professionals who do patent searching for law firms, and about 20 searchers based in academic institutions. We are employed in performing patentability, freedom-to-practice, and validity patent searches for Fortune 500 / multinational companies, leading universities and major IP law firms. In recent years, PIUG members have also engaged in patent information analysis as a strategic innovation tool." Needless to say, patent research careers can be quite diverse.

*Society of American Archivists (SAA)*

www.archivists.org

With over 4,000 members, SAA is an extremely active organization in terms of member education, publications, development of policies and standards, and taking a leadership role in the emerging electronic records environment. Check the SAA website for a list of the society's sections and roundtables, career information, and numerous information resources related to archives work. Substantial discount for student members.

*Special Libraries Association (SLA)*

www.sla.org

Go-to source for professional support and development among primarily U.S.-based information professionals in special library and alternative LIS roles. Most effective when you join and become active in your local chapter and/or one of SLA's multiple special interest divisions and sections. Publishes the now-online *Information Outlook*; members can check out the "Manage Your Career" section for job and resume posting as well as information about career planning and competencies.

*Strategic and Competitive Intelligence Professionals (SCIP)*

www.scip.org

Competitive intelligence (CI) is an important component of business research across all industries and businesses. SCIP members comprise both independents and CI specialists who work for businesses, so there is a broad range of experience and knowledge to share within the group. Check the website for fee-based education resources and certification information. Steeply discounted student membership fees for full-time students only.

*Theatre Library Association (TLA)*

www.tla-online.org/

Since 1937, TLA has supported librarians, curators, and archivists working with collections in the areas of theater, dance, performance studies, popular entertainment, motion pictures, and broadcasting. It achieves its mission of "development and promotion of professional library expertise and standards" through annual conferences and other meetings, publications, book awards, an electronic discussion group, and affiliation with related organizations. The TLA website provides information about the organization, the profession, performing arts libraries, archives and museums, publishers, and resources specifically for students. There is a modest student membership discount, but the dues are already exceptionally inexpensive.

## Online Resources

*61 Non-Librarian Jobs for LIS Grads*
>   http://infospace.ischool.syr.edu/2011/12/23/61-non-librarian-jobs-for-librarians/
>   From then-student Mia Breitkopf, this 2011 post identifies 61 LIS-related job titles that sometimes included "librarian" in their description (but often did not). Although Breitkopf included hyperlinks for each of the jobs, understandably those postings are no longer live. Her list, however, provides a great starting point for job search terms beyond the traditional LIS titles. See also Breitkopf's "61 Tech Geek Jobs for LIS Grads," at http://bit.ly/1KYRTwV.

*Careers in Federal Libraries*
>   https://groups.google.com/forum/#!forum/careers-in-federal-libraries
>   Federal librarian Nancy Faget has organized this popular and highly engaged group (nearly 2,400 discussion threads/job posts), which provides a terrific entry into seeing what federal library jobs may be open, as well as information about applying for those jobs. According to Nancy, not only are there a good number of federal library job openings, but they also pay well—so if you're willing to consider relocation, this is a resource you'll want to check out.

*Data Science: What's in It for the New Librarian?*
>   http://infospace.ischool.syr.edu/2012/07/16/data-science-whats-in-it-for-the-new-librarian/
>   An Information Space post from the Syracuse University iSchool, this introduction to how data science might be an apt career fit for LIS professionals does a great job not only of sketching out the opportunities but also, through the comment thread, of asking how the relevant skills can/will be integrated into the MLIS and iSchool curricula. (Key resource)

*Education & Careers*
>   www.aallnet.org/mm/Careers/lawlibrarycareers
>   Excellent, content-rich collection of articles and overviews of a career in legal librarianship.

*Embedded Librarian*
>   http://embeddedlibrarian.wordpress.com
>   From embedded librarianship thought leader David Shumaker, this blog presents his thinking and research results related to embedded librarianship and also aggregates key information from others. (Key resource)

*"Emerging Careers" Archived Posts*
>   http://hacklibraryschool.com/category/education-curriculum/emerging-careers/
>   A collection of Hack Library School's career profiles describing nontraditional and/or emerging career paths. (Key resource)

*The Evolving Value of Information Management*
>   http://ftcorporate.ft.com/sla/

Subtitled "The five essential attributes of the modern information professional," this 2013 report is the result of a collaboration between SLA and *Financial Times* Corporate that sought to identify what they described as the "evolving value of information management" (and managers) in organizational environments. An excellent overview of the potential threats and opportunities for this career path. (Key resource)

*The Future of Knowledge Work*
http://intel.ly/16E0NOG
Although not specific to LIS careers, this fall 2012 white paper by Tim Hansen of Intel provides a useful framework for considering the future of information work within organizations. Subtitled *An Outlook on the Changing Nature of the Work Environment*, its five main points address changes in the nature of employment and employee expectations, dynamic (and impermanent) team structures, "virtually" located offices, collaboration between employees and their smart systems, and "servicification," that is, consumerization via services.

*Keywords for Job Searching*
http://inalj.com/
On the I Need a Library Job (INALJ) site, check out the list of terms found under the left column "Keywords for Job Searching." Some of the titles are familiar, but others such as community manager, conflict information strategy, data visualization, digital content curator, futurist, and infomatician represent new potential nontraditional career paths for most LIS professionals. (Key resource)

*Librarians: Get a Job in Data Science, Makes Lots of Money*
http://bit.ly/1juwpWE
From then-student Mia Breitkopf, this post for Syracuse University's School of Information Studies "Information Space" blog is a terrific introduction to data science work, including what it involves, relevant job sites, and keywords to use when searching for data science positions. Although written in 2012, much of the information is still relevant and, at the very least, a solid starting point for further exploration of this career path.

*Library & Information Science Jobs You Can Get Today*
http://librarysciencelist.com/library-information-science-jobs-you-can-get-today/
This June 2013 post lists and describes 30 jobs, many of which may be found in a traditional library setting but entail doing unusual types of work. Although the jobs listed have undoubtedly been filled by now, the listings provide interesting overviews of some nontraditional work.

*LLRX*
www.LLRX.com
Founded and published by the prolific Sabrina Pacifici (who also authors the daily BeSpacific law and technology news blog), LLRX aggregates a wide range of news items related to legal, social, and technology issues. In addition to signing up for the LLRX RSS feed, you may want to check the website for the subject-specific resource collections on competitive intelligence, information management, government resources, and other key topics.

*Manage Your Career [SLA]*
https://www.sla.org/career-center/
Although SLA no longer offers the wealth of career articles and coaching available through its Career Center in previous years, it does provide a handful of career articles plus searchable job postings, an alerting service, the ability to post your resume, and a number of job-hunting webinars through the "Manage Your Career" page. One of the most useful ways to use this resource is to explore the names of the open positions for a sense of alternative job titles, for example, information management center analyst; director, taxonomy, and indexing; manager of knowledge and library services; senior KM content coordinator; biopharmaceutical information specialist. (Key resource)

*An Overlooked Opportunity: Working for Vendors*
http://lj.libraryjournal.com/2013/03/careers/how-to-become-a-21st-century-librarian/
This brief piece, a sidebar accompanying the *Library Journal* article "How to Become a 21st Century Librarian," highlights the often-forgotten but numerous and varied career paths vendors offer to those with LIS skills.

*Update to "Choosing Law Librarianship: Thoughts for People Contemplating a Career Move," LLRX*
www.llrx.com/features/lawlibrarianship.htm
Written by law librarian Mary Whisner in 1999 and updated in 2008, this excellent article will still resonate today for those contemplating a career in law librarianship. Whisner addresses all the key issues, including pay, characteristics of the work, and the importance of both law and library degrees to career success.

*Visualising Data*
http://visualisingdata.com
An aggregation of data-visualization sites, reports, and other resources for those trying to quickly get up to speed on this increasingly important information skill. The place to start for data-visualization information.

*Who Needs a DAM [digital asset management] Librarian?*
http://digitalassetmanagementnews.org/features/who-needs-a-dam-librarian-part-i-come-out-come-out-wherever-you-are/
A terrific four-part series from DAMNews editor Deborah Fanslow on the growing opportunities for LIS-trained digital asset managers. If you are at all interested in digital asset management as a career choice, be sure to bookmark the DAMNews site (http://digitalassetmanagementnews.org) and sign up for its RSS feed. A phenomenal resource.

*Why Your Team Should Appoint a Meta-Knowledge Champion*
http://digest.bps.org.uk/2014/09/why-your-team-should-appoint-meta.html
This article from the online Research Digest of the British Psychological Society points to yet another way that information specialists could easily repurpose their skill set to add value in an embedded or integrated role. Reporting on findings from research undertaken at the Rotterdam School of Management at Erasmus University, The Netherlands, the article describes the "meta-knowledge champion" as the person who's aware of everyone else's expertise and able to

apply that knowledge at the point of need to further the team's strategic goals. A new role for which to volunteer – and then turn into a job?

# Notes

1.  ALA Library Fact Sheet 1—Number of Libraries in the United States, accessed at www.ala.org/tools/libfactsheets/alalibraryfactsheet01.

2.  "2012 SLA Salary Survey," Special Libraries Association, 2012, accessed at https://www.sla.org/shop/salary-survey/.

# 5
# Independent LIS Career Paths

*If you ask me what I have come to do in this world*
*... I will reply: I'm here to live my life out loud.*
—Émile Zola

So far, we've considered traditional librarianship and the broad range of jobs within school, public, and academic libraries, as well as the incredible diversity of nontraditional LIS career possibilities. In addition, almost any aspect of information work can be done as an independent.

This path can be as simple as doing the work you've previously done as an employee, but doing it instead as a newly minted contractor. Or it can mean starting a new product or service business—alone or with colleagues—based on expertise you've gained along the way as an LIS professional.

In addition, there are many different approaches to working as an independent. You might work with a single client, for example, being a contract substitute librarian for one library district. Or you might become a "solo," a one-person shop offering your services, for example, as a freelance indexer to publishers around the country.

On the other hand, you might want to build a business that includes multiple employees, thereby extending your company's ability to handle a large number of clients and projects simultaneously. Or you might decide you'd rather not take on the management and overhead of employees, so as an alternative you decide instead to join a loose network of information pros who come together on a project basis, participating based on the expertise needed on specific projects.

Alternatively, you might prefer to sign up with a "temp" agency that specializes in information work. This strategy lets someone else worry about the marketing, management, and client relationships, while you simply show up and do the work (performing at the highest level of excellence, of course!).

The bottom line is that all the choices are completely up to you: what work you do, how you do it, what markets or clients you go after as well as, occasionally, what clients you fire, what you charge, and how you grow/expand your business, if this is a goal for you. These are but some of the major choices you'll make as an independent.

## What Work Would You Do?

Consider all the things that traditional librarians do, from cataloging to reference to indexing to BI to research. All of these can be—and have been—done on a contract or consulting basis, either for traditional libraries, special libraries, or organizations lacking the specific expertise in-house. (Remember, in an era of corporate library downsizing, outsourcing key activities to competent LIS contractors is one of the best ways for organizations to continue to get the necessary work done.)

Then consider those activities described for the nontraditional path—these are all candidates for freelance or contract work as well. The emphasis on strategic management of knowledge assets means businesses increasingly need people who know meta-tagging, know how to build taxonomies, how to research international market opportunities, how to research and write white papers, how to do CI, and how to analyze and summarize key information. A lot of this work is done on a project basis by outside contractors . . . such as, potentially, you.

Or, think about doing these same sorts of activities within a broader context. For example, your expertise in marketing libraries might turn into a consulting business developing marketing plans for nonprofits and cultural institutions. Years you spent designing and implementing your academic library's web portal could translate into a business developing websites for alumni associations or career colleges. A successful track record as a BI librarian might launch you on an independent path as a corporate or association trainer or an online teacher or a freelance creator of online tutorials for businesses.

Other examples might include freelance cataloging; creating and maintaining research guides and online tutorials for virtual libraries; social media marketing, which takes both research and writing skills; developing and managing online communities for clients; launching an information brokerage or contract research company; providing current awareness services for start-ups in emerging industries; being a consulting editor for one of the library-focused publishing companies; or doing freelance prospect (i.e., donor) research for a nonprofit.

Independents have pursued careers as freelance book-talkers and/or storytellers, manuscript evaluators and consulting acquisitions editors, adjunct faculty (classroom based or online), library building consultants, organizational development consultants, writers (books, articles, online content, marketing/communications, white papers, ghost blogging), workshop and seminar presenters, and grant writers. Colleagues have set up and maintained technical libraries for local tech firms, cataloged personal libraries for wealthy clients, specialized in market research or patent searching, taken on systems and networking projects, built reputations as freelance legal researchers, provided research training to specialized groups, done trend analysis for marketing companies, written position papers for non-profits, worked as freelance genealogists, edited manuscripts for LIS publishers, and even become private investigators—all based on skills they've developed as LIS professionals.

Regardless of what service you offer, you may want to keep in mind the differing perceptions of the terms freelancer, contractor, and consultant. Generally, in the business world, someone who does freelance work is assumed to be doing an occasional activity whose performance standards have been assigned and are monitored by project managers. A contractor is someone who may be involved in more complex, higher-level activities that may also involve a long-term project or assignment. A consultant generally comes in at a strategy level, identifying the parameters of a problem and recommending its solution. Sometimes the consultant also implements the solution, although often this is completed either by internal staff or by contractors.

In general, freelancers and contractors will simply be asked to sign a standard contract for their work. Consultants, on the other hand, will be expected to develop a proposal that outlines their responsibilities, timelines, deliverables, and fees.

## How Would You Work?

Depending on which of these paths you choose, your workplace environment can vary wildly. For example, if you work for clients, you may have a working environment that combines home-office space with time spent in your clients' offices. Some of the best-known independent info pros who've chosen the solo option have worked successfully from their homes for years.

If you'd rather build a business that includes employees, you'll probably find it easiest to lease office space that will accommodate your team (in fact, many residential zoning laws forbid operating such a business from home). If you're part of a collaborative network, you may all choose to work from your homes or may instead decide to share space and an administrative staffer. And if you're temping, your working environment will change with each new assignment. Some of this work may be virtual, some on-site.

As you think about an independent option, think also about the preferred working environments and arrangements you explored in Chapter 2. If you had the choice (which you do), would you prefer to work from a home office or share office space with other independents? Would you prefer to work regular, consistent 9–5 hours Monday through Friday? Or would you rather take Wednesdays off for skiing, yoga, or golf—and then work several evenings a week to round out your 40 hours? Or would you prefer that be 20 hours? The choice would be yours.

Given the option, would you prefer to work for national clients, which would probably entail a substantial amount of business travel, or for local organizations, which would keep you closer to home on weekends, but possibly also limit the number and size of potential clients?

Would you prefer to work solo or as part of a loose network of colleagues with complementary skills where you can hand off work to each other? Or perhaps as part of a more tightly integrated, collaborative team that can take on larger opportunities and projects as a group? Or perhaps you might choose to contract with an agency that places you on temporary projects and also relieves you of the stress of ongoing marketing responsibilities.

Would you plan to work a full-time schedule or work part-time? Would you be willing to work 24/7 to meet last-minute client deadlines or instead choose to work only on those projects and activities not likely to interfere with other personal commitments?

These are among the choices you have as an independent to shape the structure and flow of your work life.

## What Market Would You Target?

Again, there are many options here. Would you focus on the library market or on clients outside the library world? Specialize in nonprofits or work only with the telecommunications or healthcare or education industries? Would you specialize in working with government agencies and develop an expertise in navigating the red tape necessary to secure large and lucrative government contracts? Would your product or service be applicable across a broad range of organizations or would you be targeting a small niche market?

The answers to these questions will determine how large or small your market segment will be, with corresponding benefits to each choice. A broad-based target market means you'd have lots of potential customers, but reaching them would drive your marketing costs proportionately higher. You might also have greater competition going after a large target market, and it might be more difficult to differentiate your service among those being offered by others. Also, the more competitors in the marketplace, the likelier that your potential clients would expect you to compete with lower prices.

A niche market, on the other hand, offers the benefits of a more tightly focused (and thus less expensive) marketing effort, an easier opportunity to build your brand visibility and reputation, and probably less competition with correspondingly less pressure to lower prices. However, a niche market has one very important drawback. That is, if your product or service is tied to the health and well-being of a particular market segment, and that segment suffers a downturn, so will your business. This is also one of the benefits of targeting a national market rather than a local one. If your focus is on local clients, and your regional economy goes into recession, you have no other markets to turn to, at least in the short term.

If your preference is to target a niche market, whether regional, industry specific, or a particular type of organization, it's still possible to protect against downturns. By keeping an eye out for how your product or service can bridge to new markets and taking initial steps now to create those bridges in terms of market knowledge and contacts, you'll be well prepared should the need arise.

## What Would You Charge?

Again, many variables: do your prices need to reflect a competitive environment? Are you working in a geographic location where fees are generally higher or lower than the national average? Would you charge nonprofits less than you charge for-profits? Would you base your fees on what you need to earn to cover your monthly overhead, on what the market will bear, or on an hourly charge basis that includes your invisible costs such as training/professional development, association memberships, marketing time, and other expenses?

"How do I price my services" is an ongoing topic among independents, as we struggle to find a formula that is logical, defensible to clients, and applicable in every situation. Oh that it were possible! Instead, we usually end up developing guidelines that shape our pricing approaches to various types of projects.

One of the biggest questions is whether to price by the hour or by the project. Generally, services marketers recommend that you price by the project (after having established for yourself the hourly rate that you need to cover). The challenge for novices—OK, for experienced independents as well—is to correctly estimate how many hours a given project is likely to take. When you're first starting out, you'll pretty much be guessing. But the more often you've done a certain type of work, the more familiar you'll become with the process and time involved. This will make projects more predictable, and your time estimates much more reliable.

One way to solve this dilemma for those new to contract work is to do a small, representative piece of the project and see how long it takes. For example, if your project entails processing a corporate archive, try test-processing a small but representative set of materials to get a sense of how long it would take to process this selection and what sorts of issues might arise. This then allows you to extrapolate to the entire project and more realistically estimate the time involved. If, for example, one box of documents took you 3 hours to process, and there are 50 boxes, you can estimate that the project may take you 150 hours. Add a 10% "unforeseen disasters" margin, to bring you to 165 hours. If you charged $50/h, your baseline estimate for the job would be $8,250 plus whatever percentage profit margin you've established for projects. Your total project fee would represent your baseline cost and your profit margin (presented as a single fee), plus "approved expenses."

Of course, when you get into the project, you'll undoubtedly encounter all sorts of challenges that didn't surface in the first run-through, and you'll wish that you'd bid more. But every time you do another project, you'll have a better sense of what to look for—and what contingencies to plan for in your estimate.

Another common approach for business researchers is a "do not exceed" budget, which may range from $500 to more than $2,500, depending on the client's request. The purpose of this type of budget is to allow the researcher to explore a given topic and appropriate resources to see how much information exists and how readily available it is. At the end of, say, a $500 expenditure of time and database costs, the researcher gets back to the client with his or her findings. This is usually either the information sought, or an assessment of what information is available and next steps (and associated costs) in obtaining that information.

Although there are no perfect answers for pricing that will apply in all situations, the best coverage of pricing issues can be found in Bates's *Building & Running a Successful Research Business, 2d ed.,* Chapter 15, "Setting Rates and Fees," as well as in Alan Weiss's *Value-Based Fees: How to Charge—and Get—What You're Worth* (both described in "Resources" section).

## How Would You Get Clients?

This is the really challenging one. Most of us feel fairly confident that we can do the work a client asks of us—once we have that client. But actually *getting* that client is a whole different matter.

Services marketing is, to quote a book title, "selling the invisible." As is the case for all independents regardless of profession, assume marketing efforts will generally take up a substantial amount of your workweek (at least 40%), especially when you're just starting out. And assume you'll be trying all sorts of things to get your message out, establish your brand, and increase your visibility within your target market.

What kinds of things might that include? You'll network tirelessly, attending business luncheons, speaking at professional group meetings, presenting at conferences, and volunteering in the community or with organizations relevant to your market. Some independents find cold-calling effective, while others avoid it at all costs.

An informative, polished, and professional-looking website is imperative, as are business cards and possibly "leave behind" minimal print collateral (e.g., a trifold 8½ × 11 brochure). In addition, many independent info pros send out a monthly or quarterly e-newsletter with content relevant to their target audience as a way of staying "on their radar." Another option is to find pro bono work that allows you to demonstrate your skills to your target audience and connect with their key issues in a way that showcases your value to potential clients before you're ready to ask them for paying projects.

Your social media presence and engagement will also be an important part of your marketing strategy. At the very least, you'll want to have a thoughtful, complete, engaging LinkedIn profile and join and engage with relevant LinkedIn groups—often an amazing source of knowledge, possible project partners, and potential clients. In addition, you may want to have a presence on Facebook, Twitter, or other social media platforms depending on your time, preferences, and target audience.

Paying close attention to how you "package" your deliverables (e.g., the reports you create for your clients) is another way you impress your clients and establish the quality of your professional brand. Your goal always is to add value to your deliverables, not only to reinforce the proposition that you are highly competent but also to emphasize the importance of your contribution to your client's goals. By extension, the key here is to focus not simply on delivering data, but also on building relationships. The more work that comes to you through existing clients, the less time you'll need to invest in developing new clients.

As with pricing questions, there is no right marketing strategy that fits every circumstance. You'll simply try them all to see what works most effectively for your particular service and market. But the key here is that marketing is a huge commitment for any independent, and if you don't think you'd be able or willing to undertake it, then an independent option probably isn't for you.

# How Would You Create and Maintain Your Support Community?

One of the downsides of being an independent can be that generally you're working on your own *a lot*. Although some people thrive on this solitude, others find it can quickly lead to feelings of isolation and loneliness. It's easy to feel—and be—out of the loop of tips and trends and water-cooler conversations, where so much informal knowledge is shared. The trick is to create your *own* water-cooler space.

True, they may be virtual, but online communities, LinkedIn groups, and electronic discussion groups offer an extremely effective way to reach out and connect with someone . . . or lots of someones. Joining one of these online forums, whether public or private, offers you the opportunity to build connections with peers, benefit from the knowledge of others doing work similar to yours, and share your expertise with an appreciative community.

Another alternative is to become active in a local chapter of a key professional organization, which will encourage you to engage in regular meetings and group projects. (Volunteering to do the newsletter immediately makes you the most well-connected person in the organization!) Or organize an informal group of colleagues in your area that gets together weekly or monthly to swap war stories, raise questions or problems, and brainstorm solutions. Schedule regular lunches with former coworkers and individuals in your network or consider taking or teaching a class in your area of interest to build new relationships with those who share your passion.

If you're a student, another way to create and maintain your future support community is to take a leadership role among your fellow students now, so that you can continue to connect as alumni after graduation.

Although it takes more time and effort to be part of an active community when you work alone, with a little creativity, it *can* be done. Doing so will not only help you feel less socially and emotionally isolated, but will also allow you to stay current with the best thinking going on in your field.

## And Don't Forget to Think About . . .

Those were the really big questions that all start-ups face, but certainly not the only ones. If the independent path is an option you'd like to explore, then it's time to start researching the next set of questions and noting your answers in your career journal. They'll form the underpinning of your business and operations plans, so think through carefully your answers to the following questions:

- How will you get your first project and then convert that project into an ongoing client?

- Who/what is your competition, and how will you compete against them?

- How will you establish and maintain your brand?

- How will you describe your product or service to others in 50 words or less? If you strike up a conversation with a stranger who expresses interest in what you do, you'll want to be sure you've got a great response. As Mary Ellen Bates has noted, this is easier if you first find out a bit about your fellow conversationalist so you can tailor your description of your work and value proposition to his or her situation. (Keep in mind, however, that the trick here is not to sound like a lion that's just spotted fresh prey. . . .)

The good news is that there are several excellent books available to help you work through each of these issues. The reality-check news is that until you've thought all of these issues through and are confident that you've addressed (and have go-to responses for) each one, you're probably not ready to launch.

# Portable LIS Careers

One of the things to consider if you're contemplating an independent career path is whether or not you want your business to be "portable." If you're an employee, your portable job options might include telecommuting, being a "virtual" employee, and/or doing contract or short-term project work that allows you to organize your work schedule around your need to be geographically flexible. Not all employers are open to these options, but if this is important to you, it's something to discuss with a potential employer *before* you take a job rather than after (when you've lost your negotiating leverage).

Creating portable work can be much easier to do if you're an independent, because with the effective use of communication and collaboration technologies, a substantial amount of client work can be done from any location. This can be, in fact, one of the major benefits of becoming a solopreneur—if you've set the expectation with your clients that you work remotely, then it's much easier to work from wherever you want, whether that's while you're attending a professional conference, moving to a new city, or hanging out at the local Starbucks.

Many clients may want to meet you in person, but a brief "get to know each other in person" trip to wherever they're located is a small price to pay for the flexibility a portable business can offer. After that, online communication tools such as Skype, GoToMeeting, Google Hangout, and other similar technologies can usually sustain a good relationship.

What sorts of LIS jobs fit into the portable career option? Pretty much anything that doesn't require you to be on-site or meeting with a client on a regular (e.g., weekly) basis. That includes business research, writing, editing, market research, prospect/donor research, online teaching or training, indexing and abstracting, social media/content marketing, taxonomy building, and online contract reference work. As is the case with any independent work, your job will be to line up clients, but you already know how to do that, right? Network, network, network!

---

### So You Want to Start a Research Business

One of the most popular independent options of interest to students is that of information broker. This is no surprise—many of us went into the LIS profession because we loved research. We thrive on the hunt for information, and the process of research is a delightful challenge that has kept many of us looking for answers well beyond when a sane person would have done the sensible thing and gone to bed. If you're one of those "I'm not gonna quit 'til I find the answer!" types, does this mean you were born for a career as an information broker? Maybe yes, maybe no.

As Mary Ellen Bates points out in *Building & Running a Successful Research Business: A Guide for the Independent Information Professional, 2d ed.* (CyberAge Books/Information Today, 2010), being a successful information broker means you are good at both research *and* being an entrepreneur. Among the skills she identifies as critical to this type of work:

• Subject expertise in your practice area, or, if you intend to be a research generalist, an ability to master new topics quickly (think of this as the ability to "learn on the fly" quickly and at the point of need).

- An understanding of how to effectively package information to best meet the needs of your client.

- Research skills, to include phone interviewing, mastery of commercial databases as well as print and Internet-based resources, and an ability to navigate government resources.

- Time and workflow management skills (to keep your head above water when all those projects land on the same day, with the same deadline).

- Business skills (negotiating, marketing, selling, cash flow management, and often most importantly, the ability to insist on being paid as agreed).

- Business operations knowledge (basically, how businesses work and what it takes to be profitable).

Like other types of independent work, being a successful information broker depends not only on knowing how to find, package, and present information, but also on how good you are at running and growing a business.

## Income and Education

There is a much greater range of incomes for independents than for those who take either traditional or nontraditional LIS jobs. The reason is the high number of variables, including:

- What type of product/service you offer

- How much your clients value and will pay for your product/service

- How *often* and how regularly they will value and pay for it

- The type of market you target (e.g., high-tech Fortune 500 companies *vs.* nonprofits)

- The size of your potential market

- Whether that potential market is growing or contracting

- Where your client base is located (as with traditional/nontraditional salaries, generally clients in large urban areas are willing to pay higher rates than those in small rural areas)

- How much work you're able to land

- How long you've been in business

- How much time you spend marketing, and the effectiveness of your efforts

- How many hours you're willing to work

- How committed you are to regularly updating your skills

- How effectively you can up-sell, that is, convince a client to hire you for additional and more profitable work

- How good you are at building "trust relationships" with your clients, so they see you as a key part of their success strategy rather than just as an occasional contractor

- How effectively you manage your time

- How effectively you manage your accounts receivables—in other
words, are you willing to insist that you get paid in a timely manner?

Within those—and other—variables, the income can range from zero to six
figures annually. The key thing to remember, however, is that *you* are the
one who controls most of these variables. The choices you make will determine almost all of your outcomes, including your income—which, theoretically, is what you're shooting for when you decide to become an independent.

Although many independents note that it's wise to assume *at least* two
years before you'll be bringing in enough money to support yourself on your
income, it may take longer than this—or less time, if you launch with a
high-volume, existing client. Also, keep in mind that whether you're billing
$50 or $150 an hour, you're also covering a multitude of expenses that were
previously your employer's responsibility. A good rule of thumb is to figure
that between taxes and business expenses, your net "take-home" pay will be
just a bit more than half of the amount you bill out.

Job prospects are potentially huge—outsourcing, contingent/contract
workers, and individuals brought on board on a project basis are trends that
are growing exponentially. But again, *how* huge independent "job prospects"
are depends on how effectively you market your service, how many clients
need your services right now, and how rapidly you can profitably expand
that market, among other factors. It's all part of the basic independents'
mantra: while your opportunities are only limited by your imagination, the
outcomes are all up to you.

In terms of education, as an independent, you'll need three kinds of
knowledge: the specialized expertise for which you charge your fees; the
requisite business acumen to start, manage, and grow a business; and an
understanding of effective marketing practices. It's critically important that
you don't assume having the first kind of knowledge will give you a pass on
having the other two. So take a class or two in entrepreneurship through
your local chamber of commerce or community college. Read marketing
books, join the AIIP, and peruse the electronic discussion list's archives for
invaluable marketing tips and techniques. Brainstorm with other independents, research "services marketing," and attend conference presentations
on doing business as an independent. And if your social media/branding
skills aren't top-notch, add this to the list of areas in which you'll need to
develop an expertise.

Once you have confidence in your entrepreneurship and marketing
skills, your challenge will be to stay ahead of the curve in your area of expertise as well as with emerging trends for your market. You may want to consider expanding your area of expertise to a related field—for example, you
may want to extend your basic business research practice by also adding a
specialization in CI, and you'll need to grow that skill base. Or you may want
to expand your basic cataloging and classification skills with an expertise in
taxonomy building. Both of these new skill bases will require you to learn
new disciplines—and to find the fastest, most cost-effective way to do so.

Also, you'll need to stay abreast of advances in your office technologies,
including online collaboration tools, search engines, digital presentation
software, information visualization tools and techniques, and other types
of technologies. Unlike when you are employed, you'll be doing all of this on
your own time, so you'll need to develop a time- and cost-effective approach
for mastering your ongoing learning curve.

# Exploring Independent Career Paths

Becoming an independent is such a big step, it's a good idea to try it out before making a life-changing, long-term commitment. Try one or all of the following activities to "get your toes wet," recording your responses in your career journal. Did you enjoy the work? Were you engaged in the process and happy with the outcome? Would you be willing to learn more about it and to do so on an ongoing basis? Would you feel comfortable marketing that type of product/service to others? Here are some ways to begin answering those questions:

- Try interning with a local information broker or one you can work with online.

- Create web content on a voluntary basis for a local nonprofit whose mission you support.

- Subcontract on a "moonlighting" basis for a contract cataloger.

- Research your potential market—including players, trends, issues, and a SWOT (strengths, weaknesses, opportunities, threats) analysis—and write up your findings as a trial client project.

- Apply to become a book reviewer for a publication like *American Reference Books Annual* or *Library Journal* or write articles for other publications to build your knowledge of information sources and develop your writing skills and process.

- For the local public library, create an online tutorial that helps seniors find great "encore career" resources.

- Volunteer to do the kind of work you think you might want to do professionally so you can start to learn more about the skills involved, understand the time it takes to do this type of work, and begin building a portfolio of project experience and credentials in your potential practice area.

- Find or create opportunities to try out your dream work via your existing job, even if it means working extra hours for no pay.

- Do a marketing plan and test it. To pull together a marketing plan, you'll need to determine, at a minimum, who will purchase your service and why. You'll need to segment your market, so that instead of broadly targeting, for example, special libraries or business start-ups, you'll narrow your pitch to just that slice of the market that has a *compelling need* for your service. This could mean targeting corporate librarians who've recently had to downsize staff or business start-ups, for example, in the biotechnology industry.

Once you've segmented your market and discussed your proposed service with several potential clients, you'll have a better sense of (1) what marketing message will resonate, (2) who and where within given organizations decision-makers are (this is your target focus), and (3) probable pricing assumptions. You'll also have a better sense of whether or not you'll be able to market day in and day out.

Although this is a very brief overview of doing some rudimentary market research, the point is to help you understand how important marketing activities—and market knowledge—are to your success. Can you easily approach people and talk about your service? Are you comfortable coming up with a strategy for marketing your service? Are you willing to network, network, network? For most independents, marketing is the really tough part. But it is also the make-or-break component: if you can't market yourself, then it will be extremely difficult to succeed as an independent.

Additionally, if you're a student, consider . . .

- Joining the AIIP, taking advantage of its discounted student memberships. Besides giving you the opportunity to access its wealth of online professional resources, this will allow you to sign up for AIIP's discussion list, which provides an incredibly valuable compendium of insider tips, savvy advice, and best-practice suggestions worth many times the price of membership.

- Interviewing independent information professionals in your area and then writing up your findings for your student newsletter; check the publicly available AIIP membership directory (www.aiip.org/AboutAIIP/directory_home.asp) to find independents who live nearby.

- Taking every research class you can and, if possible, getting hands-on experience with the big three: Proquest Dialog, Lexis-Nexis, and Factiva (Dow Jones).

- Taking at least one business class for one of the electives in your grad program—consider marketing, management, project management, business communications, or organizational behavior.

If your test runs tell you that although you love the work, the marketing would drive you nuts, then you're probably better off considering either subcontracting to another independent (only if you already have great skills in their business specialty and will work for a lowered rate) or doing freelance work in addition to your regular employment. At the very least, this will allow you to continue to build a portfolio of projects and assignments without jeopardizing your professional standing (or your mortgage), and it may also provide an opportunity to start building visibility and a client base before you take the independent leap, should you eventually decide to do so.

The reality is that some people find working as an independent to be an ideal fit with their personalities, while others find that despite their initial assumptions, it's the fastest route to personal and professional misery.

In fact, most successful entrepreneurs share several key characteristics. After going through your self-assessment process, you should be able to determine how many of these fit your profile and preferences. For example, entrepreneurs generally have:

- A strong willingness to take (informed) risks and still be able to sleep at night (usually)

- An expectation that their efforts control their outcomes
- A willingness to take the initiative
- Strong self-discipline
- Effective time-management and self-organization skills
- An ability to quickly master new knowledge
- A willingness to work *very* long hours when necessary
- A willingness to take on all aspects of the business, from business strategy to marketing to client relationships to clerical work

Ideally, independent information pros should also have:

- An ability to deal with irregular income
- A strong professional network of colleagues with a variety of skills and contacts
- A willingness to travel for business as needed
- A desire to stay ahead of the curve regarding emerging trends, technologies, products, and potential market opportunities
- A comfort level with change, accompanied by a willingness to try new things
- A willingness to put their personal lives on hold if project/client deadlines intervene
- An ability to juggle multiple projects without losing control of them

In addition, according to authors Jim Clifton and Dr. Sangeeta Bharadwaj Badal in *Entrepreneurial Strengthsfinder* (Gallup Press, 2014), successful entrepreneurs are likely to have many, if not all, of the following talents:

- Business focus (your decisions are based on driving profit)
- Confidence (you have a high level of emotional intelligence, e.g., strong self-awareness and understanding of others as well as a belief in your ability to succeed and a willingness to take action based on that belief)
- Ability to think creatively (you're able to think creatively about both existing and new ideas and products; you're comfortable exploring options and creating solutions)
- Ability to delegate (even though many independents perform most of their business activities themselves, it is truly important to recognize what could or should be outsourced for the most effective use of your time—and if you're still micromanaging, that doesn't count as delegating!)
- Determination (you're not deterred or derailed by setbacks)
- A high comfort level with independence (you rely on yourself to achieve your goals, have a strong sense of responsibility, can multitask, and are highly competent when it comes to managing your business)
- An ongoing drive to seek knowledge (the knowledge you're seeking here, per Badal, is related to growing your business, rather than

doing research for a client or, like so many of us, seeking knowledge just for the fun of it!)

- An ability and willingness to promote yourself to others (you're comfortable talking up your business, i.e., you're able to build your business through face-to-face networking and interaction)

- An ability to build lasting, trust-based relationships (an absolutely critical element of building your business; as noted previously, you want to move clients into a "trust relationship" position where they rely on your judgment and are happy to recommend you to others)

- A high comfort level with risk (you're able to assess and manage risks, emotionally as well as from a business perspective)

Bottom line: launching as an independent is a risk that entails a tremendous amount of hard work for an uncertain payoff. But it can also be incredibly rewarding, a wonderful way to live the life you want to live, and the best way to maximize the financial return on your professional skills. You're always dealing with something new (although this carries its own level of anxiety), you never have to ask permission for a day off (although you'll find yourself frequently working nights and weekends, at least in the beginning), and you'll rarely get bored. And given today's employment climate, this career choice may turn out to be the best route to lifetime employability.

## Getting Started as an Independent

If, after exploring all the questions we've raised, you still feel like this is the career path for you (or one you'd like to at least consider), there are a number of ways to move forward—some slow and steady, others a leap off the cliff. Consider one or more of the following approaches:

- **Building an initial client base through volunteering.** This will bring you projects you can point to, "clients" who can attest to your skill and professionalism, and an expanding network of connections in the community. It can also let you hone your expertise in a safe environment, that is, one where the expectations aren't quite so high as they would be with, say, a $25,000 project at stake.

- **Doing your independent work as an after-hours sideline in addition to your day job.** Has someone gotten wind of your special expertise and asked you to take on a project in your spare time? If you can devote the time to it and there is no conflict of interest with your current employer, this approach allows you to build your expertise, client base, and portfolio with very little associated risk. You may want to encourage this by letting everyone you know that you're available to take on small projects (that can be done during nonbusiness hours) in your area of expertise.

- **Interning with an independent practitioner.** Find someone who's doing what you want to do and see whether it would be possible to work with them for a specified time period, doing activities that will let you hone your skills while benefiting the practitioner's business. Agree up front that no clients of the organization with whom you're interning will ever be approached by you, and be prepared for the fact that you'll probably be working for no pay because the practitioner will have to train you to some degree.

- **Working as a subcontractor for another independent.** Although this approach doesn't push you to start developing your marketing muscles, it's nevertheless a good way to start building up a portfolio of projects if you can find an independent information pro who's willing to take you on. Assume that this option will be feasible only if you're ready to "hit the ground running," that is, you already have professional-level skills in the practitioner's area of specialization. As noted previously, agree up front that no clients of the business with whom you're subcontracting will ever be approached by you. (A major benefit here: you may learn marketing strategies by observing how the independent you're working with markets his or her business.)

- **Talking your employer into outsourcing your current job—to you.** One of the most popular ways of getting started as an independent is to turn your employer into your first client. This makes sense because they know the caliber of work you do, know they can rely on you to perform, and know you understand the organization and its priorities (and, oftentimes equally important, its politics).

- **Jumping into the deep end.** If you feel you've done your homework, understand your market, have completed all the business start-up planning and administrivia, and are ready to launch your service, then put everything else aside and go for it. Although this is a much less risky approach if your household has a second income to rely on, for some people "taking the leap" is the only way to go.

---

### Why You Might Love Being an Independent

If you love the freedom and independence available only to someone who's self-employed, and you're able to deal with the financial uncertainty of no steady paycheck, then you might thrive on the life of an LIS independent. For whom is this career choice most comfortable?

Given the marketing requirements, unless you're a subcontractor or working for a temp agency, this path is best for outgoing people (or those who can easily fake it) comfortable with risk-taking, multitasking, and constant change. You need to be willing to seek out and extend yourself in professional/social situations, respond quickly to multiple client needs and deadlines, and deal with the day-to-day administrivia that is a part of every business.

But if you have a reasonably high level of self-confidence, are comfortable taking the initiative, and don't mind the challenge of a nonstop learning curve, then the rewards of an independent career are likely to far outweigh its challenges for you. You have the freedom to work on projects that interest you and to set your own professional agenda. You may work way too many hours, but it will be *your* decision to do so, and you will reap the rewards of your efforts.

In fact, this is one of the key considerations of an independent path. You're in charge, you can do whatever you want—as long as you understand that you and you alone are entirely responsible for your business's well-being. Its reputation depends on how well you perform every day both as a specialist in whatever it is you offer to clients *and* as a business owner.

If you thrive on that kind of challenge, then you just might find an independent career to be a perfect fit.

# Resources

## Books

Awe, Susan C. *The Entrepreneur's Information Sourcebook: Charting the Path to Small Business Success, 2d ed.* Libraries Unlimited, 2012. 285p. ISBN 1598847864.
The second edition of this practical sourcebook continues its previous strengths: thoughtful evaluations of hundreds of print and electronic resources (free and fee based); helpful screenshots of relevant websites; and an organization that reflects the natural steps you're likely to take when contemplating going independent (e.g., Are You an Entrepreneur; Research, Statistics, and Information Gathering; Start Up; and Your Business Plan, among others). Along with excellent advice on the start-up process, Awe also provides (new to this edition) a solid overview of the role of social media for marketing, networking, and increasing visibility.

Bates, Mary Ellen. *Building & Running a Successful Research Business: A Guide for the Independent Information Professional, 2d ed.* CyberAge Books/Information Today, 2010. 500p. ISBN 0910965859.
Don't even consider becoming an information broker without reading this book first. Those who have heard Bates speak at LIS conferences will recognize her voice here: smart, funny, realistic, and supportive. Bates walks readers through the entire range of issues related to starting, running, and growing the business, plus takes you through a "day in the life" scenario that provides a realistic view of what this career choice really looks like. She makes it clear that if you're thinking about this line of work, you'll need to master both your core marketable skills *and* the competencies necessary to be an entrepreneur (see, e.g., "The Project from Hell," p. 177)—and then provides the insights necessary to do so. An invaluable source for both students and practitioners. (Key resource)

Bates, Mary Ellen, *The Reluctant Entrepreneur: Making a Living Doing What You Love.* Niwot Press, 2014. 216p. ISBN 061597595X.
Whereas *Building & Running a Successful Research Business* was written specifically for information professionals seeking to build practices based on their skills as researchers, *The Reluctant Entrepreneur* takes a broader approach and is meant for anyone providing any type of professional services to clients. (As Bates puts it, that includes therapists, consultants, accountants, and graphic designers as well as freelance taxonomists, consulting content strategists, and independent information project managers.) Because of this different perspective, the new information and insights are an expansion, rather than a repetition, of those found in *Research Business.*

Clifton, Jim and Sangeeta Bharadwaj Badal. *Entrepreneurial Strengths-Finder.* Gallup, 2014. 158p. ISBN 1595620828.
An exploration of the psychology of successful entrepreneurs, including their key behaviors and personality characteristics. In addition to identifying and describing the 10 talents of successful entrepreneurs, the authors elaborate on what each talent looks like in action, provide examples of noted businesspeople who exemplify that talent (and how they do so), and follow up with coaching advice on how to incorporate or strengthen that talent in your own career or business. This is a short read and geared more toward entrepreneurs looking to build companies rather than to solopreneurs and independents, but still useful as a reality check before going on your own.

de Stricker, Ulla. *Is Consulting for You? A Primer for Information Professionals.* American Library Association Editions, 2009. 101p. ISBN 0838909477.
From well-known library and information consultant de Stricker, this brief primer first addresses the realities of a consultant's life and whether or not that would be a good fit for you, and then moves on to how to get established and "get down to business." See especially chapter 5, "Business Planning: Is There a Market—and a Living—for Me?" before quitting your day job.

Palmer, Kimberly. *The Economy of You: Discover Your Inner Entrepreneur and Recession-Proof Your Life.* Amacom, 2014. 239p. ISBN 0814432730.
Supplemental businesses, otherwise known as side-gigs, are a terrific way to test out your entrepreneurial mettle while also providing an alternative revenue stream, should one be needed (hello, pink slip). Palmer provides information about the career trends driving this increasingly popular option, tips for identifying side-gig ideas, juggling your full-time job and side-gigs, and other logistics and tactical issues. As one who has thrived by combining full-time "day jobs" with a variety of side-gigs my entire career, I can heartily endorse both Palmer's message and advice. (Key resource)

Sinetar, Marsha. *To Build the Life You Want, Create the Work You Love: The Spiritual Dimension of Entrepreneuring.* St. Martin's, 1995. 210p. ISBN 0312141416.
Sinetar gained attention in the late 1980s for her popular *Do What You Love, the Money Will Follow* (Dell, 1989). In *Build the Life You Want,* she focuses on the spiritual aspects of an independent path and the various ways in which our careers (and their transition points) may lead us to it. Affirming that it's possible to be an entrepreneur without abandoning your personal values, this is a classic work, written before the advent of social entrepreneurship and the concept of building meaning and purpose into our careers.

*Start Your Own Business, 6th ed.* By Inc, the Staff of Entrepreneur Media. Entrepreneur Press, 2015. 766p. ISBN 1599185569.
The fact that *Start Your Own Business* is in its sixth edition provides a good indication of its usefulness to would-be entrepreneurs. Check here for information about finances, legal issues, business milestones to anticipate, how to target the appropriate market, and more.

Weiss, Alan. *The Consulting Bible: Everything You Need to Know to Create and Expand a Seven-Figure Consulting Practice.* Wiley, 2011. 288p. ISBN 0470928085.

Weiss's books are legendary among independents for their practical hands-on advice and counsel. *The Consulting Bible* is useful even for those who would be happy billing out substantially less than seven figures, as it addresses so many questions that independents of all sizes deal with every day. Topics include the role of a consultant, trends in consulting driven by changes in the corporate hiring landscape, landing clients, pricing, growing your business, building sustainable client relationships, and many other strategic topics. Other equally valuable books by Weiss include *Million Dollar Consulting, 4th ed.* (McGraw-Hill, 2009); *Value-Based Fees, 2d ed.* (Pfeiffer, 2008); and *Getting Started in Consulting, 3d ed.* (Wiley, 2009). (Key resource)

## Articles

"Nation Gains More than 4 Million Nonemployer Businesses Over the Last Decade, Census Bureau Reports" United States Census Bureau, May 27, 2015. Accessed at https://www.census.gov/newsroom/press-releas es/2015/cb15-96.html.
    The most current numbers on solopreneur and "mom and pop" businesses in the United States, representing a substantial and ongoing increase in nonemployer businesses. A fascinating overview of who's working independently, in what locations, and what types of work they're doing.

"There's an App for That." *The Economist* 414, no. 8919 (January 3, 2015): 29–32. Accessed at www.economist.com/news/briefing/21637355-freelance-workers-available-moments-notice-will-reshape-nature-companies-and.
    A fascinating, scary overview of the coming workplace, shaped by freelance or contingent workers. The tagline: "Freelance workers available at a moment's notice will reshape the nature of companies and the structure of careers." For those wanting to create a career or business as an independent information professional, this will be a trend to watch for potential opportunities.

## Periodicals

*Connections.* Association of Independent Information Professionals, 1986–. Quarterly. ISSN 1524–9468.
    www.aiip.org
    *Connections* is available to AIIP members only, but the current issue can be read by going to the AIIP website and selecting Discover > AIIP Connections. This will give you a good sense of the types of issues of interest to the membership.

*EContent.* Information Today, 2004–. 10/yr. ISSN 1525–2531.
    www.econtentmag.com
    *EContent* is intended for "decision-makers in the media, publishing, technology, and mobile sectors." It's also a great resource for anyone who works with econtent in any of its various iterations—for example, purchasers of ebooks, licensers of databases, and information professionals who use digital content in their jobs. Especially valuable for those independents whose work includes digital content development.

*Fast Company.* Fast Co., Inc., 1995–. Monthly. ISSN 1085–9241.
www.fastcompany.com
Imagine hanging out with a friend who is smart, funny, hip, and knows all the coolest people. OK, so sometimes she's a little bit *out there*, but she still comes up with enough interesting ideas to keep you hooked on those Saturday brunches . . . that's *Fast Company.* It covers cutting-edge business trends and ideas, showcases the insights of thought leaders, and almost always has something useful for career strategists. More engaging than intellectual, *Fast Company* is a great resource if your career focus is on the business world.

*Information Outlook.* Special Libraries Association, 1997–. Monthly. ISSN 1091–0808.
www.sla.org/content/Shop/Information/index.cfm
This now-digital publication is available to members as part of their membership benefits. There is substantial overlap between special librarians and independents in the resources they use, the knowledge and expertise they share, and often as clients and service providers for each other. *Information Outlook* is, consequently, not only a good tool for independents in their day-to-day practice, but also a good resource for staying abreast of potential clients and their issues. Because members also have access to an archive of back issues, many of which touch on resources or issues of interest to independents, being able to glean relevant information from *Information Outlook* may provide a good reason for joining SLA.

*Online Searcher: Information Discovery, Technology, Strategies.* Information Today, 1993–. 6/yr. ISSN 1070–4795.
www.infotoday.com/onlinesearcher/
The result of combining *Online* and *Searcher* magazines in 2013, *Online Searcher* content is geared toward those in "academic, corporate, government, law, medical, public library, knowledge management, web development, and freelance environments." The publication is written by and for information professionals, edited by well-known industry observers Marydee Ojala and Barbara Quint, and covers such topics as managing online research projects, client/employer research, new research technologies and tools, industry trends, and strategizing new information services. The website provides title access to past issues, some of which are available for free, others for a fee. A must-read for business researchers.

## Associations

*Association of Independent Information Professionals (AIIP)*
www.aiip.org
The primary resource for anyone considering a career as an independent information pro. AIIP is a very active, knowledge-rich organization whose members are legendary for their willingness to share best practices, business tips, product recommendations, and any other type of information that will help fellow members succeed. Membership in the organization brings access to the AIIP electronic discussion list, perhaps the most valuable learning tool available for independents, and a community of colleagues who will cheer your every success. Check the website for career information, publications, and information about the organization and its events. Steeply discounted student memberships. (Key resource)

*Special Libraries Association*
www.sla.org
As noted earlier, there is substantial crossover between the issues, interests, and goals of SLA and AIIP members. Consequently, many independent info pros who belong to AIIP are also SLA members and attend both annual conferences. SLA offers the benefits and diverse communities of a large professional group, while the much smaller and narrowly focused AIIP provides an amazingly collegial and supportive environment for its members. Both can play an important role in the success of an independent.

*Strategic and Competitive Intelligence Professionals (SCIP)*
www.scip.org
Competitive intelligence (CI) is an important component of business research across all industries and businesses. Many IIPs include CI as part of their service offering; some specialize only in CI. SCIP membership comprises both independents and CI specialists who work for businesses, so there is a broad range of experience and knowledge to share within the group. Check the website under CI Resources for salary information, white papers, articles, career information, and several overviews of the CI process. Steeply discounted student membership fees, but for full-time students only.

## Online Resources

*AIIP Discover*
www.aiip.org/Discover
This section of the AIIP website offers "Getting Started as an Independent Information Professional," a bibliography of resources on Info-Entrepreneurship, and additional information helpful for those independents just starting out or considering doing so.

*Bates Information Services*
www.batesinfo.com/index.html
Links to a vast number of resources Bates has compiled on life as an information researcher, consultant, trainer, and author. See especially the materials under the "Writing" and "Coaching" tabs, as well as the free ebooks found under the "Store" tab. For those who wish to learn more, Bates also offers a popular coaching service for information entrepreneurs.

*Considering an Online Business? Read This First*
www.entrepreneur.com/article/241981
From consultant Steve Tobak, this *Entrepreneur* post is a bracing (but truthful, based on my experience) reality check for content specialists (many of whom are LIS professionals) who think that starting an online business would be simple, easy, and a guaranteed revenue stream. Consider Tobak's advice to be wise counsel on how to succeed, rather than necessarily a reason not to try if this is where your passion lies.

*How to Get Paid for What You Already Do for Free*
http://bit.ly/1C02Aen
This idea-sparking post, subtitled "Tips for brainstorming, researching and designing a business," provides a useful starting point for thinking about what sort of information work (product or service) you might

want to consider should you decide to go independent or start a sideline business.

*The Independent Information Professional*
www.aiip.org/Content/Documents/Document.ashx?DocId=33869
An overview of the various types of independent information professional careers, including those involving general business and industry, legal research, the healthcare industries, public records, banking and finance, government and public policy, and science and technology. An excellent starting point if you'd like to get an overall sense of what IIPs actually do. (Key resource)

*Information Broker FAQ*
www.marketingbase.com/faqs.html
A quick overview of the market for info brokers, skills and attitudes needed, typical services offered, working as a part-time info broker, and more. From information-brokering mentor and coach Amelia Kassel, this page provides useful and practical information for those considering the profession.

*Me, Incorporated: We're All CEOs at the Company-Of-One*
www.careerealism.com/all-ceos-company-of-one/
From Joellyn Sargent, this October 2014 Careerealism post provides a brief but realistic overview of the initial steps involved in getting ready to go independent; especially important is her advice to start thinking like the boss—the person in charge of your future—even while you're still an employee.

*Presentations: Mary Ellen Bates*
www.slideshare.net/MaryEllenBates/presentations
Slide presentations accompanied by voice-over audio from Mary Ellen Bates on an extremely wide variety of topics related to succeeding as an information professional, whether employed or independent. Anyone who has heard Bates present on search tips, business strategy, marketing, or any number of other high-impact topics will appreciate having another chance to catch up with her insights; those who've never heard her present will find a library here of invaluable tips.

*Steps in Starting Your Own Business*
www.rileyguide.com/steps.html
A useful collection of resources (business plans, tutorials, advice, government agencies, tools, and more) under the headings of "Steps in Starting Up," "Finding Help," "Funding for Your Business," "A Little Legalese," and "Setting Up the Office." From the Riley Guide people.

## Freelance, Project, and Part-Time Work Sources

*Elance*
www.elance.com
For freelance writers, marketers, designers, mobile developers, data scientists, translators, project managers, and programmers, among others. If you're interested in using your information skills in the writing or content development area, it's encouraging to note that when last checked in December 2012, the categories of writing jobs, content writing jobs, and copywriting jobs were all trending up. However, keep in mind that individual projects typically pay very little.

*Flexjobs*

www.flexjobs.com

A reputable site for finding freelance gigs, project work, remote/tele-commuting opportunities, and part-time jobs. Although the focus is not specifically on information work, many LIS skills lend themselves to the types of opportunities listed here. In addition, many of these may provide a great way to test out your abilities as an independent.

*MediaBistro*

www.mediabistro.com

Information professionals interested in writing, editing, or content development may find MediaBistro offers some interesting opportunities. The site provides a freelance marketplace for professionals in social media, advertising and public relations, TV and video, publishing, design, and technology. In addition, the MediaBistro folks offer online writing and editing courses, job postings, and multiple blogs within each of the company's practice areas.

*ODesk*

www.odesk.com

Enter "research" into the job-search field and you'll find a number of interesting variations—for example, a grant-funding researcher, a blog researcher/ghost-writer, and an ebook researcher/writer. The pay is notoriously low here, but if you'd like to test out your skills a bit before seriously considering going independent (rather than actually trying to make serious money), ODesk could be a good option.

# 6

## Understanding, Describing, and Documenting Your Value

*If you don't know what you bring to the table, you won't get a seat there.*

—Dan Schwabel

You've explored your unique interests, aptitudes, and preferences. You've looked at traditional, nontraditional, and independent career options that build on your LIS professional skills. Now it's time to consider how those skills match up with the career opportunities you might want to pursue. To do that, you'll need to rethink, reframe, and rephrase how you interpret—and present—those skills.

In the library profession, we generally think of our skills in terms that connect with readily understood and categorized positions: for example, reference, readers' advisory, cataloging, circulation, network administration, archives, and collection development.

These positions are essentially "predefined" for us. For example, we expect that good reference librarians know how to answer questions asked by patrons, students, faculty, and employees. They know how to interview patrons to clearly understand their questions, know the range of information resources that are appropriate to the task, and are able to use them effectively and successfully to deliver the correct answers. Top-notch reference librarians are usually also adept at:

- Teaching others how to find and use appropriate information resources.

- Preparing print and online tutorials and guides on specific subjects.

- Creating and presenting workshops and seminars on information topics of value to their audiences.

- Continually monitoring multiple sources to learn about (and how to use) new information resources.

- Evaluating competing information resources and providers and recommending which to use, license, or purchase.

- Evaluating online resources for authority, credibility, and usefulness.

- Creating a supportive, welcoming dynamic to diffuse the library "intimidation factor" for patrons.

- Creating online content for the library's web portal for special communities of users.

- Tracking down information that might seem impossible to find to others.

- Listening for the nuances within a patron's question that indicate a different direction—or answer—might be warranted.

- Maintaining a positive attitude toward patrons despite the occasional challenges of dealing with the public, students, coworkers, and bosses.

All of these attributes are taken for granted as part of the job description for "reference librarian." However, any one of these could also be a key skill in other types of jobs, including those in nonlibrary environments. It all depends on how you frame them.

Each of the activities noted earlier for reference librarians involves a skill that has value across a broad range of organizations and opportunities. A good reference librarian has a dynamite combination of information and people skills, as do most individuals in the library profession. However, your ability to both understand *and frame* those skills effectively will determine how easily you transition from one professional opportunity to another as you move through your career.

Reframing your skills is a process that asks you to *identify and understand your skills in a broader context.* In addition, you need to:

- **Reconsider the language you use to describe your skills.** You must describe what you can do in terms that resonate with your audience, which means you need to understand and describe in *their* language.

- **Rethink and repurpose what you can do with your skills.** What roles, responsibilities, and opportunities would your skills prepare you for if there were no libraries?

- **Develop confidence in your skills—and the value they bring**. Because most traditional LIS jobs are predefined, or very specific regarding what activities and responsibilities they entail, we rarely have to push much beyond our "competence zone." Reframing your skills has as its goal, however, getting you into *new* opportunities—where you'll need confidence in both your skills and your ability to navigate unknown space.

# Understanding Your Skills

What do information skills look like? For starters, most MLIS graduates have at least a baseline level of expertise in the five core areas of

- Finding and/or acquiring information
- Organizing and/or managing information
- Working with the public
- Using information, communication, collaboration, and social media technologies to further the goals of the organization, including libraries
- Managing teams, projects, and, in some cases, organizations

But take those core skill areas and look at them a bit more closely, with an eye toward describing them to a nonlibrarian. What might they look like? For starters:

**Finding and/or acquiring information.** These are research skills, which entail being able to understand and refine a question; identify, evaluate, and use appropriate resources among the often thousands that exist; analyze and synthesize the information discovered; and if appropriate, present well-written, articulate, focused summaries and recommendations. Research skills can be broad based or centered on an advanced subject expertise you may have developed.

In addition, those doing acquisitions have developed skills in purchasing, license negotiating, and vendor relations. Many special librarians have experience in negotiating enterprise content purchases. Information professionals involved in collection development are skilled in the ability to understand, evaluate, and choose among the various types and formats of available resources and are also comfortable working with teams of colleagues to develop collection strategies.

**Organizing and/or managing information.** Yesterday's reasonably predictable job of "cataloger" has now expanded into an extremely diverse role that ranges from traditional materials cataloging to creating taxonomies for digital products, to understanding the critical role of metadata in digitization initiatives. But the core skill underlying all of these roles is the ability to create and/or apply standardized systems that organize—and allow for the efficient retrieval of—information.

Great catalogers and other LIS information organizers are extraordinarily attentive to detail, adept at creating conceptual relationships, and attuned to how users locate and retrieve information. Additionally, their understanding of cataloging and classification systems often comes with a high level of technology and systems expertise.

**Working with the public.** Depending on where they work, LIS professionals deal with many "publics"—patrons, students, faculty, coworkers, and/or clients, to name a few. Traditional public services work may include working the reference desk (in person or online), offering readers' advisory, doing BI, delivering outreach programs, running children's story hours, organizing corporate end-user training sessions, or proctoring exams for local online learning students.

Given this broad range of activities, info pros working in public services areas must possess strong communication skills, an ability to deal effectively with many different types of personalities, and an ability to think on their feet in response to an ongoing barrage of questions and information demands.

**Using technologies to further the goals of the organization, including libraries.** More and more traditional library work is based on the use of key technologies to accomplish a multitude of goals. These include tools for communication on demand, online group collaboration, web design and development, systems implementation, and data management and analysis. In addition, many librarians develop exceptional social media skills, navigating this space in ways sufficiently strategic to rival any corporate social media marketer.

These abilities are easily adapted to other environments, including for-profit, nonprofit, and independent work. Information technology drives, supports, or underlies nearly every function in today's organizations; consequently, it becomes a matter of deciding what organization, industry, or type of work you would like to pursue.

**Managing teams, projects, or organizations.** Many information projects are based on the effective management of teams and projects. In addition, library directors and deans, school librarians, and heads of organization information centers are all responsible for managing at least department-level enterprises, regardless of size. They establish organizational goals and priorities, set performance expectations, allocate resources, create budgets, deal with personnel issues, manage external relationships (with bosses, boards, and donors, among others), and respond to an exciting variety of crises, craziness, and (on a good day) opportunities.

Effective LIS managers must have solid leadership capabilities, an ability to both motivate people and hold them accountable, and a willingness to shift focus in response to changing circumstances. They understand each functional area that reports to them; so, for example, even if they don't know how to catalog a book, they understand the process, the skills required, and the issues involved.

All of the skills and abilities described for these five key areas are vital to the traditional work that LIS professionals do within the library field. But for those who want to broaden their options beyond traditional LIS career paths, they can all also be valuable to other roles both within and outside of the profession. For individuals who would like to explore career options outside of traditional library environments, these skills can be effectively "repurposed" for broader application.

These capabilities can be valuable to government agencies, nonprofits, business start-ups, large corporations, professional associations, and myriad other employers—or clients. The key is to understand how to frame or describe not the *titles* of the jobs you've held, but rather the *value* of what you can do.

# Describing Your Skills

How would you describe your skills to nonlibrarians, no jargon allowed?

You can find information—credible, reliable, actionable information—fast and often cheap. You know what makes for good online content and can often create it yourself. You can teach, and design and deliver both online and face-to-face training. You expertly organize large collections of things so that others can find and use items in the collections and are great at customer service and coaching. You work effectively in team-based and collaborative environments, usually possess excellent communication skills, and demonstrate a strong sense of community service, regardless of the specific community. Some LIS professionals possess extraordinary analytical skills, while others excel at creating highly innovative outreach programs. All of these skills are demonstrated in the jobs you do or have done.

In order to translate these terrific LIS skills and experience into broader opportunities, however, it's necessary to *describe* them in language that resonates with the individuals who provide those opportunities. That means

- Using business terminology to describe LIS activities (e.g., "created user-friendly, actionable guides to best-in-class topic resources" instead of "created pathfinders")

- Focusing on the value and benefits you bring rather than the titles you've had (consider "led the development and launch of the first program to support adult learners in the community," rather than "director of adult services")

- Emphasizing outcomes and results rather than activities and roles (e.g., "developed collaborative programs with several local nonprofits that resulted in a 20% increase in program participation" rather than "ran outreach programs")

For example, someone who's worked as a systems librarian in an academic library might emphasize his or her history of leading collaborative teams that created technology solutions; project management skills that resulted in a new system implementation on time and under budget; review and evaluation of five vendor proposals that resulted in negotiated cost savings of 15 percent to the organization; or creation and leadership of a campus-wide integrated teaching technologies group that monitored and introduced advances in teaching technologies.

Leadership, team building. Project management, budget and resource oversight. Vendor evaluation, contract negotiation and licensing, cost reductions. Taking initiative, leading collaborative projects, focusing on emerging opportunities. Phrasing skill descriptions in terms of results, accomplishments, and value added allows them to resonate with *any* employer, not just the traditional library human resources person (who would, by the way, also find them exemplary).

It's also an effective way for you to recast how *you* think about your capabilities. One of the things many of us do is downplay the value of what "comes naturally" to us (or comes naturally after multiple grad-school courses). If you're a whiz on the Internet, but you figure this is just part of your job and you're good at it, chances are you're not going to think of this as a particularly valuable or noteworthy skill. But the reality is that a whiz on the Internet can bring exceptional value as a business researcher, CI specialist, donor prospect evaluator, or any number of tactical roles.

So get into the habit of acknowledging what you're good at, with a focus on what your skills have accomplished. Don't be shy about this; you *do* bring value, and it's up to you to highlight it in language that's meaningful in the nonlibrary world. Still shy about this? Recruit a friendly colleague who understands what you do and will happily describe to you your greatest assets. And when you think about or describe those assets, understand that they potentially contribute value to many types of organizations, both within and outside of traditional librarianship.

# Repurposing Your Skills

Information skills (often library skills in disguise) are in demand. But to connect your information skills with the range of potential opportunities, you need to rethink the application of those skills and get comfortable "repurposing" them.

For instance, a research capability would enable you to also excel at these value-added activities:

- Investigating people, issues, organizations, and industry trends
- Undertaking primary as well as secondary research
- Designing research projects
- Creating and delivering an executive information service
- Providing data analysis, synthesis, and evaluations/recommendations
- Researching and assessing donor prospects
- Creating presentation content
- Providing market forecast and trend information and tracking
- Preparing an assessment of market opportunity
- Providing current awareness/alerting services
- Creating newsletter content
- Writing abstracts and summaries of key business publications
- Creating customized web content
- Preparing company, market, and/or competitive profiles
- Undertaking patent research
- Researching and analyzing sales prospects
- Developing initial information components for scenario planning
- Providing baseline information for SWOT (strengths, weaknesses, opportunities, threats) analyses
- Writing internal and/or external topic briefings or white papers
- Working with the information technology team to provide technology assessment

Or consider the ability to organize and manage information and information systems. Increasingly critical to the success of organizations, this may go way beyond the "knowledge management" descriptor. For example, an information professional with expertise in this area might appropriately highlight his or her ability to

- Analyze and map business processes
- Design systems and processes for supporting internal knowledge transfer
- Oversee the development and application of topic-specific taxonomies
- Evaluate and choose among vendor-provided storage, access, and retrieval options

- Align technology analysis/implementation with organizational strategic goals
- Develop training materials and provide system training to users
- Implement best-practice project management tools and processes
- Monitor emerging technologies and issues related to business intelligence management
- Collaborate with other departments to develop an integrated, enterprise-wide intranet
- Plan, implement, and document a system-wide information architecture
- Develop databases to support operations, such as customer relationship management or Sarbanes–Oxley compliance
- Lead project teams
- Create the infrastructure of internal or external communities of practice
- Organize and undertake an employee skills inventory

Or perhaps you've spent your career in public services. Your ability to navigate an information interview, your strong verbal and written communication skills, your ability to work supportively and effectively with all sorts of personalities, and your familiarity with teaching patrons the intricacies of various information resources mean your skills might easily port to these related opportunities:

- Customer service management
- Product development
- Market research
- Focus group facilitation
- Vendor representative
- Sales
- Training and development
- Teaching
- Instructional design
- Online teaching
- Outreach/program development
- Creator of information literacy programs
- Online librarian
- Information and referral program manager for a government agency

Strong research and writing skills transfer easily into policy analysis; a systems network background can bridge to work developing corporate intranets. Reference and user services translate into product development and customer service roles for information product vendors, while working with library donors and friends' groups would be equally effective for a multitude of nonprofits.

Library managers have the most easily repurposed skill set, because effective managers are critical to the successful running of all organizations. So a library manager who can demonstrate a successful track record of leadership, staff development, budgeting, community relationships (regardless of what that community may be), crisis management, and the host of other challenges that come with day-to-day management can easily transfer these skills into other organizations, whether from one type of library to another, or from a library environment into a business, nonprofit, or government agency.

## Transferable *vs.* Translatable Skills

The key concept here is *transferable skills*. These are skills that bring value to many environments, rather than being specific to a given organization. Although you may have learned and practiced them in the context of library work, they can be applied to new types of library work or to new nonlibrary work opportunities. As noted earlier, these can include technology skills, an ability to work with customers/the public, management expertise, communication skills, and overall information research and/or management abilities.

However, while the key *concept* may be transferable skills, the key *activity* is translating them for the non-LIS world. The easiest way to explore repurposing your skills is to start reading job descriptions, both library focused and nonlibrary, for industries or organizations that interest you. While you're exploring, check out the wording they use to describe various positions and line up your skills against their specifications. Adapt their language to describe your capabilities. That way, potential employers who don't understand what a Library Specialist Grade IV is capable of will still be able to understand the value you bring to their specific organization.

One of the easiest ways to translate your skill set is to look for keywords used in job descriptions, especially those that are clearly simply a different way of describing activities and competencies with which you're familiar through your LIS work. Not sure if your writing skills translate into a consumer content developer role? Then start researching additional similar job descriptions for more detail.

Another way to quickly get a handle on non-LIS (but related) job titles is to use two LinkedIn features: Edit Profile and Jobs. When you select the "Profile > Edit Profile" option from the drop-down menu, you'll be given an option (down the page a bit) to add Skills & Endorsements. When you start to type in a term, LinkedIn will automatically display the key terms searched on related to that skill. You'll immediately be able to see what employers call the skills they're looking for. The other LinkedIn function you'll want to explore is the Jobs feature. When you put in keywords or titles you think might be relevant, you'll see jobs that match (or almost match) your keywords. By looking at these job descriptions, you'll start to recognize the language you'll use to describe your own skills in non-LIS environments (as well as getting a good feel for who's hiring).

### An Initial Process for Mapping Transferable Skills

Considering transitioning from a traditional LIS job to a job outside the familiar library roles? One of the biggest challenges you'll face is figuring out how your traditional skill set "maps" to non-LIS positions.

In an effort to create a group of questions that could be replicated for each LIS role, I decided to take one job—reference librarian—and see how it could be taken apart as an LIS role and then parsed into non-LIS opportunities. A caveat here: I've never actually *been* a reference librarian, but have colleagues who've been willing to share their reference-librarian experiences with me, so this represents my best-guess interpretation of basic reference-librarian skills.

Here's the process I would go through to map this role:

**Job title:** Reference/research librarian

**Core job skill:** Research

**Job skill components:** (1) Mastery of research process; (2) ability to conduct successful reference interview; (3) ability to identify, evaluate, and choose best, most authoritative information resources to answer question; (4) ability to successfully use those tools to answer patron questions.

**Additional "soft skill" business strengths:** (1) Customer relations; (2) interviewing; (3) interpersonal communication; (4) ability to identify or understand "the question behind the question."

**Business value-add:** (1) Analysis and synthesis; (2) research results presentation and packaging for client; (3) specialized topic knowledge (e.g., biotechnology); (4) specialized resource knowledge (e.g., public records or patents). *[Note: these are skills that would make your basic reference skills more valuable to a non-LIS employer.]*

**Shift in approach:** In a business or organization setting, your research will generally be used for decision support, so you will be expected to provide very targeted information and data as concisely as possible—think bullet points; also, research will often be only one component of your mandate—you may also be relied on to analyze, synthesize, and "package" the information so key points are readily identifiable.

**Potentially translates to:** Business or data analyst, business or information researcher, market research, business or product development support/research, CI specialist, donor or prospect researcher (in general, all of these titles would include descriptors such as "analyst," "researcher," "specialist," or "coordinator").

**Additional potential roles:** Focus group facilitator/leader; environmental scanning specialist; business trends analyst; customer service, content curation, writer, online content developer.

**Who would use these skills:** Almost all businesses (most likely in these departments: marketing, sales, business development, product development, corporate communication, and/or community affairs), large nonprofits (especially for donor research), marketing and PR agencies (research for their client projects), organizations that use content for marketing/branding purposes.

**Considerations:** (1) Think about which aspects of reference work you most enjoy to determine which of these career paths might be most appropriate for you—for example, if you especially enjoy the people interaction part of reference work, then you might be most interested in jobs like market research, focus group facilitation, or customer service; (2) think about whether or not there's a subject area you'd like to specialize in if you choose to pursue the research field; (3) if your writing skills aren't solid, you'll want to practice them until they are.

Although this process has been used for just one LIS role, research/reference librarian, it may help you map any number of LIS skill sets and competencies into new nontraditional or non-LIS roles.

## Creating Your Portfolio Career—and Career Portfolio

One way to begin building your confidence factor around your transferable skills is to reconsider your work history, with an eye toward noting your track record of growth, accomplishments, and contribution. In other words, reframe your career into a "portfolio" perspective.

Most of us have a tough time saying great things about ourselves in an interview. You don't want to come across as a braggart, but on the other hand, you really *did* nail that last project, and against overwhelming odds. How can you convey that information with confidence in an interview situation, when you're likely to be feeling nervous and unsure of yourself?

One great way to overcome this challenge is to create something in advance, when you're not feeling pressured or nervous—and that something would be your professional portfolio. Whether a physical or online collection of materials, your portfolio can speak for you, showcasing the best achievements of your career, describing them clearly and thoughtfully, and documenting them with supporting evidence (including others' recommendations).

Think of your career portfolio as an inventory of projects, accomplishments, contributions, innovations, initiatives, and other cool things you've done along the way. They don't necessarily have to be library related, but you want to focus on activities that demonstrate a growing capability to assume responsibility; analyze information and use it effectively to make strategic decisions; and identify and implement solutions to problems/challenges. Look back over your career history: when did you demonstrate leadership, great communication, team management skills, and knowledge growth? (By the way, grad school is a great place to start building all these portfolio elements!)

Once you start thinking through how to reframe your career history along these lines, you begin to understand how LIS skills can transfer—and be valuable—both inside and outside traditional library environments. Approaching your career from this perspective moves you from "this is what I know" to "this is what I can do with what I know," which then moves you to "and this is why I'm such an incredible asset." Recasting your career into a portfolio-based approach also gives you an extremely valuable tool with which to shape your career and its opportunities.

The physical expression of your portfolio can be anything that works for you—from your career journal to an outline of key themes and activities to a graphic or visual map of work you've done, projects you've worked on, skills you've mastered, and the connections among them. The point is to use a method that helps you identify the connections and themes central to your work life.

**Creating a value-focused resume.** Time to take out your career journal and get ready to start taking notes, because translating your portfolio into a written document entails rethinking both the information you provide and the way in which you organize it. A value-focused resume differs from a standard one by showcasing skills mastered and applied, outcomes achieved, and solutions initiated rather than titles held. A quick overview of the differences between the two would be:

| Standard Resume | Value-Focused Resume |
| --- | --- |
| Job parameters | Accomplishments |
| Activities/tasks | Outcomes/results |
| Position/title | Projects |

Essentially, a value-focused resume documents demonstrations of competence.

## Reviewing Your History

To begin to "translate" your career history into a professional portfolio, consider what activities you've engaged in that match the following descriptions and fill them in (either on this page or in your career journal).

Took responsibility for _____

Led the creation of _____

Assembled and managed team that _____

Organized and executed _____

Wrote the _____

Changed the _____

Designed the _____

Assessed and evaluated _____

Spoke on behalf of _____

Researched and recommended _____

Created program to enhance _____

Initiated community outreach program _____

*. . . that resulted in . . .*

. . . cost savings of _____

. . . increased donations in the amount of _____

. . . expanded visibility for _____

. . . new opportunities for _____

. . . higher patron usage levels for _____

. . . greater attendance at _____

. . . this new program _____

The idea is to demonstrate an ability to contribute to an organization's goals and the professional effectiveness to do so successfully, whether those organizations are libraries or other types of enterprises. And be sure to note in your journal if there are other achievements not included here, whether part of professional or volunteer activities.

# Designing Your Portfolio

As you mine your career experiences for portfolio entries, you'll want to focus on transferable skills. They will be of two kinds: discipline-specific skills such as reference or serials management or cataloging, and professional cross-disciplinary ones such as leadership or project management. Any potential employer will immediately understand the value of your cross-disciplinary skills. However, as was noted previously, you'll want to describe your library-specific skills with a broader context, so resume reviewers will immediately understand those skills' applicability to their specific job openings.

Putting together a written document that represents your professional portfolio will help you work through the four key areas of reframing your skills—identifying and understanding your skills in a broader context, shifting the language you use to describe your skills, rethinking and repurposing what you can do with your skills, and developing confidence in your skills and contribution. The overall goal is to demonstrate both to yourself and others the breadth and depth of your skills—and your value.

As an example of the difference between the traditional and value-focused approaches, consider the following job history descriptions: one a traditional chronological rendering of jobs and job descriptions, and the other a value-focused approach that highlights achievements.

Another way to approach this would be to describe your "engagement experience." An example would be:

*Information strategy. Have worked with nonprofits and corporations to help them determine how to align internal and external information resources with their strategic goals. Goals included increased visibility*

## Traditional Resume Job History Overview

| 2011–Current | Director, Corporate Information Services<br>Responsible for managing corporate information resources (print and electronic), performing research as requested, managing vendor contracts, and assisting with company website as needed. |
|---|---|
| 2006–2011 | Assistant Director, Knowledge Center<br>Assisted director in overall management and maintenance of company library, responsible for collection development for engineering department. |
| 2000–2006 | Information Specialist, Community Nonprofit<br>Did research project, answered questions for staff and public, maintained resource library. |

**Value-Focused Resume Job History Overview**

| 2011–Current | Director, Corporate Information Services<br>Led the creation and launch of a company-wide business intelligence portal that enabled product design, customer service, and marketing teams to elicit and receive feedback from key customers; the resulting "feedback loop" was so successful that it has now been integrated into all product development initiatives. |
|---|---|
| 2006–2011 | Assistant Director, Knowledge Center<br>Created company-wide knowledge-sharing initiative among staff engineers that led to the organization's first online community of practice; based on the success of this COP, the engineering department won its first-ever "company innovators" award. |
| 2000–2006 | Information Specialist, Community Nonprofit<br>Developed the first information collection on microenterprise opportunities in community, which helped increase the number of microenterprise start-ups by 20% per year from 2000 through 2005. |

*in the marketplace, higher membership numbers, greater consumer interest, positioning as a thought leader or industry authority, or new revenue streams.*

***Content development.*** *Have developed successful print, presentation, and online content to drive organization's strategic goals. Content has included articles, white papers, speeches, knowledge guides, online tutorials, online reference tools (timelines, glossaries, industry overviews, etc.), resource directories, and communities of interest.*

***Research.*** *Have conducted primary and secondary research for nonprofit and corporate employers, especially in the areas of education, business, competitive intelligence, trends forecasting, and information services.*

As you can see, the portfolio approach clearly tells prospective employers what you're capable of and in what ways you'll be a valuable contributor to their organization. You can then follow this intro material with a chronological listing of jobs if appropriate.

# Growing Your Portfolio

What if your career so far hasn't offered you much of an opportunity to demonstrate competency, or participate in any interesting projects, or come up with any cool solutions? Then it's time to get started, using one of the many ways to "bulk up" your portfolio. Keep in mind that you're also bulking up your experience and expertise, and the confidence that goes with that, as you add bullet points to your portfolio.

The first place to check for portfolio-building opportunities is your current job. Volunteer for projects just getting started, where your skills can make a valuable contribution. As you do so, keep in mind your time frame. Sally Gibson, head of the Cataloging, Acquisitions, and Processing Department at Illinois State University, makes the wise point that you should "volunteer for short-term projects if you do not plan to stay in your current situation for very long. This way, you will have the opportunity to see a project through from beginning to end."[1]

See whether there are any workflow issues that could benefit from new more streamlined processes—and design them. Decide to become the local expert on some aspect of your job (or an area of professional interest) and then share what you learn with your colleagues and/or professional community. Seek out opportunities to collaborate with peers from other departments to develop interdepartmental initiatives where useful. Ask your supervisor what he or she feels would enhance the success of the department (or its efficiency, or morale, or visibility, etc.), then lead a brainstorming session with like-minded colleagues to identify (and then implement) solutions.

Let others know you're looking for professional growth opportunities and be willing to say yes even though it may mean more work for no increase in pay. OK, *usually* it means more work for no pay increase, but keep in mind that you're basically investing in your career, in the same way you would be if taking a class to increase your skills. Essentially, you're building a career base from which to launch multiple professional opportunities.

If your workplace doesn't lend itself to portfolio building, look next to your professional associations (including graduate student groups). Once again, volunteering is key. Taking on the organization newsletter can demonstrate your ability to write and edit, to lead team projects, to work with publishing and e-mail software and platforms, to meet deadlines, and to coordinate group efforts. Becoming program chair demonstrates an ability to manage multiple, ongoing projects with constantly shifting personnel and logistics challenges, an ability to deal calmly and effectively (on a good day) with last-minute crises, and an ability to envision, organize, and execute programming ideas that align with the goals of the organization.

If you're looking for an opportunity to demonstrate your leadership capabilities, run for executive office. As president or president-elect, you'll have an opportunity to suggest—and then follow up on—new initiatives, processes, or opportunities. Or consider becoming the group's webmaster, where you may be creating valuable new online content to support a membership drive, or reorganizing the site to create a best-in-class knowledge portal, or implementing technology fixes that enable new interactive site capabilities. Or create a new role—chief learning officer—and develop a professional development agenda for which you identify and organize access to key information resources for members.

The opportunities to contribute are endless and can be at the local, state, regional, national, or international level, depending on your interests. But it's up to you to take the initiative to make a difference and create "portfolio-worthy" outcomes.

On the other hand, if LIS-related professional organizations aren't your passion, consider volunteering in something that *does* matter to you, again going for maximum impact from the skills you contribute. Create a web presence for your local League of Women Voters, do donor research for the American Red Cross, help your town's synagogue (or church or temple or mosque) create a theology library, develop information resources for the local women's microenterprise lending group.

Do an information guide for new pet owners for the local Humane Society, teach a class on Internet research at the senior center down the street. Research and write a position paper for your favorite political candidate. Solicit donations for a career resource library at the local teen center and then create it, or volunteer to spend one day a month teaching high-school seniors how to find financial aid resources. Use your LIS skills to contribute to a cause you believe in, whether by doing research, organizing existing information, creating an information collection, helping create a web presence, or some other professional-level activity. This will allow you to start using your skills to build a better world while also strengthening those skills and documenting your ability to create value with them.

If you're an LIS student, consider these options for growing your portfolio entries:

- Join or start a student chapter of a national organization and volunteer for a position that lets you demonstrate or broaden an existing skill.

- Whenever possible, consider your class projects and assignments to be "trial runs" of professional-level projects and imagine how you would package and present the information within a nonlibrary environment.

- If possible, structure your internships, practicums, and/or capstone projects so that they are project-based and enable you to either demonstrate or broaden a key competency.

- Consider taking courses outside the MLIS curriculum to add unique skills to your knowledge base and use assignments from those courses to create portfolio-worthy papers, assessments, trends analyses, or similar types of documents that reflect your interests.

Most importantly, keep in mind that what's important in the long run is not what courses you've gotten A's in, but how many ways you can strategically apply the knowledge you've gained.

As you go about building your portfolio, look for ways to demonstrate key professional strengths, including the ability and willingness to

- Take initiative
- Create innovative solutions
- Make effective, well-reasoned decisions
- Identify, analyze, and draw actionable conclusions from information
- Effectively use print and verbal communication skills to achieve goals
- Monitor and make the best use of financial resources
- Participate in place-based and virtual teams
- Collaborate across departmental boundaries
- Organize and execute projects on your own
- Lead and/or manage teams, projects, or initiatives
- Learn as needed—in other words, yes, you have an existing capability, but you can also grow quickly to adapt to new opportunities
- Invest yourself for the benefit of others

## Benefits of a Portfolio Approach

Taking a portfolio approach to your career delivers a number of benefits.

For those of us who have had, shall we say, somewhat *eclectic* careers, it's a way to bring together what might seem like disparate, disconnected pieces of jobs and activities into a cohesive whole. I've worked in many jobs for many employers in a number of different industries; yet from a portfolio approach, what counts is the projects I've worked on in each of those jobs. Have they demonstrated an increasingly strategic role? Have they showcased an ability to take initiative, manage complex projects, bridge professional communities, expand my knowledge to meet the needs of the opportunity? This type of professional growth may not jump out at a potential employer or client from a traditional resume—and in fact, you may not have noticed it yourself if you've been thinking of your career as simply a series of job titles. A portfolio approach gives you a different perspective.

Another benefit is that by reframing your career this way, you're more likely to see themes or connections that might not have been otherwise clear to you. Focusing on the things that have been rewarding to you, what do the projects you've worked on or the various types of work you've done have in common? Were they all focused, for example, on designing processes? Or being a change agent in peoples' lives? Or developing information content? This can be an important part of your self-assessment exploration, because it will help you highlight threads of continuity you may want to develop in more depth.

Putting together your professional portfolio will also help you identify areas where you might bulk up your skills, education, or experience to fill in gaps—or further develop potential areas of opportunity. Based on this examination, for example, you might decide a lateral move that doesn't provide more money or a higher-level title is still worth going after because it offers oversight of a terrific project or will help you learn valuable new skills.

A portfolio approach can also help you expand your career by *bridging* into new areas rather than by *recareering*. What's the difference? Recareering is when you pretty much walk away from the professional base and expertise you've built over the years and begin an entirely new career from scratch (translation: you're the lowest one on the totem pole again). Bridging, on the other hand, allows you to extend the reach of your existing career by using the skills and competencies demonstrated in one arena—or type of library, or professional discipline—to another. By focusing on building up and out from the base you've already assembled, you avoid having to start paying all those dues all over again. A portfolio approach can help you identify those transferable skills and eventually document them to a future employer.

Lastly, taking the time to pull together a portfolio-type overview of your career will help you understand more clearly where you are today and where you want to be headed. By understanding the overall shape and direction of your career so far, you'll be in a better position to assess what investments of time, effort, and intellect will get you to where you want to go.

---

### The Art and Science of Landing the Job

Cover letters, portfolio resumes, interviewing skills—how effectively you present yourself to a potential employer often depends on your ability to master these key tools. Happily, there are some terrific resources to support that mastery. Consider:

Tony Beshara's *Unbeatable Resumes: America's Top Recruiter Reveals what REALLY Gets You Hired* (AMACOM, 2011). Although not specific to LIS jobs, Beshara's advice is practical and based on his experience as a successful placement specialist. Especially helpful is that he goes beyond traditional resume advice and includes the job application situations more and more job hunters are dealing with today, for example, video resumes, social networking, and applying online with automated systems. A great resource for understanding what might be wrong with your resume and how to make it right.

Wendy S. Enelow and Louise M. Kursmark's *Cover Letter Magic: Trade Secrets of Professional Resume Writers, 4th ed.* (JIST Works, 2010), a comprehensive, step-by-step guide to creating successful cover letters—basically, everything you could ever want to know about cover letters (and more) but all useful information. Related titles are Susan Britton Whitcomb's *Resume Magic, 4th ed.* and *Interview Magic 2d ed.,* from the same publisher.

Because social media is a pretty important part of job searching and professional positioning (i.e., marketing yourself to potential employers) these days, Kristen Jacoway's *I'm in a Job Search—Now What??? Using LinkedIn, Facebook, and Twitter as Part of Your Job Search Strategy, 2d ed.* (Happy About, 2012) can be a useful resource for charting out your social media job-hunt strategy. A quick read that presents more than 100 resources and tips for using social media tools to advance both your job search and your career.

For additional practical advice, although from outside the LIS community, consider perusing the "Career Resources" section of Monster.com (see especially the articles under "Resume Resources" and "Top Articles in Career Advice"). Also check out the excellent resume, cover letter, and interviewing articles at Quintessential Careers (www.quintcareers.com), listed in the Job-Hunting Tools, Career Tools, and Career Categories on the site's left-side menu.

Lastly, you may want to check out Jay Conrad Levinson and David E. Perry's *Guerrilla Marketing for Job Hunters 3.0: How to Stand Out from the Crowd and Tap into the Hidden Job Market Using Social Media and 999 Other Tactics Today* (Wiley, 2011), which, although a bit more "in your face" than most of us are likely to be, nevertheless offers solid advice and lots of it. The book covers creative ways to approach personal branding, key elements of a successful attitude, and tools and tactics for "cracking the hidden job market"; coaches you through your research plan, provides a resume writing and cover letter boot camp, and lays out the why-to's and how-to's of networking; walks you through LinkedIn and other social media tools and tactics, then describes how to get in front of the people you want to meet with.

Also, if you're a student, consider asking your faculty and/or student advisers to help you set up a mock interview day, where local practitioners help students practice and refine their interview skills through simulated interview situations. It provides a priceless opportunity to become familiar with the types of questions you'll be fielding (as well as asking) in a safe environment where the goal is to coach you to success.

# Resources

## Books

Handy, Charles. *The Age of Unreason*. Harvard Business School Press, 1998. 288p. ISBN 08758443018.
   The book that predicted the de-jobbing of the workplace as a social and economic phenomenon. Handy, a British organizational management expert, argued that the historical workplace of stable jobs and lifelong employment was going to be replaced by a working environment characterized by constant, random, and discontinuous change. He predicted the emergence of a new class of workers called "portfolio professionals" whose work would be project based, networked, and decentralized. A fascinating work upon whose ideas many others have built.

Hoffman, Reid, Ben Casnocha, and Chris Yeh. *The Alliance: Managing Talent in the Networked Age*. Harvard Business Review Press, 2014. 224p. ISBN 1625275773.
   Hoffman and Casnocha, who wrote the best-selling (and very actionable) *The Start-Up of You* in 2012 for individuals strategizing career development, approach a similar topic in *The Alliance* but from the employers' point of view. Essentially, what do employers need to do to create a realistic, trust-based relationship with employees in a world where loyalty in either direction is no longer part of the equation. It's useful for employees to read as well, however, because it will help them identify and negotiate for job relationships that benefit both stakeholders.

Kashdan, Todd B. *Curious? Discover the Missing Ingredient to a Fulfilling Life*. Harper Perennial, 2010. 336p. ISBN 001661198.
   In Adam Bryant's book *Corner Office* (St. Martin's Griffin, 2012), he interviewed dozens of CEOs to determine, among other things, what they most valued in employees. "Passionate curiosity" was considered one of the most important characteristics, one that outweighed age considerations for all who commented on it. Psychologist Kashdan presents arguments for the importance of curiosity to a fully-lived and rewarding life, but curiosity may also be considered an important strength to highlight as you document your value. A fascinating book.

Reinhold, Barbara Bailey. *Free to Succeed: Designing the Life You Want in the New Free Agent Economy*. Plume, 2001. 258p. ISBN 0452282519.
   *Free to Succeed* is hardcore "how-to": lots of checklists, charts, statistics, and exercises—to be expected of an author who's also a professional career coach. But much of her advice is both thought-provoking and actionable, even though its focus is not specific to the LIS profession. Although in dire need of updating, *Free to Succeed* nevertheless remains a useful resource for brainstorming ideas and possibilities.

Shontz, Priscilla K. and Richard A. Murray. *What Do Employers Want? A Guide for Library Science Students*. Libraries Unlimited, 2012. 118p. ISBN 1598848283.
   In order to determine how best to showcase your value to LIS employers, it helps to understand how to match your value to their needs. Shontz and Murray have given you a great start here, especially if you're a student or recent grad. A terrific starting point for your initial LIS job search. (Key resource)

Slim, Pamela. *Body of Work: Finding the Thread That Ties Your Story Together.* Portfolio/Penguin, 2013. 240p. ISBN 1591846192.

> Besides the fact that Slim leads off with one of the all-time great quotes ("Life isn't about finding yourself. Life is about creating yourself."—George Bernard Shaw), this is a wonderful guide to finding the threads of continuity that can be discovered in even the most eclectic career. The author focuses on the concept of "bodies of work" in a way that aligns with and supports a portfolio-based career approach. An interesting, useful, and highly engaging exploration of underlying individual career themes. (Key resource)

## Articles

Markgren, Suzanne. "Ten Simple Steps to Create and Manage Your Professional Online Identity: How to Use Portfolios and Profiles." *College & Research Libraries* News 72, vol. 1 (January 2011). Accessed at http://crln.acrl.org/content/72/1/31.full.

> Another excellent resource from Susanne Markgren, this article provides a walk-through of the steps necessary to create an effective online portfolio, as well as the reasons why this is so important to your job-hunting and long-term career goals. (Key resource)

"Portfolio Careers: Is the Latest Work Trend Right for You?" Learnvest for *Forbes*, February 27, 2013. Accessed at www.forbes.com/sites/learnvest/2013/02/27/portfolio-careers-is-the-latest-work-trend-right-for-you/.

> A great starting point for understanding portfolio (or project-based) careers as well as a related career approach—"slashers," who create sustainable careers based on simultaneously pursuing multiple career and revenue opportunities.

Zimmerman, Eilene. "Making a Living, One Project at a Time." *New York Times*, August 25, 2012. Accessed at www.nytimes.com/2012/08/26/jobs/making-a-living-one-project-at-a-time-career-couch.html?_r=0.

> Describes the emerging employment category of "career project professionals," a group that chooses to work short term on specific projects in their areas of expertise. This is an extreme iteration of the portfolio-based career, where one's portfolio of accomplishments opens up opportunities to work independently on a series of short-term projects.

## Online Resources

*Attention New Librarians and Career Changers: Identifying and Conveying Transferable Skills*

> http://ala-apa.org/newsletter/2005/04/17/attention-new-librarians-and-career-changers/
> An ALA-APA *Library Worklife* article by Julie Todaro, this is an excellent, very comprehensive overview of the concept of transferable skills as well as those most common/applicable to LIS professionals. Even though this was written years ago, Todaro's key points and concepts are still highly relevant.

*Suzanne Markgren's Online Portfolio*

> http://smarkgren.wordpress.com/
> An outstanding example of an online professional portfolio compiled by author (*Career Q&A: A Librarian's Real-Life, Practical Guide to*

*Managing a Successful Career)* and academic digital services librarian Suzanne Markgren.

*Making the Shift: Using Transferable Skills to Change Career Paths*
LISCareer.com, March 2010. Accessed at www.liscareer.com/taylor_transferable.htm
An outstanding overview from Deborah Taylor of the steps necessary to define and apply transferable LIS skills. See especially Taylor's Transferable Skills grid, which lays out skills by Area [of LIS activity], People, Things, and Info/Data. (Key resource)

*Only 7% of Job Seekers Do This, But Everyone Should*
http://bit.ly/1xtsC30
The thing that they should do, according to writer Lea McLeod, is build a personal website to strengthen their reputation and visibility. In addition to citing the benefits of this approach, McLeod outlines the steps necessary to create your personalized website.

*Transferable Job Skills*
www.quintcareers.com/transferable_skills.html
Part of the Quintessential Careers site presented by QuintCareers, this resource brings together five practical articles on identifying and showcasing in-demand transferable skills. Three of the articles deal with shaping cover letters so that they most effectively highlight your transferable skills, while the two others speak to their strategic value to your career and provide a detailed list organized by category (communication, research and planning, human relations, organization/management/leadership, and work survival). Not specific to LIS careers, but applicable information nevertheless.

*Transferable Skills*
www.lisjobs.com/CareerQA_blog/?s=transferable+skills
From Career Q&A with the Library Career People, this collection of questions and answers about using transferable skills to open up additional LIS career opportunities offers terrific insights in how to make the most of your own transferable skills. (Key resource)

*Transferable Skills: Bringing Your Skills to a New Career*
http://careerplanning.about.com/od/careerchoicechan/a/transferable.htm
An About.com article written by Dawn Rosenberg McKay, this piece from her *Career Planning* guide covers what transferable skills are, how to identify your own transferable skills, and understanding how you can most effectively use and sell those skills to a prospective employer. See also the many related articles on transferable skills linked from Ms. McKay's.

*Using Portfolios and Profiles to Professionalize Your Online Identity (for Free)*
www.liscareer.com/markgren_portfolio.htm
Another helpful article from digital librarian and LIS career expert Susanne Markgren, this is an excellent overview of the what, why, and how-to of e-portfolios.

# Note

1. Author correspondence with Sally Gibson, December 27, 2014.

# 7
# Thriving on Change

*I am not afraid of storms, for I am learning how to sail my ship.*

—Louisa May Alcott

In careers as in life, change brings opportunity. In fact, if you have a good understanding of who you are and what you may want to achieve (which you do by now!), change can be a tremendous ally.

In 1934, Austro-American economist Joseph Schumpeter published his landmark study of entrepreneurship, *Theory of Economic Development: An Inquiry into Profits, Capital, Credit, Interest and the Business Cycle* (Harvard University Press). Although economists of the day generally dismissed any role for entrepreneurship as a major macroeconomic influence, Schumpeter asserted that periods of technological innovation and the entrepreneurial activities associated with them created "waves of creative destruction." Old ways of doing things were swept away, but were replaced by dynamic new processes and solutions, not to mention businesses, industries, and job opportunities.

Well, yes, change *also* brings disruption, confusion, uncertainty, and often a sense of loss. No wonder it's so easy to default to our "duck and cover" response—if I ignore it, it just *might* go away. By now, however, most of us have realized that's probably not the most effective coping strategy, and many of us are learning to take a different approach. Like so many things, that involves reframing—specifically, reframing what change can mean in your life.

If we take Schumpeter's vantage point, change offers opportunities where none previously existed. The trick is to learn how to spot them and then how to align your skills with those opportunities. As Mary Ellen Bates

149

has suggested, "learn to think like an entrepreneur," and that bit of wisdom applies whether you're employed or an independent.

Before you begin this chapter, take out your career journal and think back through moments of major change in your career. Note them in your journal, and we'll come back to them in a bit.

# Positioning for Opportunity

It has been said that good luck is the result of preparedness meeting opportunity. Good career luck is no different: if you systematically prepare for the opportunities that changes in the profession create, then you're in a much better position to recognize and respond to them.

A lot of this is simply training yourself to be aware of the world around you, but with an eye toward circumstances that could benefit from what you know, or know how to do. It also helps to think through some basic approaches to monitoring your environment that will help you target opportunities that most closely align with your individual goals.

As you start exploring your own changing landscape, think about the following approaches to help organize your process.

**Understand what to look for.** A number of business experts, economists, and futurists have weighed in on which change categories are most likely to produce economic opportunity, including management thought leader Peter Drucker in his *Innovation and Entrepreneurship* (HarperBusiness, reprint ed., 2006). Arguing that opportunities for change could be categorized and then monitored, he identified emerging trends, technology advances, changes in established processes, and changes in what he termed "industry and market structures" among other defining events or trends that were likely to create opportunities for innovation and/or entrepreneurship.

William Bridges, author of *Jobshift: How to Prosper in a Workplace without Jobs* (Perseus, 1995) and one of the first experts on change and transitions, included among his hit list a roadblock or a bottleneck, a shortage or limitation, or a chronic weakness. He also suggested that any interface between groups having different values, languages, or outlooks would necessitate new solutions.

Do any of these resonate in the library and information worlds? Consider

- An economy that has resulted in unprecedented numbers of jobseekers over the past several years
- Downsizing and layoffs at all types of libraries
- Outsourcing of key operational functions
- Increases in non-MLIS hiring for traditional library jobs
- An onslaught of new information, collaboration, and communications technologies
- Data challenging text as a primary information resource
- "Born digital" and self-publishing growing faster than print or traditional publishing
- Social media channels providing new pathways for disseminating information, both credible and not
- The aging of the profession (still), although so far we've seen no rush to retirement

- Organizations closing their libraries, but reassigning or hiring information workers as key departmental team members

- The merging (if chaotic) landscapes of the education, information, communications, and entertainment industries

- The now-ubiquitous expectation of 24/7 accessibility of information

- Radically changing expectations of what a library is—and does—in its community, whether that be a school, higher education institution, town, or organization

What opportunities do these changes represent? With funding from the BankAmerica Foundation, the San Francisco Public Library has created a Jobs & Career Center that includes not only dedicated space but also events, resources, and tutorials.[1] Many other public libraries have launched similar initiatives. (New product.) Although the trend to retire corporate libraries continues, more and more organizations are embedding or integrating their information pros in functional teams, where they are key assets. (New role.) Although more users can access information directly, this has created a stronger teaching/coaching role for librarians than ever before. (New service.) Outsourcing information functions creates a need for contractors and independents to step in on a project basis. (New business.)

In fact, each one of the changes noted earlier either has created or will create opportunities within the profession—ones new and different from those we're familiar with, but opportunities nevertheless. True, they are opportunities that are most likely to push us outside of our comfort zones, but to quote Facebook founder Mark Zuckerberg, "The biggest risk is not taking any risk. In a world that's changing really quickly, the only strategy that is guaranteed to fail is not taking risks."

## Thinking about Change

OK, time to practice your change-framing skills. Take out your career journal and write down as many examples of the following types of change you can identify in your own professional environment:

An unmet market (or organization) need

Example(s): _____

Upcoming or anticipated events (regulatory, demographic, technology based) or trends that will necessitate new solutions

Example(s): _____

A product, service, or process in need of improvement (keeping in mind that process innovation—or simply figuring out how to do something better—can be as valuable as a product or service innovation)

Example(s): _____

These may apply as well to opportunities related to your current employer, industry, or community as they do to starting a new business. (Needless to say, some organizations are more responsive to new ideas than are others.)

Once you've identified all the changes you can think of, put your notes aside for a moment; we'll return to them momentarily.

**Target your areas to monitor.** There are three places to monitor for change: in your own environment, in that of the constituencies served by your organization or business, and in the world at large. For example, your own environment might be public libraries, its constituencies a community of seniors, young adults, homeschoolers, entrepreneurs, adult learners, and book club members.

Or your own environment might be the corporate library of an aerospace engineering firm, and its constituencies defense contractors, research and development (R&D) firms, government agencies, and regulators.

Or your environment might be an academic library, serving constituencies of traditional undergraduate students, graduate students, nontraditional students, full-time and adjunct faculty, and possibly alumni.

Or perhaps your environment is that of an information broker, and the constituencies you serve are local small businesses, or law firms specializing in environmental issues, or high-tech start-ups in the biotech arena.

The point is that changes to the environments of your constituencies can easily have as much impact on your professional life as changes specific to your immediate environment. So it only makes sense to pay as much attention to what's going on in *their* lives as in yours. Changes there can be as likely to produce opportunity for you as those at your fingertips.

Beyond that, be aware of the world at large. Just because iPods started out as cool toys for early adopters and adolescents doesn't mean they're not already beginning to play a role in how we deliver reference services. Keep your mind open to taking that creative leap of imagination and look for connections—especially for those *outside* the LIS profession that may become solutions or opportunities *within* it.

**Set up a monitoring process.** Staying attuned to changes in your world and others involves monitoring information, looking for specific types of "signifiers," and thinking creatively about possible impacts and opportunities. Your primary tool is an environmental scan, the same process we looked at for identifying knowledge needs.

Think about identifying context: extrapolating meaning and possibility from emerging patterns. As noted, your environmental scan should include resources both inside and outside of the LIS profession. But as part of your scan, look for information about new vocabulary, technology issues, and developments in your areas of specialization; about emerging trends and patterns; about disruptive ideas and technologies and events; about doors that are closing as well as those just opening.

Then take it to the next level. Based on the information and trend data you gather, extrapolate where those trends and ideas and disruptions might lead. Who will need what you can do—or what you'll soon know how to do? What position or role can you create that may not yet have a name or description? And what will you do to stay ahead of this curve?

Where to look? Periodicals, print and online, generally form the basis of an environmental scan, but blogs and other online news/information sources have added a new and often very useful type of information feed. Conferences are always a great resource for identifying emerging trends and technologies; even if you can't attend, many of the presentations will be available online after the event. Special "trends" issues of business publications are a great source of forecasts for key technologies, regulatory issues, potential international impacts, demographic trends, and other market influences; analyst reports when available are also valuable for their analysis and forecasts. Another source of trend indicators is professional associations, which often do annual forecasts on issues of interest to their membership. In addition, social media platforms such as LinkedIn, Twitter, and, increasingly, Facebook provide an easy way to see what thought leaders in your areas of interest have on their radars. And Alltop.com (a blog curator) can help you quickly scan key bloggers across hundreds of wide-ranging topics, while any number of alerting options will push relevant items to your in-box.

What's the best way to get into the habit of looking for opportunity in change? Practice, practice, practice. Read the local business journal with a goal of identifying three potential employers or clients and the strategic contribution your skills could make to their organizations. Cruise *Library Journal* with a goal of recognizing the top five innovative ideas or programs or products. When you attend conferences, look for cutting-edge programs that address emerging challenges in your area of specialization, then follow up with speakers to delve even deeper into their insights and thoughts about future ramifications.

**Anticipate the future.** Take a look at the publications that do annual forecasts, including business titles, science and tech publications, and social science– and futures-oriented issues like *The Futurist*. Explore their predictions and try to identify a threat and an opportunity for information professionals in as many forecasts as possible. How might you—and the profession—position for each? Build scenarios: if this outcome happened, what would it mean to me? Do I think it likely? How would I position my career to prepare for this?

Read job postings, look for changing parameters for traditional jobs, and new positions with possibilities for LIS professionals. Where there's a match between your skills and an unusual position, think through what makes this type of work valuable to the employer, then consider for whom else it would be valuable as well. Can you pitch this role to other potential employers, or this service to potential clients?

Read for questions as well as answers. Perhaps the most important questions are "what impacts might this have" and "upon whom?" Again, look for changes happening in the profession, in the communities you serve, in your target constituencies or industry (if in corporate), and in the market of your target industry. Look for who needs your skills but doesn't know it yet.

As you scan your environment, consider how your current breadth of expertise will help position you for the changes you see. Does your environmental scan turn up more strengths than weaknesses, more opportunities than threats for your skill set? If so, you know you're on the right track.

**Make change work for you.** Go back to the change events, possible outcomes, and positioning strategies you identified. As you consider these circumstances, think about aligning your skill set with them to see where there's a match. Do you have technical skills and industry knowledge that make you the best person to create a new, networked market research process for your employer? Does your knowledge of languages position you to create outreach programs for a new immigrant community? Does your track record working with local nonprofits make you the perfect person to head up the new social innovation center? Could your knowledge of South America and international business information resources perfectly suit you to join the company's launch team working on introduction of its new product in Brazil?

The purpose of paying attention to these types of circumstances is to help you think about which ones might offer you an opportunity to create something new—a service, product, program, solution, or position—that takes you in the direction of your career goals. Whether you aspire to a traditional, nontraditional, or independent path, or even an eclectic combination of all three, being able to identify the opportunity in change helps you move toward that future.

# Creating Your Change Strategies

*You gain strength, courage, and confidence by every experience in which you stop and look fear in the face. You must do the thing you think you cannot do...you learn by living.*

—Eleanor Roosevelt

Most of us associate change with loss; understandably so. Change disrupts our familiar routines and patterns. Change can create chaos in our ordered lives and destroy the easy flow we've come to rely on. It brings on that winning combination of "loss of the familiar" and "fear of the unknown," often with the inspiring subtext of "your job is on the line." Easy to see why change so often elicits our duck-and-cover response.

During change, we're often going into unknown territory where we basically don't have a clue what we're doing. We're all familiar with the phrase "comfort zone," and we know that one of the challenges of change is that it pushes us out of our comfort zones. But most LIS professionals set very high performance standards for themselves, so the more important issue is that change pushes us beyond our *competency zones.*

When you're used to generally feeling like you know what you're doing, willfully going into a situation where you feel clueless is not usually an opportunity that most of us jump at. However, when you're facing change, this is often exactly what you *must* be able to do in order to take advantage of those opportunities. To quote Helen Keller, "avoiding danger is no safer in the long run than outright exposure. Life is either a daring adventure or nothing at all."

In fact, your ability to approach change from a positive perspective is critical to the success of your efforts to grow your career over a span of years and decades. Even so, like so many things, your ability to move from old change responses to new ones is probably along the two-steps-forward-one-step-back continuum—some days you'll be on top of your game, other days beneath it. But consistently making the effort to approach change from a position of confidence rather than fear is key to building the career you're capable of.

Are there strategies you can put in place to diffuse the intimidation factor of being in unfamiliar territory? Are there ways to become more comfortable with the risk-taking that new opportunities entail? Are there coping strategies that will help the desire for gain outweigh the fear of loss? Actually, there are many. For starters, consider the following approaches:

**Embrace *beginner's mind*, and get comfortable with not knowing.**
When you're an adult and you're used to being good at your job, you're also used to a high level of competency. Having to start all over again, to be in a place where you don't know what you're doing, can be unnerving at best. Yet this is exactly where change frequently lands us. Without a willingness to move out of our competency zones, we can't grow. If we can't grow, we can't adapt to change, can't take what choreographer Agnes de Mille called "leap after leap in the dark." Instead, we need to

get beyond our initial embarrassment at not knowing in order to reach the openness, lack of ego, and humility that defines *beginner's mind*. Only then can we position for the opportunity inherent in the changes around us.

**Develop a sense of adventure.** Okay, so most of us are probably not going to rush right out and take up sky diving. And I have to admit, no way in the world am I going to eat raw fish. But most of us could stand to cultivate a bit more openness to life, and this is just the opportunity change offers us.

Yes, it's easier and less disruptive to stay with the familiar, to say no thanks, to avoid the unknown. But if we never take a flyer, if we never cultivate a sense of adventure, then life becomes pretty predictable pretty early on, and our souls become old and tired well before our bodies (or professional abilities) do. Change provides the adventure of new opportunities if we have the courage to embrace it.

**Work on being more open to opportunities for growth.** Often the older we get, and the more we've experienced, the easier it is to say no. But what if instead our knee-jerk response was "what the heck, let's try it and see what we can make happen?" Not "we already tried that and it didn't work," but "what can we do differently to change the outcome?"

Albert Einstein pointed out that an apt definition of insanity is doing the same thing over and over again and expecting different outcomes. Why not open up to change and see what happens. Respect your need for stability, but push yourself outward when you can. Baby steps are still steps forward.

**Create your own change.** One way to do just that, to push yourself outward, is to actively initiate change in your life so that you create a sense of familiarity with your own personal change process. Whether it's something like changing your morning routine or where you go on vacation or how you celebrate the holidays or where you live, making changes that *you* have initiated allows you to create a change process that supports you through transitional periods in your life.

Do you need to mourn the loss of familiar routines before you can enjoy a new situation? Is there some ritual of letting go of the old and committing to the new that is meaningful to you? Do you need to involve friends to support you through change decisions? Or, like me, do you need to read every book ever published on a given change you're contemplating before you take the leap? Whatever your individual change process is, it helps immensely for you to become familiar with it in a safe environment, that is, one that you've created, before you have changes thrust upon you from the outside.

We all have different ways of coping with change; if you start initiating changes now and start understanding what your most effective strategies are, it makes it less likely that changes coming at you externally will derail you.

**Honor your sense of humor.** Learn to laugh at yourself and not take yourself so seriously. Librarians have never been known for their raucous sense of humor—in fact, we tend to take anything related to librarianship *extremely* seriously. This may also tend to make us also take *ourselves* very seriously, which is a real negative when it comes to embracing change.

If you can laugh at things (and yourself), life and relationships flow more easily, change is less threatening, and you don't get as bogged down in making sure you're in control of the world. When life seems to be spiraling out of control, laughter can be the thing that saves your sanity and keeps you centered.

**Get used to letting go.** One of the toughest things about change in your professional life is that it often entails the loss of something you've become attached to. It can be relationships you've come to enjoy, work you've developed an expertise in, a paycheck you've relied on. But the reality is, things change, and your only healthy option here is to accept that and not take it personally.

I read somewhere that in the Afghan language, the verb "to cling" is the same as the verb "to die." Yet for most of us, it's simply part of our natures to want to keep close to us those things we've come to care about. Unfortunately, it's the nature of the world that change will often result in their loss. We can be angry and bitter about this or we can recognize and understand the immutable flow of life, and of our professional lives, and simply accept it.

**Be patient with the unfolding, rather than rushing to closure.** How many of us read the last few pages of the mystery before we start the book? How many of us want to close in on a decision before all the options have been put on the table? How many of us start filling in the test answers before we've finished reading the instructions? How many of us are still trying to figure out how to have the patience to be "in the moment" rather than planning for the conclusion?

Change is, among other things, an extended process that unfolds in its own time, as do our reactions to the changes we're confronting. It can be frustrating for those who want to quickly move to resolution—okay, my life has changed drastically, I will give myself three days to process my emotions around this, and then everything will be "back to normal." Needless to say, this strategy rarely works in real life. Instead, if we're lucky, we finally begin to understand that rushing through life and insisting on controlling its outcomes is counterproductive—it takes away the flow of moments that need time to develop into wisdom and clarity.

**Develop your strategies for dealing with chaos.** One of the most interesting points that Alvin Toffler made more than forty years ago in *Future Shock* was that the people who dealt most successfully with ongoing and chaotic change in their lives always had some corner of calm and order that anchored them.

It might be a ritual like spending all morning on Sundays reading the *New York Times*. For someone else it might be having a cup of tea at 4:00 every afternoon. For others it might be a yoga or meditation practice adhered to faithfully every day. But the point is to have some routine or ritual or space that is consistent, orderly, and sustaining. That way, as chaos swirls around you, you can remain as grounded as possible.

**Let go of perfection.** Anyone who has ever taught a class of library students has seen the debilitating effects of perfectionism writ large. I don't know if it's hardwired into our profession or we develop it as we go along, but we all seem to be so focused on doing a perfect job of whatever we're doing that we often have no energy or initiative left over for any broader perspective. Change is especially unnerving for perfectionists because by its very nature it means you have to do something new, which you don't yet know how to do, so you can't be perfect at it.

We *have* to be willing to fail, to be wrong, to make mistakes without losing our sense of self esteem. It's simply the only way you'll ever be able to move forward with the world. Writer Anne Lamott says it best: "perfectionism is the voice of the oppressor, the enemy of the people. It will keep you cramped and insane your whole life."

**Learn your risk-taking style.** Initiating change always entails a level of risk. I'm not talking about stuff like bungee jumping here, I'm talking about risking the really important things—your job, your self-esteem, your mortgage, or perhaps even more distressing, the respect of your colleagues.

Some of us find the easiest way to take a risk is by simply closing our eyes and leaping off the cliff. Others will want to have prepared ten contingency plans for every possible negative outcome. Others, and I count myself among them, will practically research something to death until they are sure that the risk they are taking is an *informed* one, that they have weighed every single piece of information in order to minimize the potential downsides associated with a given action.

Whatever your risk-taking style is, it will help you manage your fears around change if you have explored and understood how you most comfortably or effectively deal with it.

**Invest yourself in the process, not the outcome.** Yes, there is the whole Zen thing about the journey being more important than the destination, and on our more enlightened days, many of us can totally connect with that approach. However, there's also a very practical reason to look at our professional lives this way—very few of us control the money, which means that we also don't control the outcomes.

Instead, focus on the work itself, and how you can grow professionally from it. Establish your personal learning agenda and a set of goals for yourself—for example, work on your management or team-building skills, focus on practicing process innovation, or identify some other skill that you want to develop or improve. That way, no matter what the long-term outcome of your work situation, you will have made progress toward your *own* goals. You'll never control the outcomes; too many variables. But if you invest yourself in what you can learn/connect with/build during the process, the outcome becomes almost a minor part of the equation.

**Feel the fear, but keep moving forward.** I have never gone into a new situation where I was responsible for the success of a venture without being flat-out terrified. And since every job or project I've taken on for the past twenty years was something that I'd never done before—and several of them something that *no one* had ever done before and I was essentially making them up as I went along—that's a lot of being flat-out terrified.

But if we let ourselves be limited by our fears, that means we never give ourselves the opportunity to expand beyond what we can do comfortably today. Change and the unknown may scare the daylights out of you, but you can make a decision that you're just not willing to let that stop you. The reality is, fear doesn't go away. But we can learn to manage it, so on a good day it's not debilitating, and on a great day we can harness its energy to take us to exhilarating heights of accomplishment.

**Develop an expectation of personal resiliency.** Change is going to bring a lot of setbacks with it. We are going to mess up, fall down, and just generally flail about as we try to figure things out. Life's messy that way. But you can make a decision that you can retrench, recover, and move forward. You can know that you're smart, capable, and *important* to your communities, so you need to show up with your best stuff every day, even on those days when you have no clue what you're doing. If we can commit to resiliency rather than wasting our energies on perfectionism, then change can become our tool rather than our nemesis. Where are you going to put your energy? Better to learn to navigate change than waste time and lose focus by fighting it. If you decide that you are the type of person who finds a way to grow in any situation, you will be. This is a combination of frame, attitude, and will. It can become a matter of principle to us that although setbacks may detour or distract us, they will never defeat or derail us.

We don't have a choice about whether or not to accept change, or deal with it, or be touched by it. Our only choice is in how we respond—will we take the initiative to lead the opportunities embedded in the changes hitting us, or will we let others determine our options? Will we deal positively, assertively, *confidently* with change—or be clobbered by it? The alternative may not be death, but very possibly it's worse—it's marginalization, where our contributions are no longer needed or valued. For those of us in the LIS profession, the fear should not be of failure, but of invisibility.

Looking for opportunity in change is not meant to deny the fact that in a dynamic—OK, chaotic—environment, there will be some serious dislocation going on. People lose their jobs when things change, and there's not much we can do to stop it. What we can do instead is to assume this may happen and be prepared for it. That portfolio you were working on? One of its purposes is to remind you to be prepared for disappearing jobs. That way, rather than being stuck in neutral, you can focus *your* energy on moving forward with change.

# The Learning Edge

*Anyone in any industry will tell you there's new stuff to learn every week these days. So you have to say, "What information and people do I have at my disposal? What questions do I need to ask? How do I gauge whether I've really understood?"*
—Salman Khan, Founder of the Khan Academy

As we've seen, reframing your professional experiences through a portfolio lens lets you showcase the patterns and major accomplishments of your career to date. It can help you identify areas of interest that you might want to pursue further, or directions in which you might want to extend your professional "reach" (e.g., bridging your reference skills into doing a column on business information resources for the local business journal).

This reframing process will also, however, help highlight gaps in your knowledge base, areas where you may want to actively reframe how the world perceives your skills and what you can do, and/or a need to more actively build your professional support community. What do you need to learn, how do you need to position your skills, and with whom do you need to build relationships in order to grow your career? These three elements will help build the underlying foundation of your resilient career.

In fact, a commitment to continual learning is one of the most powerful ways of using change to open up new career opportunities. New knowledge is often critical to being promoted by your current employer; it provides a competitive advantage when you are applying for a new job, and it's frequently the key to bridging existing skills into a new professional arena.

In some areas, such as academic librarianship or highly technical special librarianship jobs, a second master's degree in addition to the MLIS is often part of the job description, or at least highly preferred in job applicants. In addition, many LIS pros who've been in the workforce for a while consider graduate degrees in related fields such as knowledge management, technical communications, instructional design, or GIS as a way of opening up new job opportunities. Many LIS professionals in the corporate environment find that having an MBA gives them an extra element of credibility in conversations with senior executives.

But even if your career aspirations don't depend on another degree, you should still assume that ongoing learning will be a pretty regular part of your career plans. In the words of Grace Anne DeCandido to MLIS graduates at SUNY Albany, "You have your degree, but you make your education every day. One of the great joys of being a librarian is that it is the last refuge of the renaissance person—everything you have ever read or learned or picked up is likely to come in handy."[2]

When thinking about your own career, the questions to ask involve what sorts of skills and knowledge add value to your professional "asset base," what options exist for expanding your professional expertise, how you personally learn most easily and effectively, and what steps you can take to ensure your knowledge stays up to date—if not ahead of the curve.

## What Do You Need to Learn?

Two terms familiar to planners in all organizations are *gap analysis* and *SWOT analysis*. A gap analysis is an assessment of existing resources *vs.* resources needed to achieve a stated goal, and identification of the gap between the two. From a career perspective, this means you would list your current skill set and knowledge base, identify the skills and knowledge necessary for potential jobs you'd be interested in (think job posting sites), and determine what skills fall into the gap. This becomes the basis for your learning agenda.

In a SWOT analysis, you identify strengths, weaknesses, opportunities, and threats. In terms of your career, your strengths and weaknesses would be based on which of your skills you have confidence in and which could use some work (or are nonexistent). Your opportunities and threats would focus on what career paths might be open to you based on your existing or future skills, and what paths might become closed to you if your knowledge doesn't keep pace with information and technology advances.

Either one of these approaches will help you develop your personal learning agenda, a set of learning goals that will map out what things you want to learn more about in the coming months/years, and how you will go about learning them.

What types of skills or expertise will add value to your professional portfolio? These will differ for everyone, since your aspirations will probably be quite different from those of your friends and colleagues. However, it may help to think about them in the general categories of

- Discipline-specific professional skills and areas of expertise

- General professional skills

- Business skills common to all organizations, including nonprofits, government agencies, and libraries

- Personal competencies, described by SLA as those "attitudes, skills and values that enable practitioners to work effectively and contribute positively to their organizations, clients and profession."[3]

**Discipline-specific professional skills and areas of expertise.** This area focuses on the core skills associated with LIS professionals. This might include reference and/or research; organizing information; putting together technology-based information systems; developing knowledge collections; creating web content; providing BI, and similar types of activities. But it may also include advanced subject expertise in a specific discipline, say Japanese history or chemical engineering or law. Skills in web portal or intranet design and implementation, CI, taxonomy building, and information architecture would be considered "discipline-specific" areas of expertise.

**General professional skills.** These competencies support your ability to perform your job responsibilities effectively, regardless of what they are. These skills can be honed in graduate school as well as on the job—yes, there really *is* a payoff to all those group projects! Some of the most important (and useful) professional skills include:

- Communication skills: verbal, written (including print and online), and listening

- Teaching/training/coaching skills, which include not only subject knowledge but also an understanding of how to help others learn

- Presentation skills, which encompass the ability to create effective slidedecks, to speak confidently and persuasively to groups large and small, and to speak to the media on behalf of your organization when appropriate

- Time management, which includes a clear understanding of the limitations and prioritization imposed by an 8-hour workday

- Strong in-person and virtual collaboration skills, which can include both team participation/leadership and cross-departmental engagements

- Leadership skills, including the ability to inspire, motivate, set priorities, model accountability, and practice self-leadership in your own life

**Business skills.** Based on an understanding of how organizations (not just businesses) operate, these skills are often critical to professional advancement. However, they are rarely covered in any depth in most MLIS programs, which leaves most of us scrambling to pick up this knowledge "on the fly." These skills may include:

- An ability to analyze and concisely synthesize information, and the ability to draw from it and effectively present your conclusions to senior executives.

- Solid business acumen: an understanding of your organization's strategic goals, the arena within which it operates (be that social services or bioengineering), and your proactive role in helping to implement key strategies.

- An ability to analyze and improve business processes, both in your department and throughout the organization.

- An ability to create and execute an at least rudimentary budget; you may dislike working with spreadsheets, but not being able to do so is fast becoming a form of professional illiteracy.

- Strong project management skills, with an ability to effectively manage the key resources of time, personnel, and money against stated objectives and deadlines.

- Familiarity with basic strategic planning approaches (understanding that each organization usually has its own unique variation of these processes), and an ability to plan for your department as well as an ability to contribute to enterprise-wide planning activities.

- An ability to manage staff fairly, consistently, and with an understanding of current performance-improvement practices.

- An ability to manage vendor relations, including developing requests for proposals (RFPs), evaluating proposal responses, and negotiating contracts.

- Strong relationship management skills, both internal (coworkers, bosses, and those supervised by you) and external (patrons/customers/clients, suppliers, donors/volunteers, etc.).

- An ability to understand—and contribute to—the organization's "big picture," rather than remaining focused solely on departmental issues.

## What Are Your Learning Options?

Once you've identified *what* you need to learn, you next need to determine *how* you're going to learn. The good news here: we live in the age of the free-agent learner. That means regardless of your circumstances, there are multiple ways to expand your skill set. It will be up to you to determine which options are best for you at any given time.

There are a number of questions to think about before you look at which choices work best for you. For example, do you prefer a formal learning experience (that is, interacting with an instructor in a face-to-face or online classroom, either with fellow students or independently)? Or perhaps an informal experience, such as working with a mentor or learning community, reading a book, taking an online tutorial? Does online learning work best for your hectic schedule, or does the learning dynamic of face-to-face classroom interaction suit you better?

Is getting official credit for your learning important for your career, or would a noncredit option work just as well for you? (Often this choice is related to employee tuition reimbursement.) Is it important that your education be delivered within the context of an MLIS program (perhaps through a continuing ed course), or is it just as useful to take courses outside the profession? For example, sometimes for purposes of building a portfolio, it makes more sense to take courses outside the library profession to demonstrate your interest in and ability to bridge multiple disciplines. (It's also a great way to start building a broader professional network.)

Once you've thought through those options, you'll want to next consider how and where: on the job, from the LIS profession, from your own professional community, from an MLIS program (as either an enrolled student or occasional, self-directed learner), or from other sources.

**Learning on the job.** Learning on the job can include on-site training programs, project work, professional development funds, and tuition reimbursement.

Workplace training is a great option when available: you don't have to pay for it, it usually leaves your nights and weekends free, and you can immediately put into practice what you've learned. Also, it's often focused on in-demand *transferable skills*, so that you can be boosting your value to the organization and bulking up your portfolio at the same time. Many organizations have a dedicated training budget for all employees, and it just makes sense to make sure you take advantage of every dollar available to you.

Your workplace is also a great place to learn by doing. Work projects give you an opportunity to develop new skills by working with experienced pros, and you'll get immediate and ongoing feedback on whether your skills are up to the task. As you create your learning agenda, think about opportunities to volunteer for new workplace initiatives based on what new knowledge or skill development they'll offer.

Professional development funds are dollars made available for activities such as conference attendance; job-related workshops, seminars, and preconferences; and job-related courses or classes. This can be an important benefit when you're building a portfolio so be sure you're taking maximum advantage of your employer's support and consider it one of the items you include in salary negotiations.

Tuition reimbursement is money paid either directly to you (the student-employee) or to an accredited education institution for undergraduate or graduate for-credit courses. You usually need to demonstrate some relationship between your job responsibilities and the course/degree program you want to pursue, but many organizations are fairly flexible here. Also, it's not necessary to take only bachelor's or graduate-level courses; if a local community college has a dynamite course in website UX design, there's no reason not to take it. Your tuition reimbursement amount may be tied to your class grade, and you may be attending class during evenings or weekends (even with online learning), but you'll have an opportunity to broaden your skills with only an investment of time, rather than money.

In the words of Priscilla K. Shontz in *Jump Start Your Career*, "Make sure you leave smarter than you started."

**Learning from the LIS profession.** It's often noted that one of the really great things about this profession is peoples' willingness to share knowledge. That means you're part of one of the world's biggest learning communities.

Find successful local practitioners who have done what you're interested in doing, take them to lunch, and ask them what the key skills are in their position—and how they learned theirs. Even if they can't take the time for lunch or coffee, most will at least be able to respond with an e-mail answer, albeit a brief one (and possibly a few weeks down the road).

Enlist one of the most valuable and easily accessed learning tools of the professional community by signing up for the best blogs, electronic discussion groups, and RSS feeds in your areas of interest. Get a sense of who's most knowledgeable, most innovative, most credible on a given topic, and track their thinking through their writing and/or presentations.

Sign up for online and regional courses, workshops, and one-day seminars through professional associations like the Special Libraries Association, the Public Library Association, or the Medical Library Association (and their regional chapters). Check out classes offered by your local library council, state library, or regional bibliographic utility, or look into regionally delivered vendor training. Consider joining a local users' group focusing on a new skill you want to develop or start one yourself. Attend preconferences at state and national association conferences and conventions.

Even if you can't attend their preconferences, conferences themselves offer a wealth of learning opportunities. A survey of their presentation topics will provide an excellent overview of emerging trends and hot topics throughout the profession or in the specific focus area of the conference (e.g., Internet Librarian). Session presentations usually emphasize best practices, current thinking, effective solutions, systems, and processes—in general, actionable information.

In addition to helping you identify thought leaders in a given discipline, conferences may connect you with experts willing to answer e-mail questions from you at a later date. Also, exhibitors and vendors are there to share information with conference attendees (well, actually they're there to sell things, but the easiest way to do that is to share information) and often offer free user meetings, product training classes, and demonstrations.

Keep in mind that, in general, all LIS and LIS-related associations have strong education and professional development mandates as part of their missions. Therefore, be sure to check the websites of any associations in your area of interest to see what sorts of education programs they offer, many of which may be available to you online.

**Learning from your own professional community.** Don't forget that your network of professional colleagues is an incredibly valuable, informal, and readily available source of knowledge and expertise. As we go through our careers, we build relationships with fellow students, coworkers, association colleagues, people we meet as fellow panelists at professional conferences, and myriad other connecting points. This community of colleagues not only is one of the most rewarding aspects of having a long career, but also offers a rich source of knowledge, counsel, and insight.

LIS professionals are legendary for their willingness to share information with each other, and learning from friends is one of the fastest, most enjoyable ways to expand your knowledge base. The only caveat: be ready to be a resource for others when *your* knowledge needs to be tapped.

**Learning in grad school.** Being in grad school is a terrific opportunity to learn—but it's up to you to set your own learning agenda in order to most effectively position yourself for maximum career opportunity. Every course you take provides two learning paths that should go forward side by side: the structured learning identified in the course syllabus, and the self-directed learning you identify for yourself.

For example, in a business research class, your learning agenda might include researching the telecommunications industry, trends in corporate information centers, or social entrepreneurship if these are areas of career interest for you. In an information ethics class, you might decide to hone your presentation or group leadership skills. In a knowledge management class, you might choose to research bioinformatics for your class project with an eye toward expanding your sci/tech expertise. Or for your paper in your information access and retrieval course, you might decide to interview several thought leaders to understand not only current practice but also future trends. You might decide to do a practicum or internship in a related field—say, publishing—in order to broaden your understanding of how this industry works.

Approach every course assignment asking "what do I want to learn with this?" rather than "what do I have to do to get an A on this?" Align every paper, project, and class activity with your personal career agenda whenever possible, and you will be both learning the core LIS knowledge and positioning yourself for your postgraduate career.

The key is to establish and follow your own learning goals along with your professor's, so that you are learning both the core knowledge as framed by the profession and the general professional skills and personal competencies that will help you create the career you desire.

**Learning after grad school.** In the old days (OK, several years ago), in order to take advantage of MLIS courses, it was necessary to show up on campus. Today, you can often choose between the options of campus based or online learning. You may also have the option of completing a course, a certificate, or a graduate degree. Few of these options are inexpensive, but they can be an effective and reliable way to expand a key skill area. Alternatively, they can offer an excellent way to bridge into new career opportunities. A certificate in CI might be used to land a job in a corporate business development group, a course in bioinformatics to position you for a health sciences information center job.

To keep costs down if employer tuition reimbursement isn't available and credit isn't an issue, consider that some MLIS programs will allow you to audit courses, for no credit, at a reduced fee.

**Learning from other sources.** Who might some of those other sources be? We've considered community colleges as one option, but there are many other alternatives. For example, you may want to explore non-LIS graduate degree programs, online providers such as Udacity, the Khan Academy, Coursera, and edX, training CDs, books, web tutorials, or private training companies not affiliated with the LIS world. And don't forget about your people resources, which could include the IT guru down the hall, your kids (who knew more about the digital surround by the sixth grade than the rest of us will ever catch up with), or a mentor who will coach you through your learning path.

There are many, many ways to expand your knowledge and skills, depending on what criteria you need to meet. If you are able to focus on the learning itself and don't need a credential or credit to document it, then consider the least expensive options first, including informal learning.

## Mapping Your Learning Agenda

Whether you're a student or an LIS professional, it's important that *you* be in charge of your learning agenda. It's one of your strongest tools for maximum career flexibility and ongoing career growth. And the best way to organize and follow through on that agenda is by creating a personal education map.

An overview of what you need to learn to continue to move toward your career goals, this infinitely changeable document should reflect the "knowledge feed" coming in through your information monitoring and outside reading. Your goal will be to identify key skills that will complement, enrich, or extend your core professional competencies in response to emerging opportunities. But for starters, and to organize your thinking, take out your career journal and start working through the questions shown in "Your Education Map," being sure to note your responses in your journal.

## Your Education Map

Consider the four skill areas—discipline-specific professional skills, general professional skills, business skills, and personal competencies. Then in your career journal, create a four-column table that focuses on the key questions: what do I need to learn, how will I learn it, when will I learn it, and how will I practice it? Your table might look something like this:

| Need to Learn | How | When | Practice |
|---|---|---|---|
| How to give more effective presentations | Read three best books on speaking and presenting, take a PowerPoint class through WebJunction, ask colleagues to critique my presentation style | One book every two weeks starting next week; PowerPoint class one week after books completed, colleague critique after every presentation, then review notes on the weekend | Find opportunity to give one presentation every other month to different types of audiences, e.g., colleagues, patrons/customers, community members |
| Grant-writing | Take grant-writing class at local community college | This fall | Volunteer to write grant proposals for local humane society and two other community groups |

Your "How" options are nearly endless. Will you attend a workshop or read a book? Join an association or sign up for an online class? Consider your job, your grad school classes—how can they be adapted to support your learning agenda? What projects will you volunteer for in order to practice a key career skill? You're responsible for your own professional growth, so put yourself in charge of your learning agenda for every new project, class, opportunity.

Explore the least expensive learning options in your community, investigate online learning programs and courses, and find out what your employer's tuition reimbursement, professional development, and workforce training policies are.

Also, if you are considering a major commitment such as a second master's degree, assume each class will take roughly 12–20 hours per week of study time and do a "test run" for a month to see whether or not you can actually carve out that amount of time without a total derailment of your work and personal lives. What will you be giving up, and is that acceptable? Equally important, will this level of commitment be sustainable over the coming months and years?

Some ideas for broadening your career skill set if you're a student? Think about . . .

. . . taking classes either within or outside your LIS program that ramp up your communications skills. These include your ability to write clearly, concisely, and authoritatively; your ability to create and deliver effective presentations; and your ability to understand and respond to gender and multicultural communications issues in the workplace.

. . . using grad school to learn how to think about the processes and skills you're using. For example, use your cataloging class to explore the broader process of organizing information, your reference class to consider the dynamic of interpersonal information exchange, team projects to think about group dynamics, motivation, etc. Consider *why* as well as *how*, build a knowledge base of abstract understanding that will position you to apply knowledge and understand patterns in new situations.

. . . using those classes that require substantial amounts of studying to practice the various learning styles, with the aim of discovering the approaches that are most effective for you.

Your goal here will be to focus your learning efforts in a way that most effectively supports your career goals, with the understanding that as those goals change, the learning agenda supporting them will as well.

As you work through your learning agenda, remember to incorporate opportunities to try out various learning styles until you find the ones that work best for you. Try to be conscious of your learning process, and how to set up the circumstances and environment that work best for you. Music or silence? Two hours every weeknight or eight hours on Saturday? Lunch hours at the library or Thursdays with your study group? Practice coaching yourself through that awkward beginning stage where you feel like you'll never figure things out. Pay attention to how your positive or negative attitudes about learning new material impact your learning effectiveness.

Make a commitment to the critical role of ongoing education in your career and put yourself in charge. Your ability to keep learning in the coming decades will determine your ability to keep working, participating, and contributing.

> *Investing in yourself is the best investment you will ever make. It will not only improve your life, it will improve the lives of all those around you.*
> —Robin S. Sharma

# Resources

## Books

Boule, Michelle. *Mob Rule Learning: Camps, Unconferences, and Trashing the Talking Head.* Information Today, 2011. 224p. ISBN 0910965927.
Heard someone mention an unconference and wondered what the heck they were talking about? *Library Journal* Mover & Shaker Michelle Boule explains what they are, why they may be a large part of the future of LIS professional development, and how to organize your very own nontraditional, self-directed group "knowledge ecosystem." Includes case studies, interviews, and examples of how other people have used these approaches successfully.

Bridges, William. *Jobshift: How to Prosper in a Workplace without Jobs.* Da Capo Press, 1995. 272p. ISBN 0201489333.
A more conceptual than actionable overview of what the world of work will look like as it transitions from jobs to projects and portfolios. A bit dated, but conceptually useful.

Brown, Brené. *Daring Greatly: How the Courage to Be Vulnerable Transforms the Way We Live, Love, Parent, and Lead.* Gotham, 2012. 256p. ISBN 1592407331.
An amazing book about letting yourself embrace vulnerability and imperfection in order to become more courageous in your choices and behaviors. The key message for information professionals, a great number of whom are perfectionists (if my students are any indication), is that perfectionism is a crippling obstacle to not only your personal growth but also the amazing professional contributions you could be making if you were willing to take the risk and dance with change. (Key resource)

Brown, Peter C., Henry L. Roediger III, and Mark A. McDaniel. *Make It Stick: The Science of Successful Learning.* Belknap Press, 2014. 336p. ISBN 0674729013.
Uses the recent advances in neuroscience/cognitive research to describe how learning occurs in the brain, and how to use that information to improve your own learning processes. Will help you figure out how to work smarter rather than harder.

Doucett, Elisabeth. *What They Don't Teach You in Library School.* ALA Editions, 2010. 160p. ISBN 0838935923.
In addition to her MLS, Doucett has an MBA in marketing and that duel framework brings a unique and very useful perspective to the practical insights she provides here. For purposes of this chapter on change, however, her description of trend-tracking (Chapter 14) is especially noteworthy, because the process she identifies can be applied equally well to libraries, careers, nonlibrary organizations, and clients. Anticipate, find opportunities, position.

Drucker, Peter F. *Innovation and Entrepreneurship.* HarperBusiness; reprint ed., 2006. 288p. ISBN 0060851139.
Renowned management consultant and author Drucker suggests that rather than innovation or entrepreneurship being serendipitous, the familiar "light bulb going on," these opportunities can instead be systematically developed. He identifies seven circumstances that enable

innovative opportunities, many of which have applicability to the LIS environment.

Dweck, Carol. *Mindset: The New Psychology of Success.* Ballantine Books, 2007. 288p. ISBN 0345472322.
Do you have a "fixed" mind-set or a "growth" mind-set? If the latter, according to the author, you see yourself as an ever-changing work in progress—and an eager and effective learner. While affirming the importance to career resiliency of a growth mind-set, Dweck also coaches readers on how to move from a fixed to a growth mind-set (lest you find yourself among the former). (Key resource)

Eads, Kenneth M. et al. *The Portable MBA, 5th ed.* Wiley, 2010. 358p. ISBN 0470481293.
The fifth edition of the book that launched the series, *Portable MBA* is included here as an example of a type of resource—the topical introduction or overview. For individuals trying to quickly come up to speed on a given subject, books like *The Portable MBA* (if well done) offer a great solution for quick "top-level" understanding. You won't have an in-depth knowledge of the topic, but you should be able to understand most of the jargon, key points, and issues under discussion—think "just-in-time" learning. Other *Portable* titles include *Finance and Accounting, Strategy, Management, Entrepreneurship, Marketing, Economics,* and *Project Management.* Quality varies among titles.

Gardner, Howard. *Frames of Mind: The Theory of Multiple Intelligences.* Basic Books, 2011. 528p. ISBN 0465024335.
The classic work on the six types of intelligence: bodily-kinesthetic, linguistic, logical-mathematical, musical, personal, and spatial. Will help you understand how you learn most effectively and tailor your studying and learning processes appropriately. This edition includes an updated introduction by the author, but otherwise features the 1993 text.

Harlan, Mary Ann. *Personal Learning Networks: Professional Development for the Isolated School Librarian.* Libraries Unlimited, 2009. 96p. ISBN 1591587905.
Although written for school librarians, this brief guide to developing a personal learning network provides useful how-to information for any "isolated" information professional, that is, one working without the collegial intellectual flow that comes from working with a community of other librarians or information professionals.

Heath, Chip and Dan Heath. *Switch: How to Change Things When Change Is Hard.* Crown Business, 2010. 320p. ISBN 0385528752.
An engaging amazing book on how individuals process and react to change in their lives, *Switch* will help you understand your own reactions to change and manage them in a more effective, positive manner. Since change is a constant factor for anyone growing their career in new directions, this book will be a welcome companion as you push beyond your comfort zone to increase your level of contribution on an ongoing basis. (Key resource)

## Articles

Beard, Alison. "Life's Work." *Harvard Business Review* 92, no. 1/2 (January/February 2014): 124. Accessed at https://hbr.org/2014/01/salman-khan.

An interview with Salman Khan, founder of the Khan Academy, one of the first massive, free, online learning initiatives. His answer to the question of what key concepts everyone should learn to succeed in today's workplace: "The one meta-level thing is to take agency over your own learning."

Katopol, Patricia. "Managing Change with Environmental Scanning." *Library Leadership & Management* 29, no. 1 (January 2014). Accessed at https://journals.tdl.org/llm/index.php/llm/article/view/7121/6317.
How to use the environmental scanning process to identify changes—for the library, for librarians, and for library patrons—that may impact specific constituencies.

Stephens, Michael. "It's about Time." *Library Journal* 139, no. 17 (November 15, 2014. Accessed at http://lj.libraryjournal.com/2014/11/opinion/michael-stephens/its-about-time-office-hours/.
Stephens, Office Hours columnist for *Library Journal* and assistant professor at the San Jose State University School of Information, argues that making time to stay abreast of the technology learning curve is critical to staying professionally relevant (despite what he describes as an understandable experience of "techno-fatigue"). To quote Stephens, "Embrace constant change... Change allows growth, and without growth we will simply be running in circles."

Stephens, Michael and Kyle M.L. Jones. "MOOCs as LIS Professional Development Platforms: Evaluating and Refining SJSU's First Not-for-Credit MOOC." *Journal of Education for Library and Information Science* 55, no. 4 (Fall 2014): 345–361. Accessed at http://papers.ssrn.com/sol3/papers.cfm?abstract_id=2541897.
An overview of results from SJSU's first MOOC test, with highly useful findings for those contemplating taking or creating a MOOC. Distinguishes between xMOOCs (focus on knowledge consumption through centralized learning platforms, emphasize individual learning and automated assessment tools—a more traditional teaching format) and cMOOCs, which emphasize knowledge creation and social learning via distributed tools "to build networks of knowledge and learners." A fascinating read for anyone interested in the potential and development of MOOCs for professional LIS learning.

## Associations

*Note: In addition to the academic programs available to the profession, all of the major LIS associations offer professional development options. These may include online short courses, satellite-delivered seminars, tutorials offered at the website, preconference workshops, certification training, and other learning opportunities. Check the association's website for specific offerings, as well as whether they are available to members only.*

*ALA Online Learning*
www.ala.org/onlinelearning/
An example of an association's professional development opportunities, ALA's professional development platform provides a "wide range of library-related online learning–covering fundamentals, advances, trends, and hot topics" within the categories of collection management, issues and advocacy, management issues for library leaders, school libraries, and service delivery in libraries. In addition, selecting

"Offerings by ALA Units" brings up education offerings from groups such as ALA Publishing, American Association of School Librarians (AASL), and the Association of College and Research Libraries (ACRL), among others.

## Online Resources

*20+ Awesome Free Online Librarian Courses*
> http://librarysciencelist.com/free-online-courses-for-librarians/
> Melissa Steele compiled this list in January 2013, and although some of the courses are no longer offered, it's a good starting point from which to launch your exploration of what else these groups may be offering now.

*Competency Index for the Library Field 2014*
> http://bit.ly/1fyFFyk
> From OCLC/WebJunction, this iteration of the Competency Index is an update of the original 2009 overview of LIS professional competencies. A great resource for identifying any skills or knowledge gaps you may want to address.

*Creating and Curating Your Digital Professional Learning Network*
> http://hacklibraryschool.com/2014/01/29/pln/
> Written for the hls blog by Michael Rodriguez, who defines a digital PLN as a web-based personal or professional learning network. A terrific how-to article that will help you reconsider how you'll gather, filter, organize, and access the hundreds of information channels that most information professionals end up monitoring. (Key resource)

*Current Awareness through RSS*
> http://americanlibrariesmagazine.org/2011/01/13/keeping-up-2-0-style/
> From library tech guru Meredith Farkas, this *American Libraries* article from January 13, 2011, gives clear instructions for setting up RSS feeds to have your current awareness sources sent directly to you via your preferred method (e.g., e-mail client, RSS reader, and personalized start page).

*Dmoz: Library and Information Science*
> www.dmoz.org/Reference/Libraries/Library_and_Information_Science/
> For an LIS blog directory of more than 178 blogs, see the listing at the Open Directory by searching Reference > Libraries > Library and Information Science > Weblogs.

*edX*
> www.edx.org
> An amazing learning resource, with hundreds of free courses delivered by, according to edX, "the best classes from the best professors and universities." You have the option of paying for course participation in order to receive a "verified certificate," but otherwise the courses are simply available for free. A great way to expand skills in new directions *if* you're a self-motivated learner.

*Learning Styles*
> www.ldpride.net/learningstyles.MI.htm
> Although this site is hosted by a commercial group, it nevertheless offers a number of tests for assessing your personal learning style(s).

A useful starting point for learning more about how you learn most effectively.

*Library 2.0: The Future of Libraries in the Digital Age*
www.library20.com
In conjunction with founding conference sponsor, the School of Information at San José State University, the annual virtual Library 2.0 conferences bring together presenters literally from around the world to present on every LIS topic imaginable. The two-day event is free, a great learning and networking event, and a terrific opportunity for individuals to present who might otherwise not have a chance to do so due to cost or time constraints. Submit a proposal!

*Library Journals, Newsletters, and Zines*
www.libdex.com/journals.html
A listing of roughly 125 publications related to the LIS world. Entries are organized alphabetically by title, many include several-word annotations to indicate audience or publishing organization, and all are linked to websites. A recent check showed that about one out of every three links is nonworking, primarily those going to the reorganized ALA site.

*Wallace, Marie, "Climbing the Learning Ladder," LLRX.com*
www.llrx.com/columns/guide69.htm
Although written over a decade ago, this column remains an excellent, user-friendly overview of individual learning approaches and how to most effectively derive value from your continuing education efforts. A great introduction to personal learning styles.

*WebJunction Learning Center*
http://webjunction.org
An "online community of libraries and other agencies sharing knowledge and experience to provide the broadest public access to information technology," WebJunction is a clearinghouse of information and best practices shared among U.S. and Canadian librarians. From a professional education standpoint, however, WebJunction's value is that it provides access to online courses and training that support LIS professional development.

# Notes

1. San Francisco Public Library Jobs & Career Center, accessed at http://sfpl.org/index.php?pg=0200001101.

2. Grace Anne DeCandido, "Ten Graces for New Librarians," Commencement Address for the School of Information Science and Policy, SUNY/Albany, May 19, 1996, accessed at www.well.com/user/ladyhawk/albany.html.

3. SLA Core Competencies, revised 2003, accessed at https://www.sla.org/about-sla/competencies/.

# 8
# Building Professional Equity

*All your professional interactions collectively communicate your brand and thus determine your career destiny.*

—William Arruda

As you build your career, you'll find that—if you've been actively engaged in growing, learning, and contributing—you're building something else as well: your professional equity.

Professional equity is made up of three elements:

- **What you know.** A combination of your "domain knowledge" (or, as we discussed in the previous chapter, your discipline-specific professional skills and areas of expertise), your general professional skills, and your business skills.

- **Who you know.** This is your professional community of connections, otherwise known as your network. The longer you work, and the more actively engaged in working with others to accomplish professional goals, the likelier your professional network will continue to grow in breadth and depth.

- **Who knows about you (and what they know).** This is what people are referring to when they talk about having a professional brand and/or brand visibility. It's the sum of many, many different touchpoints that you purposely or unconsciously create as you move through your career, and essentially it represents your professional reputation.

Think of your professional equity as three intersecting or overlapping circles that, if continually growing, will help ensure that your career opportunities are similarly continually growing.

We've looked at the "what you know" piece of your professional equity in the previous chapter; now let's look at the other two elements, which for purposes of brevity, we'll call your career network and professional brand.

# Building Your Network—Your Community of Colleagues

There are many good reasons to go to work every day, not the least of which is being able to buy groceries. But the longer your career, the more likely you'll find that the real reward of professional work is not money, but relationships—the community of colleagues who share your values, your stories, your concerns and commitments.

Through a stroke of good fortune, this same community of colleagues is also your strongest ally when it comes to helping you create a resilient career. We're not talking "rolodex networking" here—we're talking the trust that begins to build when you have an opportunity to say "how can I help?" to a coworker, or a fellow committee member, or a classmate. About the lifelong friendships that evolve out of shared professional challenges and efforts. About the goodwill that grows from your willingness to share knowledge, expertise, and credit for accomplishments.

When you seek to build a professional community by asking "how can I help you" rather than "how can you help me," you create relationships whose foundation is giving rather than taking. The goodwill and trust that builds from this not only is invaluable and intrinsically rewarding at the deepest human levels, but also becomes extraordinarily helpful when you need to expand career options. The people you know also know lots of other people—and if you've been a caring and responsive colleague, they'll probably be willing to help connect you with names, job opportunities, or potential projects.

The individuals in your community of colleagues can not only give you good career advice, but also tell you when you're entirely off base. They can be your brain trust on emerging trends and issues in an area of professional interest and give you the confidence that comes from knowing you don't have to know everything, because your diverse family of colleagues not only pretty much *does* know everything, but also is willing to share. (Because, of course, *you* have been willing to share in the past . . ..)

These close trust relationships are the "depth" element in your professional network. The "breadth" aspect derives from numerous research studies done over the past years that describe the multiple career opportunities of what's known as loose or weak connections. Building on a 1973 article by Michael Granovetter, "The Strength of Weak Ties,"[1] researchers have found that having "weak ties" among your network connections (e.g., people who are not in your same profession or whom you don't know very well—perhaps you'd consider them to be acquaintances) can enrich your career opportunities. Why? Because as Granovetter points out, your close connections probably have the same general knowledge and connections as you do, and so may be less likely to be able to connect or alert you to information or opportunities outside your professional universe. On the other hand, your loose or weak connections generally have an entirely different set of people (and opportunities) in their network, and so may be more able to broaden your universe of ideas and exposure.

Weak connections may include such disparate people as your daughter's soccer coach, the person you got to know in your online business statistics course, the vendor rep you sat next to on the conference shuttle, your fellow homeowners' association board members, your dentist, and the people you've met virtually through your favorite online charity. I would note that a professional network with a good number of weak connections can be especially valuable for those pursuing nontraditional LIS careers because often you will be the *only* person one of your weak connections knows who knows anything about finding, managing, creating, or otherwise working with information. Therefore, if someone in their network is looking for this expertise, you'll be their go-to recommendation. Although our skill set seems familiar and therefore commonplace to us and our LIS colleagues, keep in mind that to others it can look like sheer *magic*.

What are some ways to get started with network-building or expanding? First is to recognize that any time you meet someone new or reestablish a previous relationship (face-to-face or virtually), you have an opportunity to add that person to your professional community. (The operative word here is "opportunity"—you get to choose whether or not this is someone with whom you would feel comfortable being associated.) Depending on your personality and available time, you might want to consider any of these approaches:

**Face-to-face.** Although social media and texting are increasingly becoming the common means of communicating with others, for relationship-building purposes, there's nothing quite like the pretexting approach of actually sitting across from each other and talking—a great way to identify and nurture connecting points. The basis for those common threads might be having worked for the same employer, been on a panel presentation together, worked on some sort of volunteer program or initiative together, been students in the same grad program, or participants in the same job-hunting workshop.

Although face-to-face network-building usually assumes a local connection, this can also happen at conferences, when traveling, at weddings and bar mitzvahs several states over, or in any number of other circumstances. The point is to be open to the possibilities and then, if appropriate, make sure to follow up to keep the connection alive.

**Virtual.** How many of us have worked on virtual association committees and projects, and gotten to know our fellow committee members really well—without ever having met in person? With today's online collaboration technologies, more and more work gets done via e-mail, teleconferences, virtual committee meetings, and even virtual professional conferences. Colleagues have established career connections through discussion forums, association memberships, and online LIS courses' virtual team projects (a very valuable indicator of whether you'd ever want to work with someone again!), among other avenues.

Through virtual professional projects, I've had an opportunity to work with leaders I've admired for years and had a chance to get to know them and their exceptional strengths by virtually working "side by side" with them. In many ways, those bonds of shared experience and expertise are nearly as strong as they would have been if we'd been meeting in person.

**Social networks.** There are now dozens of social network sites set up to do nothing but help us connect with one another (well, actually, they're set up to generate billions of dollars in ad and data-sales revenue, but you get the point), and their goal is to make sure that we are addicted members of the over-sharing society. Nevertheless, used judiciously, these networks (especially LinkedIn and, increasingly, Twitter and Facebook) can be effective tools for building and sustaining your professional relationships.

In fact, one of the benefits of a site like LinkedIn is that through your profile, you can tell the world at large enough about yourself that other people will be able to identify connecting points or what you may have in common. Were you alumni of the same school or employer, do you share an interest in medical informatics, digital marketing, early childhood literacy, or entrepreneurship, are you both volunteers for the same charitable foundation? Building relationships—and a rich professional network—is about finding what you have in common as the starting point for creating mutual benefit. Then, the goal is to continue to nurture those connections so that the bond between you remains resilient, even if only an occasional connection or one made from a distance.

## Nurture Your Professional Ties

Nearly every day brings an opportunity to build the relationships that woven together make up your lifelong professional community. The key is to approach this not so much as an investment in your career success but rather as one of the richest rewards of life: being in a position to support others. The central question is—what can I do to help?

Consider the following "short list" of ways you might be able to help a colleague:

- Passing along information about a job opening
- Sharing your expertise to help someone do their job better
- Brainstorming ideas with a colleague needing to develop new solutions
- Providing introductions and connections among colleagues
- Recommending someone for a job
- Bringing someone in on a committee
- Publicly applauding someone's efforts or accomplishments
- Pinch-hitting for someone on a professional commitment
- Sharing information of value you've come across in your work
- Contributing your expertise to a colleague's social cause
- Mentoring younger (or older!) colleagues
- Publicly sharing credit with everyone who has contributed to a successful effort

Now you try. Take out your career journal and think back through your career so far. Note in what ways people have helped you in your career, and whether or not you have been able to return the favor. Now think about ways you can imagine helping others, based on what or who you know. This reciprocity is the heart of building a professional community that allows you to contribute to the success of others. It's also what allows them to participate in yours.

# Maintaining Your Professional Network

In much the same way my eyes glaze over when someone tells me I need to bulk up my social media presence (more on that in a bit), you may be feeling like the effort involved in building a professional network—or even maintaining the one you've already got—is simply beyond your bandwidth. If that's the case, think about ways to use the activities in which you're already engaging (or are committed to) as low-effort network-building opportunities. For example,

- Running out for lunch or post-work coffee to catch up with a former colleague, your treat.

- Commenting on or "liking" a social media post from a connection that just flew through your e-mail alerts.

- Sharing an article or blog post you just read with a connection you know will find it interesting, useful, or actionable.

- Posting an update on LinkedIn congratulating someone in your LinkedIn network for a recently noted accomplishment.

- While you're making your travel arrangements, reaching out in advance to someone you met at last year's conference to see whether they want to catch up at this year's conference.

The idea is to make sustaining your professional network not only as painless as possible, but also as positive an experience as possible for those who *comprise* your network.

# Micro-Networking: Making Small Talk

Many of us equate walking into a room full of strangers with, say, getting a root canal. (OK, some of us even feel that way about getting on the down elevator on the 35th floor with a complete stranger and trying to figure out how to break the ice.) Do you have to? Sometimes, when it comes to your career growth, the answer is yes. So how can making small talk become a bit easier for you?

One way is to practice your conversational skills with a friend. Brainstorm some opening questions you'd be comfortable asking a stranger and then practice those opening lines with each other until you know (1) you can feel comfortable saying them without sounding like a robot and (2) you'll remember them. Ask people about themselves rather than telling them about you. Being genuinely interested in people and their stories and knowledge is the best basis for building connections with new acquaintances. To quote the late Stephen R. Covey's *7 Habits of Highly Effective People* (Simon & Schuster, 1990), "Seek first to understand then to be understood." People will appreciate your interest in them, and you'll learn both who they are and what you may have in common. Again, practicing some opening questions can make this easier for you.

Also, realize that any given meeting room (or that down elevator) probably includes people just as uncomfortable with introducing themselves to strangers as you are. That person standing alone is probably dying for someone to come up and say hello to him or her. Practice being the one who takes the first step and asks the first question—you never know what opportunities your moment of courage will open up.

Another tactic is to briefly say a bit about yourself ("Hi, I'm Frieda Farnsbarger and I'm at the conference to learn more about user experience—what brings you to the conference?") in order to give the other person a "hook" with which to get started. Of course, if you want your new friend to actually *remember* your name, it's best to have business cards on hand. If your employer doesn't furnish you with business cards, they can easily and inexpensively be created by online companies such as Vistaprint (www.vistaprint.com) or Moo (http://us.moo.com). In fact, it's a good idea to always have business cards with you.

Last, look for ways to help. Talking with people about their lives or jobs or passions also gives you an opportunity to determine whether there are ways you can help them in some way. Building bonds by finding ways to help each other is not only rewarding for both of you, but also a time-honored approach to building a mutually beneficial network.

## Establishing Your Professional Reputation

As you expand your knowledge base and build your professional network, the next challenge to growing your career is to take charge of how you—and your skills—are viewed in the world. This is your professional reputation or brand.

How many times have we heard that perception is everything? Consider, then, this comment from a review of Louis Rosenfeld and Peter Morville's first best-selling classic, *Information Architecture for the World Wide Web* (O'Reilly, 1998), in *The Denver Business Journal*, August 21–27, 1998:

> *With many fine thinkers in the field, the publisher's choice of two librarians for its authoritative book on the subject is a curious one. Nonetheless, the leading publisher on Internet topics provides a useful primer.*

Reality check: Rosenfeld and Morville have since written numerous influential books on multiple aspects of information organization, and the fourth edition of their *Information Architecture for the World Wide* Web was released in 2015 (a sure sign of a best-selling, classic work). Both are "fine thinkers" and thought leaders widely respected in the information profession and beyond (Morville's bio lists clients such as AT&T, Cisco, Harvard, IBM, Macy's, and the National Cancer Institute). But all this *Denver Business Journal* writer needed to see was "librarians," and he leapt to a conclusion about what the authors were (or weren't) capable of.

Or consider this moment from my days heading up a business that had created and was marketing the first virtual academic library for online students. I was being interviewed by the lead business writer for a major city newspaper for an article about the company and the product, and the writer asked me how we had created the library. When I proudly explained that we had been working with over 100 academic reference librarians and subject specialists from throughout the country, he looked at me in stunned surprise and said "Librarians? Librarians have been creating this? I thought librarians just basically got the books down off the shelf for you and then put them back. Do they really know enough to do this?"

Mindful that whatever spiffy (if gratifying) zinger I came back with was likely to see its way into print, I tried to calmly point out to him the

multifaceted and intellectually complex world librarians and other information pros navigated on a daily basis. He was amazed and clearly a bit
skeptical (although later one of our most outstanding grad students went
to work for his organization, so I have no doubt he now understands just
what an asset her skills are). This man was well-educated, a journalist
immersed in the world of information, someone we might hope would "get
it." No such luck.

The reality is that a devoted minority of the community—whether that
is the public, school, academic, or corporate community—think we're terrific,
invaluable, worth every penny invested. The rest of the world has opinions
that fall on a continuum ranging from "nice to have and worth the investment when we have enough money" to "I don't know, what do they do?" to
"we can't afford this, and everything's on the web anyway, so why would we
need it?"

The profession as a whole continues to grapple with the issue of public
perceptions, looking for ways to showcase its resources and services to its
constituencies in ways that demonstrate value. Sometimes it works, other
times budget cuts override best intentions. What this means to you from a
career perspective, however, is that it's going to be up to you to define how
you want the world to perceive you. If your target audience (i.e., potential
employers and/or clients) has a preconceived constricting notion of who and
what librarians are—and are capable of—it's going to be up to you to change
those perceptions.

The way you do this is by creating your own personal brand. In the
marketing world, a brand is the collective characteristics that the market
attributes to a given product or service. Think of Ben and Jerry's, Apple,
Nike, Target, Estee Lauder. Whether or not we use their products, we associate specific brand characteristics with each.

For commercial entities, those brand characteristics are communicated
through language, actions, visuals, sponsorships, social media, and multiple
forms of advertising, among other channels. But for individual professionals, brand "touchpoints" (literally, the points at which you engage physically
or virtually with another person) may include a multitude of intentional
*and unintentional* impressions.

For example, consider the fact that you communicate your brand every
day through:

- Your language—is it hesitant or confident, friendly or cold, arrogant
  or supportive, professional or careless? If you want to be known as
  someone who's energetic and takes initiative, passive or hesitant language will undermine that perception.

- Your clothes—does your wardrobe reinforce the way you want your
  potential employer or client to think of you? This differs radically from
  constituency to constituency, but it helps to look like the person you
  want to connect with, which may either be the employer *or* the employer's constituency (e.g., students, if you're an academic librarian).

- Your contributions—do the projects you work on/volunteer for demonstrate the professional characteristics you want to be known for?
  For example, your brand may include a commitment to community
  service, or a passion for outdoor sports, or innovative thinking.

- Your public communications—if you blog, post to electronic discussion lists, have a website, write articles, contribute to newsletters, or
  give presentations, you are creating the public's perceptions of your

brand by the topics on which you focus, the language and writing style you use, the values you espouse, and the issues you champion.

- Your grad-school participation if you're a student—are you known for bringing enthusiasm and intellectual engagement to the class, or do you make it clear you're uninterested; do you find ways to support your fellow students or avoid unnecessary contact; do you organize dynamic student programs or let others do all the work?

- Your energy—are you someone who brings positive or negative energy into a room? Does your participation in a project lift the optimism and/or confidence level of the group? Do you laugh easily at yourself and with others? Do people look forward to working with you because your good vibes energize their own best stuff?

How you present yourself to your professional world will signify to others what to expect of you and how to treat you. Are you sending a consistent message that says "I expect to be treated as someone with substantial value to contribute?" (And then do you, in fact, follow through by contributing that substantial value?)

In one of her earlier career development books, *Make a Name for Yourself* (Broadway, 2002), Robin Fisher Roffer suggested that the "holy trinity" of a great brand will always be consistency, clarity, and authenticity. Roffer made an important point, which is that branding is not representing yourself to be something you're not. It's simply making sure that the world has an opportunity to see all the terrific things you *are*. Are you creative, enthusiastic, reliable, a "go-to" person? Do you want to be known as a change agent, a social activist, a decisive leader? Do you want potential employers and/or clients to think of you as a smart and savvy strategist who can also execute effectively? Whatever you are at your best—but also most authentic—core, this is what you want to make visible to your professional environment.

Think of branding as simply taking the initiative to shape others' perceptions of your skills and abilities before they form opinions based on faulty assumptions that will limit your ability to contribute. It's an opportunity to showcase your strengths. And if the concept still feels foreign to you, go with this great anonymous quote: "Think of yourself as an undervalued asset that's about to go public." Hey, we're LIS professionals—we merit a *really* high stock price!

---

### Branding for Beginners:
### What Assets Are You Taking Public?

We all have a brand; the only question is whether or not you will consciously shape it. So why not take the opportunity to showcase your strengths?

If you're going to "go public," what professional assets and attributes do you want to go public *with*? Some questions that might help you focus your thinking here:

- What core values do you want to define your professional reputation?

- What passions?

- What talents do you want others to associate with you?

- Are there areas of specialization for which you want to be known?

Equally important, what actions over the course of your career demonstrate these brand attributes?

What if you're just starting out and don't have any accomplishments yet that document your distinct value, a question frequently asked by students? Then this simply gives you a goal to shoot for as you grow your career. In the meantime, you might want to focus on the following key brand elements, which will help ensure your ongoing employability so you can start building that impressive career:

- Easy to work with, plays well with others

- Strong team participant, whether as leader or member

- Excited about new approaches and ideas, but understand and respect the value of established ones

- Enthusiastic and energetic, not afraid of change

- Someone whose judgment can be trusted

- Confident enough in your own knowledge and skills to understand and respect the value of others

Becoming known as the person who is great to work with, who focuses on solutions, who not only values collaborative efforts but can also take direction, is a great beginning from which to start building the brand the world will know you by.

## Building Professional Equity through Associations

One highly effective way to build your professional equity—what you know, who you know, and who knows about you—is by joining *and becoming active in* professional associations.

One of your choices will be whether to become active at the local or national level if you decide to join a national organization such as ALA or SLA and one of their chapters or divisions (the local or regional group of a national organization is usually called a chapter). At the chapter level, you'll have a chance to get to know and network with colleagues in your community or region—always great for building local long-term relationships (and for job-hunting help). Becoming active as a volunteer at the national level will increase your visibility while also vastly expanding the network and potential expertise base from which you may benefit as you continue to grow your career. (On a related note, the electronic discussion lists maintained by many professional associations can be a rich and deep source of knowledge with which to continue to expand your expertise.)

Bonus points: in addition to helping you build your professional equity, volunteering with associations and especially taking leadership roles will demonstrate to potential hiring managers that you see yourself as a professional who takes his or her ability to contribute seriously. In addition, if you do a great job, you'll impress your fellow volunteers and committee members with your reliability, commitment, positive energy, and professionalism, which will make them much more willing to help you land a job. (Remember, someone who recommends you for a position is putting his or her own professional reputation on the line.)

# LinkedIn, Networking, Branding, and Your Career

When it comes to building both your brand visibility and your professional network, I recommend LinkedIn as your primary platform for three reasons: (1) it's relatively easy to master, (2) it's cheap (as in, free), and (3) it's where people like recruiters and hiring managers frequently go to look for potential employees. Also, it's very forgiving of the fact that you may not update any of your information for months on end—unlike other social networking or media platforms that require you to be constantly furnishing witty new updates on a weekly if not daily basis. (That said, if you are already using any of the other social media/networking platforms to build your professional reputation and network, by all means, keep playing to your strengths.)

**Put your LinkedIn profile to work for you.** Let's start with LinkedIn's brand-building benefits, since your starting point will be completing your profile, essentially a branding powerhouse. For example, if you're at all shy about singing your own praises, LinkedIn allows you to showcase your best stuff without having to actually *tell* someone face-to-face how terrific you are. It has been built (and is regularly redesigned) to function as an online portfolio for you, enabling you to attach extensive evidence of your skills and accomplishments.

Unlike a traditional, narrowly focused resume, your LinkedIn profile provides an opportunity for you to present a much fuller, well-rounded portrait of who you are, what you value, and what value you contribute. The following table gives you an idea of all of the different types of information you can provide, with examples of each. Note the phrase "an idea of"—LinkedIn is constantly tinkering with its formula, but as of fall 2015, profile options included the following:

| Profile Element | Notes and Examples |
|---|---|
| **Tagline** | Concise overview of your key value to a potential employer or client; about 120 characters (including spaces); use the keywords that are specific to your field or the one you aspire to—your goal here is to be *findable*. |
| | *Note:* Focus on your top professional skills, the ones that (1) you feel most confident about, (2) you most want to do more of, and/or (3) will get you the best salary, depending on your priorities. |
| | *Example:* Online content strategist and content developer for health and wellness companies, agencies, and nonprofits. |
| **Summary** | Your most important element. Assume about 75–100 words in length (two to three paragraphs max), shoot for a concise but thorough overview of your professional strengths and areas of expertise you'd like to be known for (don't showcase work you don't want to do anymore!). Be sure to use your keywords (LinkedIn will suggest terms to "Optimize your profile to get found"). Don't be shy—this is your value statement. |
| | *Note:* If you're not sure what to say in your summary, cruise through some profiles of colleagues or people in your field you know of to see how they have written about their skills. |

| | |
|---|---|
| | *Example:* Experienced content strategist and content developer, working with corporations, nonprofits, and higher education institutions to develop information resources and processes that meet strategic goals. Expertise includes print and online content development, project-based research, information project management, and creation of information strategies that drive key organizational strategic goals. Special emphasis on career-related content for undergraduate and graduate students, traditional and nontraditional. |
| | Specialties: Information/content strategies to drive organization goals; print and online content development (organization, research, writing, editing); online resource portals; career content for college students; LIS career design workshops. |
| **Photo** | Yes, you DO want to include a photo—you'll want to look professional and friendly—smile unless you have truly terrible teeth! |
| | *Note:* People tend to respond negatively to use of LinkedIn's default gray icon when looking at profiles—many have said it looks like the person is hiding something. |
| **Location** | Where you are currently located. |
| **Industry** | What industry you are in (choose from the drop-down menu). |
| **Experience** | Chronological listing and description of current and previous employment, including titles and responsibilities. Generally, each entry will be two to four sentences, and your job descriptions will showcase skills and expertise you're currently highlighting. If possible, use keywords in your descriptions that reflect the standard search terms recruiters would be using and focus on outcomes and results when applicable. |
| | *Note:* It's great to have at least one recommendation for each position—preferably from a boss, manager, or supervisor. Also, it's OK to include volunteer work/ projects if substantial or in your line of work. |
| **Projects** | Any significant projects you've worked on or are working on that have relevance to your professional focus or indicate your areas of personal commitment. |
| | *Note:* This can be especially useful if your projects in some way relate to your job aspirations. |
| **Publications** | Any publications (books, ebooks, articles, etc.) you've written—can include URL for each entry. |
| **Skills and Endorsements** | Choose up to 50 applicable skills from drop-down menu. |
| **Volunteer** | Volunteer engagements—can be both personal and professional. |
| | *Note:* This information helps "round out" who you are for the reader (or hiring manager). |

| Education | Undergrad and grad programs. |
|---|---|
| | *Note:* You'll have the option to include specific courses if this further enhances your expertise, which allows you to highlight an area of specialization; also, consider asking faculty or administrators with whom you had an especially good relationship to provide recommendations for you as a student. |
| | **"Additional Info"** |
| Interests | Can be personal or professional |
| | *Note:* If you include personal interests, make sure you're comfortable sharing this info with potential employers. |
| | *Example:* Creating resilient careers; adult/nontraditional learners; information entrepreneurship; public libraries as community-change agents; social innovation and entrepreneurship |
| Advice for Contacting You | Identify what you're interested in being contacted about; default options include career opportunities, new ventures, reference requests, consulting offers, and expertise requests. |
| | *Note:* If you're job-hunting in stealth mode, you'll want to avoid any indication that you're looking for a job. Instead, focus on your area of interest or expertise. |
| | *Example:* Interested in connecting with other LIS professionals focusing on emerging digitization technologies. |
| Organizations | Includes both LinkedIn Groups and outside organizations of which you're a member (you're able to specify what these are). |
| Recommendations | Displays recommendations others have given you. |
| | *Note:* This populates automatically, so no need to add information here. |
| Following | Identifies thought leaders ("influencers"), topics, and organizations you've chosen to follow. |
| | *Note:* Entries from those you're following show up in your "Pulse" page. |
| | **"Add Sections to Your Profile"** |
| Language | These can be great differentiators for you, so be sure to add any languages you know. |
| | *Note:* A drop-down menu allows you to specify your level of proficiency. |
| Honors and Awards | For example, SLA's "Rising Stars" or Beta Phi Mu honor society for librarians. |
| | *Note:* Can be academic, professional, or civic/community awards. |
| Test Scores | Only if relevant to a specific type of work. |

| Courses | To indicate an area of specialization or courses taken outside the normal MLIS curriculum. This enables you to draw attention to specialized expertise you may have developed as a student. |
| --- | --- |
| Patents | List 'em if you've got 'em! |
| Causes You Care About | Part of the *Volunteer* section; choose from drop-down menu.<br><br>*Note*: Can be personal or professional, but you'll want to carefully consider what you chose to disclose if personal. |
| Supported Organizations | Part of the *Volunteer* section; can be LinkedIn or other organizations. |
| Certifications | Similar to the "Courses" information, this option enables you to note unusual or additional skills that may help differentiate you from other job applicants.<br><br>*Example*: Certification as a project manager from the Project Management Institute (PMI). |
| Personal Details | Birthday and/or marital status (you can choose who may see this info). |

As you can see, your LinkedIn profile enables you to greatly expand the amount and types of information you can showcase for a hiring manager or recruiter, or for a colleague who would like to recommend you for a position. And since experts are now saying that nearly 90 percent of hiring managers will check you out online before making a decision regarding whether or not to even interview you, wouldn't you like to know that what they'll find speaks strongly on your behalf, even if they're checking you out at midnight and you're sound asleep?

**Use LinkedIn tools to build your network.** LinkedIn offers several ways to create, expand, and sustain your professional connections. First is to simply reach out to your existing colleagues and ask to link. (Avoid using LinkedIn's default invite language; it's much better to personalize your request, however brief.) Assuming your contact accepts your request, the two of you will now be officially connected and in each other's networks. You'll each be able to see who else is in your new connection's network, great information to have if you are in need of an introduction to someone your friend knows.

Second is to "capture" those professional relationships that flow through your life daily—the person you met at the conference, the new account manager for your ebook provider, the person you sat next to at the local SLA chapter dinner. Rather than simply exchanging cards, increase the benefit of those serendipitous meetings by suggesting the two of you connect on LinkedIn—send the invite as soon as possible so neither of you forgets what your connection was (translation: when and where you met).

Third is to join relevant LinkedIn groups and check out the other group members. Is there someone in the group you'd like to get to know better? You can reach out directly to fellow group members with a suggestion that you link up, as opposed to LinkedIn's regular communications protocol, which is that generally you can only directly communicate with someone you're officially linked to. (Your thoughtful, consistent participation in LinkedIn groups relevant to your professional goals and/or career aspirations will also support your brand-building efforts by raising your visibility among a wide community of potential colleagues who can benefit from the expertise you share or even the questions you ask.)

The benefits of building a broad and deep professional network on LinkedIn are numerous. You can ask first-level connections to introduce you to someone in their network who works for a company in which you're interested. You can reach out to a connection who has relevant expertise for information and insights regarding a topic you're just starting to explore. You can ask people in your network who have first-hand knowledge of the quality of your work to write recommendations that will show up on your profile. Unlike LinkedIn's endorsements feature, these recommendations or individual testaments to your value and expertise provide a powerful type of "social proof," vetting your value for potential employers. You can introduce two people who will be able to instantly learn more about each other (and their potential for mutual benefit) by viewing their respective profiles.

**Use LinkedIn Groups to build your professional knowledge.** One of the benefits of a large network of colleagues and contacts is that it exponentially expands the reach of your knowledge base. The LinkedIn Groups feature lends itself to this type of "knowledge expansion" by exposing you to potentially hundreds if not thousands of topic experts with whom you can connect through relevant groups. For example, once you join a group, you can monitor discussions, post questions, reach out to individual experts, and post requests for expertise. In addition, LinkedIn's *Pulse* feature enables you to follow thought leaders in specific areas of interest.

Although LinkedIn is currently the strongest professional tool for building all three aspects of your professional equity through one platform, this is not to say that other social media channels do not offer excellent opportunities for building your knowledge, network, and professional visibility (or that a challenger to LinkedIn's market position might not soon appear).

# Professional Equity Equals Opportunity

You can also use internships, volunteer opportunities, and your alumni network (don't just join, get active and visible) for both network-building and establishing your professional reputation. The bottom line is to pay attention to this aspect of your career. Growing your professional community and shaping how the world perceives you as a professional is as much an investment in your career resiliency as continually expanding your knowledge base—and will have just as great a return on investment. Although all three will require your willingness to invest time and effort to grow and sustain them, all are also likely to open up unforeseen pathways of opportunity that only strong professional equity can deliver.

# Resources

## Books

*Networking*

Ferrazzi, Keith. *Who's Got Your Back: The Breakthrough Program to Build Deep, Trusting Relationships That Create Success—and Won't Let You Fail.* Crown Business, 2009. 336p. ISBN 0385521332.

Ferrazzi's first book (*Never Eat Alone—And Other Secrets to Success, One Relationship at a Time*, Crown Business, 2005) established him as a master networker with a focus on authentic, empathetic relationships. This follow-up book expands on that concept to describe the importance of creating your own inner circle of trusted individuals (sort of a "super network" or brain trust) to help sustain you through the ups and downs of your career. Think of this as your go-to guys, your cheering squad on really bad days, and your reality checkers when you're about to make a *really* bad career move.

Randel, Jim. *The Skinny on Networking: Maximizing the Power of Numbers.* Rand Media Co., 2010. 156p. ISBN 0984441816.
    Looking for a quick and entertaining read on networking tactics that still covers all the bases? Randel's *The Skinny on Networking* (part of his multi-book "Skinny On…" series) is short, practical, and readable over a longish lunch hour.

Salpeter, Miriam. *Social Networking for Career Success, 2d ed.* LearningExpress, 2013. 384p. ISBN 1576859320.
    One of the best books on using the major social media tools—for example, LinkedIn, Twitter, Facebook, Quora, Pinterest—plus other social media approaches (blogging, social bookmarks, etc.) to establish and sustain both a professional network and long-term career advantage. Salpeter is the founder and owner of Keppie Careers, a career coaching company with a terrific social media presence. (Key resource)

Schaffer, Neal. *Windmill Networking: Understanding, Leveraging & Maximizing LinkedIn.* BookSurge Publishing, 2009. 382p. ISBN 1439247056.
    Wondering how to make the most of that LinkedIn profile you started a couple of years ago? *Windmill Networking* provides step-by-step guidance for how to use your LinkedIn presence to extend (or start building) your professional network. One of the best books on using LinkedIn strategically. Other recommended titles on this topic: *LinkedIn for Dummies, 3d ed.* by Joel Elad (John Wiley & Sons, 2014), which focuses on the basics rather than on strategy, and Wayne Breitbarth's *The Power Formula for LinkedIn Success: Kickstart Your Business, Brand, and Job Search, 2d ed.* (Greenleaf Book Group Press, 2013), which is especially strong for solopreneur branding and business marketing.

Zack, Devora. *Networking for People Who Hate Networking: A Field Guide for Introverts, the Overwhelmed, and the Underconnected.* Berrett-Koehler, 2010. 192p. ISBN 9781605095226.
    Focusing primarily on networking at business events, Zack proposes a process-based approach for navigating networking situations. The author, an introvert herself, does a good job of identifying the networking challenges faced by fellow introverts and then providing realistic solutions. (Key resource)


*Branding*

Ancowitz, Nancy. *Self-Promotion for Introverts: The Quiet Guide to Getting Ahead.* McGraw-Hill, 2009. 288p. IBSN 007159129X.
    Ancowitz writes from the heart: an introvert, she is also a successful consultant, writer, and speaker. Her book draws on stories from well-known business, sports, and entertainment figures, everyday

clients, and her own experiences to lay out a life approach that will help introverts find the career success their efforts merit, but in a way that recognizes how they interact with the world. (Key resource)

Arruda, William and Kirsten Dixson. *Career Distinction: Stand Out by Building Your Brand.* Wiley, 2007. 224p. ISBN 0470128186.
Organized by three broad themes: unearth your unique promise of value, communicate your brand to your target audience, manage your brand environment. Key statement: "What makes you unique, makes you successful." Lots of solid how-to advice, resources, and cool quotes.

Beckwith, Harry and Christine Clifford Beckwith. *You, Inc.: The Art of Selling Yourself.* Business Plus, 2011. 336p. ISBN 0446695815.
Best-selling business author Harry Beckwith's expertise is in how to use communication to sell (*Selling the Invisible, a Field Guide to Modern Marketing*, reprint ed, Business Plus, 2012), and here he turns his focus to helping you sell yourself via your career brand. The book is packed with brief, concise points (roughly two pages long) that each conclude with a pithy action statement. Consider this career-branding boot camp.

Covey, Stephen R. *The 7 Habits of Highly Effective People: Powerful Lessons in Personal Change.* Simon & Schuster, 1990. 326p. ISBN 406204983X.
With over 25 million copies sold, *7 Habits of Highly Effective People* has been a tremendously influential and much-quoted guide to living one's best life. The seven habits are grouped within the three categories of "private victory," "public victory," and "renewal," and are designed to help readers develop personal best-practice approaches for each area of their lives.

Clark, Dorie. *Reinventing You: Define Your Brand, Imagine Your Future.* Harvard Business Review Press, 2013. 240p. ISBN 1422144135.
*Reinventing You* stands out from other "build your brand" books in that it focuses on transitioning your existing reputation and visibility into a new professional space. Especially relevant for LIS professionals who are looking to translate/transition LIS skills into new arenas.

Hogshead, Sally. *How the World Sees You: Discover Your Highest Value through the Science of Fascination.* Harper Business, 2014. 448p. ISBN 0062230697.
Although Hogshead comes from the advertising world and her approach can occasionally feel a bit over the top, *How the World Sees You* is included here because of her unique focus on personality archetypes and how they might be integrated into your brand message. Not scientifically based, but a very useful read nevertheless. (Key resource)

Kaputa, Catherine. *You Are a Brand! How Smart People Brand Themselves.* Nicholas Brealey Publishing, 2010. 208p. ISBN 0891062130.
Winner of multiple career book awards, this book is particularly strong on tactics and tools. Many of Kaputa's ideas are unique to this book, and yet once she's suggested them, they seem like common sense (e.g., including testimonial quotes on your resume). Key concept: a strong personal brand raises the perception of your value among others, and consequently your earning power.

McNally, David and Karl D. Speak. *Be Your Own Brand: A Breakthrough Formula for Standing Out from the Crowd, 2d ed.* Berrett-Koehler Publishers, 2011. 168p. ISBN 1605098108.

One of the more reflective, thoughtful, and methodical of the branding books. Key statement: "The 'right way' to go about building a strong personal brand is to make sure your brand resonates and is relevant, in the most distinctive way possible, for those people with whom you want to build strong relationships on a long-term basis." Useful graphics clarify a number of key concepts.

Roffer, Robin Fisher. *Make a Name for Yourself: 8 Steps Every Woman Needs to Create a Personal Branding Strategy for Success.* Crown Business, 2002. 224p. ISBN 0767904926.
Roffer was one of the first women to write about the concept of personal branding, and *Make a Name for Yourself* remains relevant even though published before social media and social platforms took the branding world by storm.

## Online Resources

*Networking*

ASKING TO CONNECT ON LINKEDIN—WORDS TO USE
http://infonista.com/2011/asking-to-connect-on-linkedin-don%E2%80%99t-default-to-the-defaults/
One of the important aspects of networking on LinkedIn is reaching out and establishing "links" to others. Although the LinkedIn system provides you with default request language, it's much better to tailor your request to the individual you're reaching out to. This blog post gives examples of wording you can adapt for your own circumstances.

HOW TO BUILD YOUR NETWORK
https://hbr.org/2005/12/how-to-build-your-network
This article, written by Brian Uzzi and Shannon Dunlap and published in the December 2005 *Harvard Business Review,* is a fascinating exploration of how information—and connections—flow based on the nature of those connections (e.g., the authors call Paul Revere an "information broker"). Note the authors, "networks deliver three unique advantages: private information, access to diverse skill sets, and power." And from a career development perspective, they also often deliver job opportunities, knowledge shared among colleagues, and a highly effective way to showcase your professional persona.

HOW TO NETWORK EFFECTIVELY
www.inc.com/guides/2010/08/how-to-network-effectively.html
A methodical, well-organized overview of how to think strategically about the various aspects of your network and how to gain the most benefit from each of those aspects. Includes techniques for getting the most from LinkedIn as a networking tool.

POWER NETWORKING FOR INTROVERTS
www.introvertscannetwork.com/
From independent information professional Marcy Phelps, this "blog by an introvert for introverts" has been wildly popular with LIS students and practitioners as well as others outside the profession. The focus is on tips, techniques, and coping strategies that enable introverts to

network effectively and (relatively) painlessly. Although Phelps decided to stop writing the blog a while back, its popularity and usefulness for readers remain.

PROFESSIONAL NETWORKING AT CONFERENCES
http://bit.ly/1Cwc0Qq
From guest blogger Jacqueline Ayala, with the basic premise that "Networking on the Web is undoubtedly fundamental to being an active member of the library community, but nothing beats the in-person connections we make with our colleagues at conferences." Ayala asserts that careful planning is key to gaining the most value from attending a conference, and she provides pointers for how to do just that.

THE STRENGTH OF WEAK TIES
http://smg.media.mit.edu/library/Granovetter.WeakTies.pdf
From the May 1973 *American Journal of Sociology,* this article by Mark S. Granovetter is the basis on which much of the subsequent research on networking was built. Granovetter looked at why "weak ties," or connections to people outside your normal sphere of influence/engagement, can prove to be a highly effective way of opening up additional career opportunities as well as extending your access to knowledge and insights outside your normal professional community. (Key resource)

THERE'S A DIFFERENCE BETWEEN BEING GENEROUS AND BEING A DOORMAT
http://sciof.us/1KSHq6a
A great interview with best-selling author Adam Grant (*Give and Take: Why Helping Others Drives Our Success,* Penguin Books, 2014) on how to be a wise "giver," that is, one who doesn't become a doormat. It's about prioritizing, drawing boundaries, and other self-protection strategies identified here by Grant. Especially important when building networking relationships.

*Branding*

100 PERSONAL BRANDING TACTICS USING SOCIAL MEDIA
www.chrisbrogan.com/100-personal-branding-tactics-using-social-media/
From branding and social media expert Chris Brogan, this post is a bit out of date (2008) in terms of specific tools to use, but the key concepts and action items still hold.

ARE ANY OF THESE BEHAVIORS DAMAGING YOUR PERSONAL BRAND?
http://bit.ly/1K1ajKu
Top 10 ways to derail your online professional reputation. When 90 percent of hiring managers are now routinely checking out applicants for their online presence, it's critical to avoid damaging behaviors that will give potential employers a reason to doubt your professional judgment.

CREATING A POSITIVE PROFESSIONAL IMAGE
http://hbswk.hbs.edu/item/4860.html
Interview with Harvard Business School professor Laura Morgan Roberts on the most important elements of creating a strong professional

brand. See especially her comments about building credibility and maintaining authenticity. (Key resource)

LIBRARIAN OR INFORMATION PROFESSIONAL?
http://libgig.wordpress.com/2011/07/28/alignment-within-the-profession/
One of the more thoughtful discussions about a key professional branding question for the LIS profession—what to call ourselves. The writer, a law librarian, explores the pros and cons of self-identifying as "librarian" or "information professional."

ONE MINUTE COMMERCIAL
http://bit.ly/1HnyMbP
Ah, the dreaded "elevator speech." An essential part of networking is being able to tell strangers who you are and what you do, especially if you are in job-hunting mode. Although designed for MLIS students, this brief guide will help anyone work through creating their own self-introduction. See especially the "One Minute Commercial" template (Career Development > Network > One Minute Commercial).

*Social Networks—LIS-Related Groups*
*Note: Many social network sites have groups of extraordinary professional development value to LIS students and professionals, places where questions, answers, information, and career insights are freely exchanged and members can learn in a supportive, collaborative environment. In addition, these platforms are especially valuable to professionals seeking to build their network and/or the visibility of their professional reputation (brand). Two of the largest aggregations of potentially relevant groups are found within Google groups and LinkedIn; see next for ways to explore their professional development resources.*

*Google Groups*
http://groups.google.com/
Search on your topic of interest in the "Search for a group" search box, but be ready to narrow that topic down; a search on "libraries" brought up about 4,300 hits.

*LinkedIn Groups*
www.linkedin.com/home
From the home page, choose "Groups" from the drop-down search box menu, then enter your topic of choice. A representative selection of some of the most active (and therefore, usually most informative) groups:

- Buslib-l
- Code4lib
- Corporate Librarians
- Digital Asset Management
- Digital Book World
- Digital Libraries
- eBooks in Libraries
- Historians, Librarians and Archivists

- Information, Knowledge & Content Management Specialists
- Job Skills for Future Library Careers
- Librarians in the Job Market
- LIS Career Options (subgroup of ALA LinkedIn group)
- Metadata Management
- SLA First Five Years
- Society of American Archivists
- Strategic and Competitive Intelligence Professionals (SCIP)
- Taxonomy Community of Practice

# Note

1. M. Granovetter, "The Strength of Weak Ties," *American Journal of Sociology*, 78(6) (May 1973): 1360–1380.

# 9
# Getting from Here to There

*Judge each day not by the harvest you reap but by the seeds you plant.*

—Robert Louis Stevenson

You've self-assessed, scoped out the professional options, reframed your skill sets, and expanded your knowledge horizons. But how do you get from where your career stands today and where you want to be in the future? How do you get from here to there?

You create a strategy.

According to *Webster's Ninth,* strategy is "the art of devising or employing plans or stratagems toward a goal." It's the plan you put together that aligns your goals with the realities of your life. It's where you change the question from "can I?" to "how will I?"

Based on the Greek *strategos* ("the art of the general"), your strategy is what puts you in charge of outcomes, and your *tactics* are the action items you undertake to execute your strategy. Your strategies and tactics are what you use to achieve your goals.

Goals, strategies, tactics. If thought through carefully, these three elements can enable you to move forward methodically and consistently toward the career you want. They also will help you create your personal career agenda—targeted outcomes that shape how you approach assignments, projects, classes, and possible job opportunities.

The most effective way to put together your action plan is to create a career map that captures your goals, strategies, and tactics within a timeline of execution. In other words, what do you plan to accomplish (goals), what approaches will you take to do so (strategies), and what action items will you undertake within these approaches (tactics).

The purpose of a career map is not to lock yourself into a grid of predetermined actions, but to (1) get you to commit to yourself in writing that you can and will take positive steps to create the career future you want, and (2) start you thinking about where you'd like to go and what you'd like to accomplish, so that when opportunities arise, you have benchmarks against which to judge them.

Depending on what format works best for you, your career map might be an outline of goals/strategies/tactics, or a multicolored visual graphic of key goals and radiating strategies and tactics. Perhaps a written narrative that describes your action plan better suits you, or a detailed flowchart, or a project management grid. The idea is simply to create some sort of document or graphic that establishes what you plan to accomplish, how, and within what time frame.

For example, you might decide that as part of your career agenda within three years you want to have created a website that curates the best mobile apps and behavioral modification games for people with depression. You would figure out what you needed to do to complete that goal, for example, doing an extensive literature search for reviews and review sources, identifying major mental health app and game creators, figuring out interviews or surveys you might want to undertake—and then identify how and when you would go about doing that. Or perhaps you want to take a stronger leadership role in your profession—your career map would chart how you would do that, for example, running for office in a professional organization, and when you planned to do that.

So grab your career journal and all those notes you've been making. Run away from home for a weekend, take a mental health day, do whatever it takes to carve out some space for yourself, and start organizing your thoughts. If you're going to be an LIS professional for the next several decades, putting together your career map will be a small investment that pays you long-term dividends.

## Career Map Components

Career maps are as different as the individuals compiling them, but generally will build on all of the work you've done so far.

To recap, these areas have included:

**Exploring personal preferences.** Essentially, what work might you want to do, and how might you want to do it? *Might* is the operative word here because sometimes these answers will only clarify themselves through several years (or more) of experimenting with options and then paying close attention to your responses.

Your career map will help you identify things you can do to test your reactions to work environments, types of work, and similar preferences. Look for or create opportunities to try out various options without having to actually commit to them. Volunteering or temping can be especially valuable here.

**Considering career choices.** Traditional, nontraditional, independent, or some combination or sequence of them all?

Once you've identified career paths of potential interest, your career map is the place you'll note what activities you'll participate in to find out more about them. Will you shadow a practitioner, request an informational interview (in person or via e-mail), do volunteer work, read descriptions of this type of work, join a professional association and listen to members' war stories, join an electronic discussion group and see what issues are being discussed? How will you learn more about the possible downsides of your potential career choices? If you're considering the independent path, how will you find out more about the market for your services?

**Working on projects.** Reframing your career from the portfolio perspective not only allowed you to see your professional strengths and accomplishments, it also highlighted professional "gaps," areas where you'll want to build expertise or a track record of increasing responsibility.

Your career map is the place for you to record what types of projects you'll seek out, and why. To up your visibility, learn a new skill, add higher levels of managerial responsibility to your portfolio, work with an outstanding colleague, bridge to a new professional opportunity, position yourself with a new constituency?

**Experimenting with your change process.** You're determined to turn change from a threat to an ally...here's where you create the strategy to make good on that commitment.

**Learning.** When you did your learning agenda in Chapter 7, you identified new areas of knowledge you wanted to master, and how you would accomplish that.

Will it be formal or informal learning? Perhaps you're not certain; in that case, this part of your career map may focus on exploring and evaluating learning options. Also, how will you explore your most effective learning style(s)?

**Gaining visibility, creating your professional presence.** True, making the effort to align who you are—your values, your abilities, your smarts, and your passions—with how the world perceives you may seem like hype. But the reality is, either consciously or by default, we define how the world sees us.

What actions will you take to gain visibility within or outside of the LIS profession? To establish your professional value to colleagues and potential employers/clients? To demonstrate expertise, or innovative thinking, or strategic initiative? Your career map is where you'll set the direction.

**Building contacts.** As we've seen, building a community of colleagues will strengthen not only your career options, but also your ongoing enjoyment of your career.

In your career map, you'll get specific about how you'll expand your professional connections, if this is a priority for you. Will those relationships be within or outside of the LIS field or a combination of both? How will you help others in your community of colleagues?

How will you try out your best approaches for dealing with change? What techniques will you use? Will you read books about the psychology of change? Experiment with one small change a week, a day, or a month? What changes will you try?

**Strengthening your risk-taking muscle.** We looked at the fact that supporting your change frame is your ability and willingness to take risks. By holding you accountable, your career map will help encourage you in the right direction.

What risks will you take, so you can start getting comfortable with your ability to "feel the fear and do it anyway?" What risks will support the direction you want your career to go? Big steps or baby ones, the goal is familiarizing yourself with how you react to risk, and coaching yourself through it. The more often you do it, the less intimidating it becomes.

**Building your information base.** You're an information pro—you do information. So keeping on top of it is one of the most important skills you'll have. We've explored a number of options; your career map is where you'll get specific.

How will you identify the information you'll need to gather regarding your intended or potential career paths, and how will you gather/monitor it? What magazines will you subscribe to, what electronic discussion lists join? Will you monitor blogs, and if so, which ones and why? Will you join professional associations, attend conferences, identify and read a core collection of books on your topic? Keep in mind, your information base will probably reflect two areas: information about the profession or type of job you're interested in, and the knowledge necessary to perform the job.

## Assembling Your Career Map

To pull your career map together, first go back and review the notes, comments, and questions you've entered in your career journal. You should find ideas and actions to explore—now is the time to decide *how and when* you'll undertake that exploration.

To begin, you'll need to start by asking yourself three questions: what are my goals, what strategies will I use to reach my goals, and what tactics (action items) will I use to execute my strategies? Then, based on your answers to these questions, you'll need to take it a couple of steps further to flesh out your plan.

**Step 1: Identify your goals.** Whether for the next year or more, what do you need to accomplish to make progress toward your career goals? Consider the following possible goals to get you started and complete the statements to reflect your personal circumstances:

- Explore these three options _____
- Develop an expertise in _____
- Find out whether I want to be/do _____
- Try out these three new skills _____
- Move to [a new location] and _____

- Get a job doing _____
- Find out more about _____
- Increase my income by _____
- Learn more about _____as a possible career choice
- Other goals _____

Keep in mind that exploring is as valid a goal as deciding or acting, but if you're exploring, your focus will be on documenting your findings, whether personal preferences (I took a leadership position, how did that feel?) or information (there are a total of XX private-practice medical clinics in this region that could use my cool new consumer medical pathfinders).

**Step 2: Identify your strategies.** Strategies are broad-brush approaches for achieving a goal, such as increasing knowledge, positioning for increased visibility, or expanding skill sets. Say, for example, you have as a goal to purchase a home in the next year. Your strategies might include preparing your personal finances, researching local neighborhoods, and investigating the home-buying process to understand what to expect.

Now you try it. Return to the goals you listed in your career journal, and then for each, come up with at least three strategies that will help you achieve it. If you can't come up with any strategies, brainstorm with a friend or colleague to help get the thought processes going. Your focus is on solutions, on getting from here to there, in a realistic fashion.

**Step 3: Decide on the tactics or actions you'll undertake to support your strategies.** If goals are what you hope to accomplish and strategies are the approaches you will use to do so, then tactics are the action items supporting your strategies. You'll want to think carefully about the tactics you'll use to support each strategy; otherwise, your strategies (and your goals) are simply wishful thinking. Also, at the tactical level, you'll want to attach timelines to your actions—what will you do, and by when will you do it? This ensures accountability, so you can easily know if you are on track . . . or still sitting at the station.

Let's try this out with our goal of purchasing a home. Your three strategies include prepping your finances, researching local neighborhoods, and investigating the local neighborhoods. How might you line this out? Your approach might look something like this:

| Strategy | Tactics |
| --- | --- |
| Prepare my personal finances | Request and review my credit file from the three major credit bureaus next week; correct any errors |
| | Set up and follow a schedule for paying off my credit card balance over the next three months |
| | Create a budget that reflects my projected monthly mortgage payment and start living within those budget constraints within ten weeks |
| Research local neighborhoods | Contact local Board of Realtors within next four weeks for information they may have available |
| | Start checking out homes Saturday mornings for sale in various neighborhoods to get a sense of prices |
| | Compile a "pro-and-con" sheet to note benefits and disadvantages of each neighborhood |

| Investigate home-buying process | Check with my local public library for recent books on how to buy a home as I get closer to making a purchase |
| | Ask friends who've already been through the house-buying process to give me pointers |
| | Work with my real estate agent to put together a hit list of questions, documents, and action items I need to start working on—schedule a working lunch for next month |

Now you try it. You've identified your goals and strategies in Steps 1 and 2; now is where you set your marching orders. What actions will you take, and when? Lay out your plans in your career journal in whatever format works best for you, whether in an outline, project management approach, graphic with circles, boxes, links, and arrows, or some other creative rendering.

**Step 4: Identify what processes you'll need to establish.** Following an action plan necessitates setting up a system or process for sticking to your plan. As our often-neglected treadmills and rowing machines testify, if you don't allocate regular time to do something, it's probably not going to happen. So when you look at your career map, decide when you're going to schedule in "career time." A useful approach here is to never let Monday show up without having noted at least one career-related action item to complete that week. Create processes to integrate your career map actions into your daily life; if you can't get to them at work over your lunch hour, plan to execute at home. Your career map can be a great tool for getting unstuck: come up with one thing you can do for at least an hour a week, and you'll be moving toward the future you want.

**Step 5: Determine what resources are available to you.** Generally, your resources will include time (as in free time to devote to your action items), people (including colleagues on and off the job), your employer (who may offer training, tuition reimbursement, mentoring programs, support for conference attendance, and portfolio-expanding project opportunities), and, if you're a student, your degree program. Approached strategically, most LIS programs offer outstanding opportunities for professional growth, self-exploration, portfolio building, and career positioning, in addition to the coursework learning opportunities.

**Step 6: Decide how you'll handle obstacles to your plans.** Whether looking at goals, strategies, or tactics, it's best to assume that life will intervene and play havoc with your best laid plans. For most of us, people come first, whether family or friends, and life in all its glory is nothing if not messy. So knowing that your plans will be disrupted, displaced, and hijacked on a regular basis—and planning for it—will help you see these events as detours, not derailments.

There are lots of ways to deal with interruptions. If time or scheduling is an issue (when isn't it?), scale back your plans for the time being. Instead of trying to follow through on all your strategies and tactics, focus on just one. Rather than writing four hours a week, write for one. Instead of pursuing a second master's degree, read books on your topic of interest or subscribe to a print or online publication you can read over your lunch hour until you're able to start your coursework. If volunteering to edit the organization newsletter is not feasible given other time commitments, volunteer to write an article or two.

If financial constraints delay a goal of moving to New York and landing your dream job in a special library, simply switch your focus for the moment.

Use the time to build skills and credentials that will increase your value to potential employers when you eventually do arrive. See whether there are ways to connect with special librarians there to get a better sense of the local job market in advance of your arrival. Consider joining the New York chapter of SLA while you're waiting for the opportunity to make your move.

If personal commitments to family and friends mean those to your career are temporarily put on the back burner, decide whether to take a time-out for the moment or simply scale back but continue to move forward with your goals more slowly. If the latter, be adamant about scheduling in time for your career development activities so you don't completely lose your forward momentum.

If, on the other hand, you decide what you really need is a time-out, it helps to have a trigger firmly established in your mind for when you will reengage with your career activities. Is it when your youngest child starts kindergarten? When your friend has gotten through the breakup crazies? When your partner or spouse has landed a job? When you've finished pre-paring your mom's taxes?

The key point here is to realize that those we love will *always* need our time and attention, and human nature being what it is, they'll also be extremely good at laying claim to our every spare minute. If you want to pursue your career goals, it's critical to make a commitment to yourself of time, energy, and attention. If others are less than supportive of the time you're now spending focused on your own goals, that's understandable—but not a reason to stop your forward progress. Solicit their support, but know you can move forward without it.

# Sample Career Maps

Still not quite sure how to create your own action plan? The following are very brief examples of one-year career maps for three different circumstances:

- Someone who's fresh out of grad school, starting a new job and want-ing to prove herself as a potential leader in the organization.

- Someone who's been the business librarian for a large public library and would like to move into a special library or nontraditional role with a local pharmaceutical company.

- Someone who wants to repurpose his transferable skills, specifically, digital asset management, from a university on the West Coast to some type of large nonprofit or corporation in Chicago.

**Fresh out of grad school, new on the job**

| Goal | Find a way to establish myself in my new job as a hard-working, competent, engaged, collaborative team member who is interested in and deserving of leadership training |
|------|-----------------------------------------------------------------------------------------|
| Strategies | 1. Maintain a positive attitude, focusing on becoming known for positive energy<br>2. Consistently demonstrate through my actions the characteristics of hard-working, competent, engaged, collaborative<br>3. Invest on my own in leadership knowledge to demonstrate my commitment to eventually assuming a leadership role |

| Tactics | 1. Maintain a positive attitude, focusing on becoming known for positive energy<br>  • Sustain a positive attitude at work and seek to energize my coworkers with positive support, encouragement, and a sense of humor<br>  • During high stress or difficult times, work hard to keep team spirits up, stay centered, and stay focused<br>  • Spend at least one lunch hour per week focused on my career map action items, which will help me focus my energy away from frustration I may be feeling and instead invest it in achieving my goals<br>2. Consistently demonstrate through my actions the characteristics of hard-working, competent, engaged, collaborative<br>  • Complete all of my job responsibilities with a positive attitude, looking for ways to improve any processes for which I'm responsible if possible<br>  • Support and assist my fellow team members even if there's no immediate payoff or return for me<br>  • Collaborate with others within and outside of my immediate department to learn more about the workings of the organization and help support its goals<br>3. Invest on my own in leadership knowledge to demonstrate my commitment to eventually assuming a leadership role<br>  • Join ALA's Library Leadership & Management Association (LLAMA) or SLA's Leadership and Management Division and take advantage of their publications and continuing education offerings; after I have proved myself as an excellent contributor, sign up for the mentoring program (with my manager's approval)<br>  • Identify and monitor management and leadership thought leaders, both within and outside of the LIS profession<br>  • Attend all management and leadership presentations at conferences I can attend |
|---|---|

## Moving from public library business librarianship into a special library or nontraditional role with a local pharmaceutical company

| Goal | Bridge from public library business librarianship into information professional role for a pharmaceutical company within three years |
|---|---|
| Strategies | 1. Identify local employment options<br>2. Develop a thorough understanding of the pharmaceutical industry, its key stakeholders, and its information resources<br>3. Create a "bridge" between current job and potential pharmaceutical jobs |
| Tactics | 1. Identify local employment options<br>  • Search LinkedIn on "pharmaceutical" and my preferred geographic location<br>  • Check with local economic development group for any pharmaceutical companies relocating to my region<br>  • Check to see whether there are any pharmaceutical professional groups with local chapters to join for networking and visibility purposes |

| | |
|---|---|
| | 2. Develop a thorough understanding of the pharmaceutical industry, its key stakeholders, and its information resources <br>• Research key players in the pharmaceutical industry with an eye out for any headquartered nearby <br>• Identify and begin to monitor key trade publications and information feeds for trends, issues, opportunities, competitive analyses of companies, and so on—goal is to prepare myself for writing compelling resumes and cover letters, be able to ace interviews <br>• Identify key industry analysts to monitor, as well as conferences (and conference speakers and topics) <br>• Start mapping out an information landscape to which I can continue to add detail and notes as I gain additional information <br>3. Create a "bridge" between current job and potential pharmaceutical job <br>• Join SLA's Pharmaceutical & Health Technology Division; network with other division members to learn more about the types of pharmaceutical work available for information professionals; do informational interviews with division members to learn more about potential positions <br>• Join pharmaceutical-industry LinkedIn groups, monitor for a while to get a sense of the discussions, then start asking questions and contributing information to start building my brand visibility <br>• Create an analysis or report on the pharmaceutical industry and key companies, consider publishing excerpts for the local business journal (as part of this project, interview HR directors of all the pharmaceutical companies I profile, ask about hiring plans, and offer to send them copies of my report) |

## Repurposing transferable skills, specifically, digital asset management, from West Coast university to large nonprofit or corporation in Chicago

| Goal | Identify potential employers in Chicago who are likely to likely to be hiring for digital asset management positions |
|---|---|
| Strategies | 1. Explore and understand who the major for-profit and nonprofit employers are in the Chicago area <br>2. Determine whether I have a skills gap between my current and desired positions <br>3. Start building professional connections in the Chicago area |
| Tactics | 1. Explore and understand who the major for-profit and nonprofit employers are in the Chicago area <br>• Identify and monitor information resources about the business scene and job market for Chicago area on weekly basis <br>• Set up job alerts for at least 20 of the organizations that most interest me <br>• Check out Salary.com, the SLA (or similar) salary surveys, and regional salary surveys to determine salary expectations appropriate to the type of jobs I'm targeting and regional salary ranges |

2. Determine whether I have a skills gap between my current and desired positions
   - Identify and e-mail several information specialists doing the type of work I'm targeting and ask them about what they see as the key skills to succeeding in their jobs—complete within six to eight weeks
   - Explore the website DAMNEWS (Digital Asset Management News, Reviews, Trends & Opinion) at www.digitalassetmanagementnews.org to learn more about opportunities and potential career paths
   - See whether there are any projects I could take on in my current position that would make me a more attractive job candidate for a potential employer
3. Start building professional connections in the Chicago area
   - Join electronic discussion groups specific to my target area within next two weeks; monitor regularly and contribute my knowledge/expertise when appropriate
   - Join ALA's Business Reference and Service Section (BRASS) and establish contact with members working in digital asset management roles in the Chicago area
   - Consider subscribing to the *Chicago Business Journal* to start getting a sense of the city's business trends, players, and environment

These three strategy maps present only a few of the strategies and tactics you might use if pursuing the goals discussed earlier on a real-life basis, but they can give you an idea of how goals, strategies, and tactics work together to support progress toward your career targets.

Also, don't forget that it isn't necessary for a goal to be a specific achievement; it may be simply gaining a better understanding of something important to you, or clarifying an upcoming decision, or qualifying an opportunity on the horizon.

# Setting Agendas

In order to turn your career map into a document that takes you toward the career you dream of, it's important to always have your agenda mentally in place. Whether you're a student in a grad program, an LIS professional just starting out on a new job, a seasoned practitioner wanting to move into a new career phase, or someone who simply wants to grow in an existing job, having a career agenda helps you align key aspects of your situation with the goals you've set for yourself.

Your agenda grows out of the career map you've created and focuses on what goals you have for whatever situation you're in. There may be skills that you want to improve or pick up, a type of project you'd like to add to your portfolio, someone you'd like to build a relationship with, or visibility you'd like to gain. The purpose of your agenda is to align your individual professional goals with the organizational goals of your employer so that both advance simultaneously.

For example, assume you've been working as the company intranet coordinator, and you've just been asked to explore options for setting up an enterprise-wide content management system (CMS). This is an area where you have no expertise, but you're interested in growing in this direction. For the company, your goals may include doing a needs assessment, creating a request for proposals, evaluating potential software solutions, acquiring the right product, and putting it in place.

Depending on your career goals, you might decide that *your* agenda throughout this process would include

- Raising your visibility throughout the organization by targeting key executives for personal interviews during the needs-assessment process

- Reading up on how to do great RFPs and then asking others who've done them previously for tips and feedback on your draft, so you can build this as a new skill area

- Creating a process template for evaluating RFP responses, which you'll add to your portfolio

- Developing an expertise in project management by taking vendor training in a leading project management software platform, which you then use to implement your CMS project

- Building your leadership skills by bringing together a multi-departmental, collaborative team to support the introduction of the CMS solution solution throughout the organization

Or say you're a student, going through an MLIS grad program. The school's agenda will be delivered through a well-thought-through curriculum of courses and learning opportunities designed to help ensure that you graduate with a solid LIS knowledge base. But while you want to fully engage with your courses, you can also use your graduate studies as an opportunity to advance your career agenda as well. Some possibilities might be to:

- Use your courses to try out various processes for dealing with change or risk-taking.

- Experiment with different learning styles to determine which one (or combination) works best for you.

- Work on your writing skills to improve this important professional capability (ask for feedback specific to your writing from your professors).

- Develop an expertise in working on and/or leading group projects.

- Use assignments for self-assessment: do you prefer leading or being a team member on a group project? Working with student colleagues or on your own? Standing up and speaking to your class or being class secretary? Doing research, working with technology or taking management courses?

- Get to know your professors and let them get to know you and your interests to start building your professional community.

- Demonstrate (or develop) leadership skills by getting involved in the student group or by organizing special programs.

- Follow up with guest speakers for expert career advice and counsel.

- Use your assignments to research companies, employers, or career paths of interest to you.

The idea is to fulfill to your best ability your responsibilities to your employer (or graduate program) but at the same time look for opportunities that support your career goals, as identified in your career map.

This strategy can be especially helpful if you're in a job that isn't a good match for you but is also one you can't leave for the time being. While honoring your obligations to your current employer, you can be looking for opportunities to learn new skills, meet new people, or spend your lunch hours researching new opportunities. Push the boundaries of your position by volunteering for projects outside your defined job, by exploring ways to improve existing processes within your job, or by exploring knowledge outside your skill area by tapping colleagues' expertise. This approach will help you invest your energy in the opportunities of the future rather than the frustrations of the moment.

## Putting Your Career Map in Play

As you've created your career map, you've focused on items that are actionable—that is, realistic and measurable. You've been specific about your action items (identify three potential employers, interview five colleagues, monitor these three blogs . . .). The very concreteness of your plan is what will ensure that you're accountable to yourself.

Keep in mind, however, that it's also important to take into consideration your life circumstances and your individual personality. In other words, don't volunteer to head up the programs committee if you're never able to make it to the monthly membership meetings. Don't take on a project management role if deadlines bring on panic attacks. And if your mother-in-law has just moved in for a three-month stay, expect that there may be a few time-outs in your upcoming schedule, and cut yourself some slack.

Focus on yourself, *and the things that you can control*. If your goal is to change your boss's behavior from clueless to enlightened, it's simply not going to happen. But if instead your goal is to find techniques for working with your boss in a way that helps you move toward your professional goals rather than staying mired in anger and resentment, *that's* an outcome you can control.

Don't get discouraged if you don't achieve your goals on the first pass, if you're not making forward progress as quickly as you'd anticipated. Don't interpret this as failure, but rather use it as valuable information, an opportunity to figure out why you missed your marks. This isn't, by the way, a failure; it's simply real life showing up. Don't beat yourself up; instead plot your strategy for recognizing and handling similar situations a bit more successfully the next time they come around.

What if you decide you don't like where your career map is taking you? Congratulations! You've just gained invaluable insight that allowed you to avoid a painful career choice, and you can now shift direction to explore a different opportunity or career path that may be a better match with your interests and aspirations.

As in most of life, often in your career choices you'll be striving for progress, not perfection. The reality is, there is no perfectly "right" job or career path. There are multiple choices and opportunities to contribute, grow, and learn, and your career map will help you shape those choices in a way that most closely complements who you are and what you envision for your career.

# Using Your Career Map to Achieve Your Goals

A career map should be a useful tool for you rather than simply an exercise in daydreaming. It can be a framework within which to evaluate new opportunities—for example, does that possible new job you're considering take you toward or away from the career you want? It can be a road map of actions to take to move closer to your goals on a daily, weekly, or monthly basis. It can remind you what to do next when you've been "missing in action" from pursuing your career path for a while due to circumstances beyond your control.

Tailored to and reflective of your dreams and aspirations, your career map should not be seen as an inflexible plan but rather as a pathway. You'll still want to be opportunistic—you don't want to not respond to a terrific job or project offer simply because you didn't have it in your plans. Instead, consider your career map to be a blueprint that can be tweaked to fit both your life's circumstances and emerging professional interests. For those stuck in unrewarding jobs, a career map can be a way to keep you investing your energies and time in positive future opportunities rather than wasting both being mired in the negative energy of your current situation.

A career map is where you not only document your dreams, but also prove to yourself that they are achievable. It's how you set yourself up for success rather than failure, as you let small steps build big momentum for you.

# Asking the Critical Question

What is your definition of success?

The answer to this question will underlie all of your goals and strategies and tactics, yet it's rarely one we stop to think about. Mostly we unconsciously mirror the expectations and value frames handed down to us by family, influential friends, the profession, and often society at large, without realizing those values may not actually fit us at all.

Our culture tends to define success in terms of financial standing and professional status—how high are you on the ladder? But that doesn't need to be your definition. In a world of constant change, the real criteria for judging success might be that you were able to overcome your fears to contribute at your highest potential. It might be that you chose to stay and engage rather than go into "duck and cover" mode. It might be that you created a product or a service or a solution that sparked others' imaginations, and they took your ideas to a new level. It might be that you worked every day to use your skills to make someone's life a bit better, using the new tools and technologies at your disposal even though they had initially been a challenge.

To some extent, you may find that your answers to the self-assessment questions in Chapter 2 tell you how much you value the traditional signifiers of success in our society: pay, title, and status. Generally speaking, people who go into the LIS profession aren't usually targeting stratospheric salaries or the high-flying jobs that bring fame and fortune, although it *is* possible to earn some pretty high incomes by taking your LIS degree in nontraditional directions. If this is an important component of career success for you, then it should figure strongly in your career map.

If working for socially responsible organizations where you can make a positive difference in peoples' lives is one of your key success criteria, then you may want to focus your career goals on public library or nonprofit work, social entrepreneurship, or creating an independent path that supports this. And if your definition of career success includes the ability to continue working—and contributing—well into your senior years, then ongoing education is likely to figure *very large* in your career map.

The other reason to think through your personal definition of success is that if you use only the benchmarks of others, you may discount extraordinary successes you achieve along the journey. If, for example, one of your success components is to have made a positive contribution to the vitality of your local professional community, then the time you spend mentoring that younger colleague is, in fact, an expression of your ongoing success.

How to think about success criteria? One way to frame the question is to apply the same approach used by psychologist Abraham Maslow in his famous "hierarchy of needs" pyramid. His premise was that at the bottom of the pyramid were our most basic human needs, that is, physiological needs such as food and water—followed up the pyramid by safety needs, belonging and love needs, the need to know and understand, aesthetic needs, and self-actualization, which was defined as finding self-fulfillment and realizing one's potential. (At the very top of the pyramid was "transcendence," at which point, we can assume, career success is probably no longer an issue. . . .)

Applying this same approach to your career aspirations, what are your core expectations and needs? For most of us, the bottom rung is a job that pays a living wage, uses the skills we've trained for, and doesn't make us crazy. But what about the next tier? Is it that you have an opportunity to contribute to your organization at a strategic level? Or that your career now offers a broad range of learning opportunities? Or that the work you do allows you to increasingly invest time and energy in a second aspiration such as writing or participating in international bike races? At each new tier, the assumption is that you are meeting the previous goal and can now move onto the next level of self-defined success.

When going through this process, it's helpful to consider what would signify to you that you had reached "self-fulfillment and realizing one's potential" within the context of your career. For example, during one of my ongoing debates with myself about what I wanted my career to be about, I decided to see whether I could come up with a professional mission statement. This would be something that defined for me what my purpose would be and what contribution I could, I hoped, make.

The statement I finally settled on was "to turn information into a tool for individuals, communities, and organizations to grow, learn, and achieve their goals." Based on that commitment, self-actualization for me would be that because of my unique knowledge and skills, I was able to contribute ideas and resources and solutions where they might not have existed had I not tried. Based on this commitment, I created and teach a course in the University of Denver MLIS program in career alternatives, on which this book is based.

In fact, none of my success "tiers" have anything to do with titles or salary or job status; they have rather to do with impact. Have I been able to make a difference in peoples' lives? Have I been able to devise and execute innovative solutions? Have I been willing to learn the things that would enable new opportunities instead of falling back on familiar, but increasingly limited, competencies? These success criteria are meaningful to me, but may look like nothing so much as pretty minor goals for others whose values differ from mine.

That's why, when creating your own career map, it's important you understand that what's meaningful to you is unique to your values and aspirations—and deserves your full respect, engagement, and commitment. Your spouse, parents, coworkers, or neighbors may not share your view of success if it doesn't involve a six-figure salary or a corner office, but that's their issue, not yours. Your challenge is simply to honor and pursue your individual vision with all the passion and energy you can deliver.

# Resources

## Books

Arnold, Caroline L. *Small Move, Big Change: Using Microresolutions to Transform Your Life Permanently*. Penguin, 2014. 238p. ISBN 0143126164.
  Unlike most books on setting and achieving goals, *Small Move, Big Change* isn't written by a psychologist or productivity celebrity; instead, Arnold is a tech leader with a BA in English. That "real-life perspective" results in one of the most practical and effective books available for making sustainable changes in your life. Arnold is cognizant of the effort it takes to make those changes and wants to help you make the most of those efforts. (Key resource)

Duhigg, Charles. *The Power of Habit: Why We Do What We Do in Life and Business*. Random House, 2012. 371p. ISBN 1400069286.
  Why habits exist and how they can be changed. Using the concept of a "habit loop," Duhigg explains how habits form and how we can purposely form "keystone habits" that help us achieve our goals. A fascinating and very applicable exploration of how to change habits that keep you stuck where you are by replacing them with ones that get you moving toward your better future.

Halvorson, Heidi Grant. *Succeed: How We Can Reach Our Goals*. Plume, 304p. ISBN 0452297710.
  *Succeed* is organized into three sections: Get Ready (what are your goals and why?); Get Set (see especially "Goals for Optimists and Goals for Pessimists"); and Go (tactics for overcoming goal obstacles both external and internal). An extremely insightful book, especially helpful for those who've had difficulty following through on previous goals. (Key resource)

Heath, Dan and Chip Heath. *Decisive: How to Make Better Choices in Life and Work*. Crown Business, 2013. 336p. ISBN 0307956393.
  A big part of setting and achieving goals is making smart, thoughtful decisions based on the best information you have at the time. In *Decisive*, the Heath brothers walk you through a series of research-tested steps to help you develop your decision-making skills for both personal and professional benefits. Fun to read and reasonably easy to implement for those of us who may be "decision challenged."

Kahneman, Daniel. *Thinking, Fast and Slow*. Farrar, Straus and Giroux, 2013. 512p. ISBN 0374533555.
  Kahneman's work won the 2012 National Academy of Sciences Best Book Award, which gives an indication of how much of an impact his ideas had and continue to have in scientific circles. He explains that when we think, our brains use two cognitive systems, one that processes information and makes decisions quickly and almost automatically, and the other that operates methodically and with intense focus.

Understanding these differences can be especially useful in helping you improve your decision-making, goal-setting, and self-management efforts.

Klauser, Henriette Anne. *Write It Down, Make It Happen: Knowing What You Want—and Getting It*. Fireside Books, 2001. 250p. ISBN 0684850028.
A more right-brain approach to goal-setting and achieving than most books on this topic, *Write It Down* focuses more on the psychological, spiritual, and self-exploratory aspects of setting goals. Inspirational and motivational, while ultimately also being actionable.

McKeown, Greg. *Essentialism: The Disciplined Pursuit of Less*. Crown Business, 2014. 272p. ISBN 0804137382.
Refreshingly, McKeown's aim isn't to help you get more done in less time; instead, it's to help you focus on getting only the right—or essential—things done so that there's more time in your life for, well, life. First you must choose which items, which goals, are most important to you, then McKeown coaches you on how to whittle down the extraneous in your life to achieve that which is truly essential to you. Naturally, this is easier said than done, but McKeown does a great job of providing the guidance needed to succeed.

Murphy, Mark. *HARD Goals: The Science of Extraordinary Achievement*. McGraw-Hill, 2011. 181p. ISBN 007175346X.
HARD goals are Heartfelt, Animated, Required, and Difficult. Although I hate gimmicky acronyms as much as the next person, Murphy actually does a good job of tying these characteristics to overcoming inertia, fear, self-doubt, and other obstacles to achieving personal and professional goals. An interesting contrast with SMART goals (Specific, Measurable, Attainable, Realistic, Timely).

Oettingen, Gabriele. *Rethinking Positive Thinking: Inside the New Science of Motivation*. Current, 2014. 240p. ISBN 1591846870.
Oettingen's basic premise is that while fantasizing about accomplishing your goals will deplete you of the drive and edge necessary to complete them (your brain's already basking in the glow of accomplishment), dwelling on the obstacles between you and your goals will also deplete your confidence and commitment by depressing you. Her solution is "mental contrasting," which entails contrasting your fantasy of your bright future with the obstacles necessary to overcome to achieve that future. According to Oettingen's research, this will both energize you to act and provide an opportunity to strategize ways to overcome the obstacles. (For example, if *X* stands in my way, I'll do *Y* to overcome it.) Oettingen isn't the most engaging writer, but her reality-check message is spot-on.

## Online Resources

*A Librarian without a Library: Staying Professionally Active While Unemployed*
www.liscareer.com/shontz_activeunemployment.htm
An excellent example of how to put together a strategy to achieve a career goal, this article provides a practical hit list of action items for those who find themselves taking a temporary (from several months to several years) leave from their LIS careers. From the prolific Priscilla K. Shontz, and part of her LIS career website.

*Career Planning*
 www.liscareer.com/careerplanning.htm
 Part of the LIScareer.com Library & Information Science Professional's
 Career Development Center, this is a collection of articles by LIS professionals on career choices, alternative careers, setting career goals,
 and other useful topics. Although not updated since 2007, the existing
 articles still provide lots of good strategy ideas.

*Personal SWOT Analysis: Making the Most of Your Talents and Opportunities*
 www.mindtools.com/pages/article/newTMC_05.htm
 From the career site MindTools, this article and accompanying worksheet help you identify the key questions to ask yourself in order to
 unearth the information most useful for making career decisions.
 A great tool for making strategic decisions as you grow your LIS career.

# 10
# Improvising Your Resilient Career

*Life is a lot like jazz... it's best when you improvise.*
—George Gershwin

Years ago, Mary Catherine Bateson, daughter of anthropologists Margaret Mead and Gregory Bateson and a respected writer and cultural anthropologist in her own right, wrote a book called *Composing a Life* (Grove Press, 2001). The book seemed intriguing not just because of its excellent reviews, but also because the idea of a "composed" life seemed so amazing, with its connotations of order and purposefulness and control. It seemed almost *mythical*, given the realities all of us deal with on a daily basis.

The book was engaging, inspiring, and beautifully written, weaving the life stories of five notable women into a tapestry of survival and achievement. But it was evident that these women weren't so much composing their lives as *improvising* them, as is perhaps the case for most of us, men and women. We improvise—create solutions on the fly—because life so rarely slows down long enough for us to methodically compose our answers to its challenges.

Instead, the circumstances of our professional work frequently require us to deal with change or get run over by it. In the interests of not becoming roadkill and instead creating a resilient career, we work on our improvisational tap-dancing skills. And like most physical skills, how you think about your moves, how you visualize your actions, and how you perceive your environment determine how effectively you execute in real life.

# What Does a Resilient Career Look Like?

Given the disruption going on in the profession as well as the world around us, it's no surprise that the concept of resilience is garnering lots of attention these days. How are others defining resilience? Authors and PhDs Karen Reivich and Andrew Shatté define resilience as "the ability to persevere and adapt when things go awry" in their book *The Resilience Factor: 7 Keys to Finding Your Inner Strength and Overcoming Life's Hurdles* (Three Rivers Press, 2002). In his *Resilience: Discovering a New Strength at Times of Stress* (Hatherleigh Press, 2004), Dr. Frederic Flach defined it as "the psychological and biological strengths required to successfully master change."

Al Siebert, PhD, director of The Resiliency Center in Portland, Oregon, defined resilience as a collection of abilities such as coping well with high levels of ongoing disruptive change, overcoming adversities, bouncing back easily from setbacks, and changing to a new way of working and living when an old way is no longer possible, among others in his 2005 classic, *The Resiliency Advantage: Master Change, Thrive under Pressure, and Bounce Back from Setbacks* (Berrett-Koehler, 2005). More recently, and drawing on the emerging discipline of neuropsychology, marriage and family therapist Linda Graham's *Bouncing Back: Rewiring Your Brain for Maximum Resilience and Well-Being* (New World Library, 2013) describes resiliency as "the capacity to respond to pressures…quickly, adaptively, and effectively." (Graham also has the best quote, from her yoga teacher: "Blessed are they who are flexible, for they shall never be bent out of shape.")

And Dr. Martin E.P. Seligman, who launched the positive psychology discipline as then-president of the American Psychological Association in 1998, identified resiliency as one of the key factors that comprise (and enable) flourishing in his *Flourish, a Visionary New Understanding of Happiness and Well-Being* (Atria, 2011).

The ability to bounce back, to recover from setbacks, to ride waves of change without getting tumbled under, to shift and adapt and reinvent—these are some of the capabilities that define a resilient career. From my perspective, a resilient career is one that is:

- Agile—able to move quickly in many different directions and to quickly develop necessary skills or knowledge to do so.

- Opportunistic—committed to finding or creating new opportunities to contribute, add value, innovate, develop new solutions, or create new career paths as old ones fall away.

- Sustainable—able to engage you and reward you both financially and intellectually over however many years or decades you may want to work.

- Meaningful—enabling you to bring your core values and passions to a purpose bigger than your paycheck, whether right now or as a direction in which you're heading.

How do you create an agile, opportunistic (in a good way), sustainable, and meaningful career? By improvising it. Since none of us can know what's going to happen next week let alone next year, our best bet is to expect the best outcomes but plan for the worst. Focus on keeping your career in "permanent beta," as *The Start-up of You* recommends, and an eye out for changes possibly heading your way.

In addition, speaking as someone who's been laid off from three jobs but was then later hired by all three employers in consulting roles, focus on the actions and attitudes that will help you, as the Japanese proverb goes, fall down seven times but get up eight.

## Actions for a Resilient Career

Your day-to-day and long-term actions are what will enable you to create an agile, flexible, highly adaptable career. The following strategies, many drawn from detailed overviews in previous chapters, will help keep you positioned in the path of opportunity as you navigate the ups and downs of your career.

**Expect change, embrace it, and position for the opportunities it may provide.** Change is always disruptive, but as we've seen, it doesn't always need to be bad news—in fact, it can often be terrific news for those ready to ride the wave. Monitor you environment, pay attention, and see whether there aren't ways to use changes to move your career in a positive direction. Then be ready to act.

*Always* **have an up-to-date career agenda in place.** Yep, it's true— we *are* all self-employed. So it's imperative that you be ready to pivot into a new opportunity by exploring in advance what you need to have been doing to prepare for those possible new directions. The exercise we went through with sample career maps will help you think through this process, so that even if you don't have any specific moves you want to make in the foreseeable future, you can still be prepared for unanticipated employment changes.

**Always have an exit strategy in place.** As mentioned previously, a useful career strategy is to hope for the best, even expect the best, but plan for the worst. An exit strategy should be built around your "what next" questions: what kind of work would you like to be doing next? For whom and where? What actions do you need to take over the next several months or years in order to position yourself for those opportunities?

**Keep growing your knowledge base.** Charles Darwin famously pointed out that it was "not the strongest of the species that survive, nor the most intelligent, but the one most responsive to change." The ability to adapt is driven by the ability to learn, continuously and on demand. By constantly expanding your knowledge base (both LIS and non-LIS), you'll also be expanding your career options. Figure out what you need to learn to keep your skills competitive, then line out how, where, and when you'll do that.

**Keep growing your professional community.** Whether they're in person or online, the professional relationships you build and nurture will be critical to continually opening up new career opportunities. As you can, participate in your local or national professional associations, engage with online groups, and find ways to support others in your professional community. This last point will likely help you thrive in two ways: genuinely caring about the people in your professional universe will reward you emotionally and will also be likely to encourage them to help you should you become a job-seeker.

**Make sure your professional reputation is positive, visible, *and portable.*** As we've seen, today's online tools and social media platforms make it easy to showcase your professional strengths to the world. You'll want to establish your professional brand *outside of your employer* so that if you lose your job, you still have a professional presence. In addition, if you are positioning for a career change, make sure your branding reflects both your current competencies and your future interests.

*Never* **burn bridges.** The professional universe in which we deploy our skills may seem vast (and in reality it is), but when it comes to job hunting, that universe can become very small very quickly. Over the course of a career lifetime, you'll find that burned bridges are very likely to come back to burn *you* as you attempt to secure new job opportunities. Resist the temptation to unload your frustration, anger, or resentment on even the most deserving of targets—it just isn't worth the potential future damage to your career. When you move on from a job (even if it's a layoff), do so with grace and professionalism. It will keep unanticipated doors open for you in the future and become part of that terrific professional reputation you're building.

# Attitudes for a Resilient Career

While your actions will set the stage for a resilient career, your attitudes will be what create the agile, opportunistic mind-set, the "inner game," that enables you to adapt, improvise, and *respond* rather than react to change.

Your attitudes determine how you interpret the events and experiences of your life. Negative attitudes will keep you "stuck" in situations that drain you of energy and joy, whereas positive attitudes can help you move forward *out* of a bad situation and into the terrific career you envision. We're not talking about what the psychology experts call "delusional optimism" here, but rather the reality-based attitudes that let you control that which you *can* control and let go of that which you can't.

Some of the attitudes that will help you build your resilient career:

**Acceptance of change.** Accepting and expecting change as an ongoing part of your career (and life) lets you refuse to waste time, energy, or attention trying to resist it. Part of being able to move forward to meet opportunity is a willingness to bring positive energy to the game. We can be frustrated about changes to the LIS employment universe or we can, as philosopher Alan Watts suggested of change, "plunge into it, move with it, and join the dance."

**Acceptance of risk.** It's okay to be risk averse, to avoid taking unnecessary or uninformed risks. But avoiding *all* risk keeps you from growing and moving forward. By becoming more of a risk-taker, focusing on those risks that are smart in terms of your career and whose results you can manage if things don't turn out as hoped for, you'll be able to more easily adapt yourself to new circumstances.

**Acceptance of failure.** Richard Branson, entrepreneur and legendary risk-taker, advised others: "Do not be embarrassed by your failures, learn from them and try again." If you can understand failure as an indication of a positive, that is, your willingness and ability to stretch beyond your existing boundaries and try new things, then all you need to do is learn from your failures and keep moving forward. The reality is that someone who never fails is someone who never grows—and resiliency is based on growth. Recognize setbacks as temporary and a necessary part of your determination to get where you're going. And keep in mind that Richard Branson now owns more than 400 companies.

**Acceptance of reality.** It's just human nature to think about the way things should be, or how you wish they were. But only by letting go of those thoughts and instead focusing on the reality of your current circumstances will you be able to achieve your career (and life) goals. Seeing and accepting reality gives you the information you need to identify a challenge and decide how you will resolve it. It puts *you* in charge of making things better, instead of hoping and waiting for someone else to fix them.

**Acceptance of fear.** As many have pointed out, courage isn't the absence of fear, but rather the ability to move forward despite your fear. In order to create the career you'd like to have, you have to get comfortable with moving beyond your comfort zone. One way to do that is to start with "small wins," taking on small fears, then continue to take on larger challenges that push your confidence boundaries. Resiliency, and a resilient career, requires the courage to grow, to risk, to fail, and to rebound. Practice, practice, practice. . . .

**Commitment to self-motivation.** If you wait for others to motivate you to do the things that will bring you closer to your dreams—or even just create a better day for yourself—you're putting control of your happiness and outcomes in someone else's hands. Knowing what strategies or incentives (or disincentives) will motivate you to overcome obstacles or even just inertia will give you the life tools and confidence you need to move your career forward.

# Self-Leadership

These actions and attitudes will help you build resiliency into your career. However, there's also a critical personal competency necessary to thrive in the midst of ongoing disruption (e.g., the current state of LIS employment). This competency is self-leadership—how honestly you approach your career, how you react to circumstances around you, and what you expect of yourself.

The central element of self-leadership is the ability and willingness to make choices. For example, you can choose whether or not to explore who you are, to improve your ability to take risks, to respond to change, to position for opportunity. French writer Albert Camus stated that life is the sum of our choices; so, too, are our careers.

We can *choose* to become leaders, leaders in our own lives. Our ability to do so, however, is to a large extent determined by how we approach the idea of locus of control.

The essence of self-leadership, the concept of *locus of control*, is based on the work done by social learning theorist Julian Rotter during the 1960s. Essentially, someone with an external locus of control believes, and behaves as if, others control the outcomes of his or her life, whereas someone with an internal control locus believes that his or her own actions drive results and outcomes.

Generally, all of us frame our life events in ways that comfort us. It's how we explain to ourselves the stories of our lives. Someone with an external frame or locus of control attributes his or her circumstances to outside influences, for example, a parent, luck (good or bad), an unsupportive work environment. Life seems out of control because it is—we simply can't control all the external forces that drive our behaviors and outcomes. The result can be a sense of helplessness about your future and your opportunities, and an unwillingness—or inability—to commit to the work necessary for creating the career you want.

Having an internal locus of control, however, shifts responsibility for your circumstances to your own choices—basically, *your* decisions and actions and efforts drive the outcomes of your life. The bad news is that an internal locus of control makes it a lot harder to blame everything (or everybody) else for what's going wrong in our lives. But the really *good* news is that if you focus on your ability to drive your own outcomes, all of a sudden, life gets much more interesting. And so does your career.

What does an external *vs.* an internal locus look like in your career? Think about which of these responses best reflect your thinking:

I'm unhappy in my job because . . .

I work for an unfeeling idiot, *again*!

My workplace isn't supportive, and I need to figure out ways to meet my own professional needs.

Finding a better job is a matter of . . .

Really good luck.

Persistent effort, lots of research, and ongoing colleague connections.

My friends always seem to get better jobs than I do because . . .

Life is unfair.

I've been spending all my time hanging out in karaoke bars singing "I Love Rock and Roll," and they've been taking coding classes.

Getting more education and broadening my skill set will . . .

Only be worth it if there's a guaranteed job with a 50 percent salary increase as a result.

Continue to open up new career options for me.

Although psychologists point out that we all exhibit a range of behaviors between external and internal loci of control and that internal is not always a better option than external, when it comes to building the career you want, internal is definitely better. If you understand that your career is in fact based on choices that you control, then your possibilities are endless. It's the difference between inertia and action, between victim and victor, between stuck and successful. It's the difference between learning from your mistakes and denying them—and being doomed to repeat them over and over. It's the difference between the career that employers say you can have and the career you create for yourself through your own efforts.

A key indicator of external-locus-of control thinking is language, the words you use to describe the way things are going in your life. On our bad days, most of us have occasionally been heard to mutter these familiar, self-defeating phrases—

- I deserve to get paid more.
- I work so hard, I should be treated with more respect.
- It's unfair that I never get to work on the cool projects.
- I spent two long years in graduate school, I have a right to a good job.
- I deserve the best opportunities because of my job seniority.
- I assumed promotion would be based on superior skills (i.e., mine).

All of these phrases are based on a misperception, which is that the unspoken contract with the rest of the world we have in our heads has somehow been agreed to by the other party.

Librarians *do* deserve to get paid more. Drawing on advanced professional skills, they provide an invaluable service for the communities within which they work. However, the reality is that compensation and societal value are not always (or even often) linked, and salaries for librarians are unlikely to increase substantially unless we can figure out a way to turn librarianship into a national sport involving some sort of ball.

Hard work *should* be deserving of respect, but in real life, the two are only occasionally linked together. The general public bases respect on all sorts of criteria, but rarely on the values we think should be key. If you want someone to respect you based on hard work, you have to be doing the kind of hard work they think is valuable—and very few people have a sufficient understanding of what librarians do to be impressed by how hard we work.

Yep, after getting through those tough years in graduate school, it would be nice to land a good full-time job with opportunities commensurate with your skills. But feeling like you're entitled to one will only set you up for a terrible sense of frustration and betrayal, making it difficult to sustain the positive energy necessary to finally land a job.

The problem is that words like *deserve, should, unfair, right, expect, assumed* all set us up for self-defeating mind-sets that keep us stuck in place, wasting our energy on how things *should* be rather than how they *are*. It's human nature to vent, but when all your energy is being channeled in that direction on an ongoing basis, you've got none left over for more useful things—like tracking down a great new job. You're stalled in the ineffectiveness of external locus-of-control thinking.

Instead, consider these statements:

- I'm unhappy in my job; what am I going to do to change things?

- I'm not growing in my career; what steps can I take to move forward?

- I'd like to be making more money; what options can I identify for this, and which one(s) will I choose to pursue?

- I'm bored with my job; what things can I do to reengage and bring fresh energy to my responsibilities?

- My boss is extremely difficult to work for; what are my choices for responding to this short term and long term, and which ones will I choose?

- I need to determine what I want from my career, and then figure out ways to achieve it.

Each of these statements reflects an internal locus of control, a willingness to take responsibility for your own outcomes and a belief that you can successfully do so. An assumption that external forces control you keeps you stalled in miserable situations and makes you a victim. Becoming instead the leader in your own life lets you find—or create—what you need.

In terms of career planning, a self-leadership approach means you identify the problem, explore how you're contributing to it, accept reality (the only thing you can control is yourself, your actions, and reactions), and come up with your strategy for creating a different outcome. Or it means targeting an opportunity, creating a plan for achieving it, making a commitment to yourself to follow through on your plan, and then doing it.

# Getting Unstuck

How many times have you been party to one of those "all the reasons I can't move forward" conversations? You know, the one where everybody tries to come up with helpful suggestions for you or one of your companions, only to be continually rebuffed with reasons why any and all of them are impossible?

It's just human nature to focus on all the obstacles we're sure will keep us from doing anything about our deplorable circumstances. In fact, one of the exercises we do in my class is brainstorm all the different ways we can feel "stuck." Among the recurring issues are:

- I'm a new mom, and I'm going to be out of the workforce for a while—I know my career's just going to stagnate.
- I think I know what I might like to do, but I don't really know if I'd like the work.
- We just bought a new house, and I can't afford to leave my job for at least a year.
- I really want to go independent, but don't have the money to do it.
- I don't get any support from family or friends in terms of career growth so I can't move forward with my dreams.
- Making these kinds of changes or taking this kind of initiative is just too daunting, too overwhelming.
- I'm not good at brainstorming, so I can't come up with any good ideas.
- I feel guilty taking time to focus on my own needs.
- I'm not smart/creative/confident enough to push my career goals.
- It's too scary to make major changes.
- I'm too old to waste time pursuing a career I'd love.
- I don't know where to start.
- I don't know what I'd need to know to succeed.
- All my career "energy" is going into grad school.

Even though the basic circumstances of a situation may, in fact, be exactly as stated—for example, a new mom may be out of the workforce for a while—it doesn't necessarily follow that one's career is going to be damaged. Instead, you can practice shifting into a self-leadership stance and come up with take-charge solutions for each of the obstacles identified. Here are some examples:

Obstacle: *I'm a new mom and I'm going to be out of the workforce for a while— my career's just going to stagnate.*

Take-charge solution: *Figure out ways to stay visible, stay connected, and stay current.*

Possible action items:

- Stay active in local professional groups by volunteering—keeps you visible, networked, and on top of industry news.

- Read at least one professional publication monthly to stay current.

- Sign up for electronic discussion lists in your area of interest to stay current.

- Get online and regularly research trends in your area of expertise.

- See whether you can do freelance or project work for colleagues or local organizations—creates visibility, ongoing professional engagement, portfolio building.

- Monitor job listing sites so you can see where skill sets are heading and identify areas you may need to refresh when you're ready to return to the job market.

- Assess online learning opportunities that will allow you to continue to grow your skills without interfering with your parenting commitments.

- Target a couple of areas where you can differentiate your skills by developing areas of specialization (e.g., second language, trends in the biometrics industry, nonprofit website development).

- Work on your research skills by doing Internet or database (if free access is available through your local library) research on topics of professional interest to you.

- Work on your writing skills by turning that research into an article for a publication (print or online)—creates visibility, bulks up your portfolio.

Obstacle: *I think I know what I might want to do, but I don't know if I'd like the work.*

Take-charge solution: *Get the information you need to make that decision.*

Possible action items:

- Identify resources related to the career path, including books, electronic discussion lists, periodicals, blogs, and associations.

- Sign up for the key discussion lists and blogs, consider joining the appropriate associations, check out online articles from the periodicals, and read at least one of the books to get a sense of roles, responsibilities, issues, and so on.

- Do informational interviews with several people locally who are in a position similar to the ones you're interested in.

- Volunteer to work at a relevant local organization to get a sense of the environment this type of work involves.

- Shadow librarians in this type of job to understand what their work looks like.

- Research the position in another setting—say, academic, corporate, or nonprofit—to get a sense of how the environment affects the position and determine what aspects of the job most appeal to you.

- Research emerging issues in your potential practice area to identify how your job might change and determine whether or not that appeals to you.

- Check out LIS job postings to get a sense of the roles and responsibilities involved in the position, with an eye toward whether or not these align with your self-assessment findings.

- Consider what other professional options might also offer the type of work you enjoy doing; for example, someone who loves reference work might also enjoy running public outreach programs (public interaction) or being a CI specialist (research).

- Seek out a part-time (evenings or weekends) position that would allow you to try out the role without leaving your current job.

Obstacle: *I don't get any support from family or friends in terms of career growth, so I don't think I'll be able to find any time to pursue the career goals I've identified.*

Take-charge solution: *Let yourself assume a leadership role in your own life and believe in your right to do so.*

Possible action items:

- Understand that often those in your inner circle—friends and family—are dealing with their own fear issues and feeling threatened by your changes, so they have a tough time being supportive.

- Understand that *knowing* this shouldn't mean *accepting* it; if you lack support, become your own best cheerleader.

- Find colleagues and friends who understand how important professional growth is to you and ask them to become your brain trust (and cheerleaders).

- Stay focused on forward progress (not perfection); if you have to fight for time to invest in your career goals, then celebrate every successful effort, even if it's only an hour a week.

- Start building a community of colleagues that reinforce your passion for your career and your enthusiasm for new challenges.

- Explore your own fears about succeeding as a professional and become familiar with the "impostor syndrome" that so many high-achieving people (most often women) wrestle with.

- Start journaling; create a private space for you to write down your dreams, ideas, goals, fears, favorite quotes, and anything else that lets you stay centered, supported, and motivated on your career path.

- Put together a personal portfolio—document the things you've learned over the past 2 or 10 or 20 years, the successful projects you've worked on, the ways you've contributed to others' lives, with a focus on proving your value and ability to yourself and building your self-confidence.

- Create success opportunities for yourself, no matter how small—for example, think of a useful or interesting information project, create an execution plan, and complete it; this will help you prove to yourself your competence and ability, and start documenting a track record of initiative and success for you to rely on.

- On a day when you're feeling frightened or frustrated or unsupported, remember that your happiness is worth the effort and that you are capable of creating that happiness.

Every one of the obstacles students raised can be addressed with this type of solutions thinking. Taking a leadership role in your life doesn't mean that obstacles go away, but it *does* mean that you won't let them derail you. Instead, you'll be able to identify the circumstances holding you back and then come up with a collection of solutions to try. Some may work, some may not, but the bottom line is: you'll be the one in charge, and you'll be learning from every step you take.

To a great extent, this commitment to taking control of your career trajectory is the end goal of all the effort you've been putting into you career journal. What we've been trying to unearth is what you want in a career, so that you can then plot a strategy for achieving that end. But the "achieving that end" part is completely up to you.

Now you try it.

What are some obstacles that you feel are keeping you from moving forward with your agenda? Is it people, money, emotional issues, or time constraints? Whatever they are, write them down in your career journal and then shift your approach from one of defeat to one of solutions.

Reframe your response as an affirmative, take-charge one, then identify and write down possible action items to resolve the issue. As you do so, make sure your locus of control is internal, rather than external. One of the most important characteristics of self-leadership is to realistically recognize what you can't control, what you can, and then to focus your energies on the latter.

Why is this so critical? Because throughout your career, whether or not you move forward is based not on your ability to change others' responses, but on your ability to change your own.

### Taking Charge When You're a Student

Sometimes, being a grad student feels like your choices are completely driven by other people's agendas. But with a bit of thought and planning, you'll be able to use your time in your MLIS program to build the foundation for the brilliant career to follow. Consider these tactics:

- Use your practicum and/or internships to try out work environments and types of work, while also building new skills that add to your portfolio.

- Take classes outside the LIS program not only to gain broader knowledge but also to build a network of contacts beyond your immediate LIS professional community.

- Whenever possible, "multipurpose" your assignments to enable you to learn more about potential employers, industries, or career paths via research and/or interviews.

- Use your student status to learn from professionals—the world is generally amazingly responsive to student questions.

- Start building faculty and student colleague relationships as the beginning of your professional community.

- Stop saying (and thinking) "I can't do that" and trust yourself enough to instead go with "I'm not good at that—yet."

- Become an advocate for your own learning—as you engage with each new course, begin by determining what things *you* want to learn in addition to what the course offers.

- Invest your time and efforts in learning that is valuable to your career goals rather than in getting straight A's.

- Understand that graduate school is not an end in itself, but simply an important building block in a decades-long career.

## The Fine Art of Career Improv

In order to create a resilient career, you'll need to get comfortable with the fine art of improvisation, otherwise known as tap dancing on shifting sand, crossing your fingers and taking a leap, or my favorite, making it up as you go along. Because so much is changing so continuously, there's no permanent "right answer" for your career, one you can count on and relax into for the rest of your working life.

Instead, there will most likely be a series of opportunities, either unanticipated or ones you've created, that you can choose to grow into or walk away from. That's one of the great things about self-leadership: you get to decide. Sometimes the time's just not right to make that leap.

But consider that a resilient career is built on saying yes more often than no. Examples are:

- Stepping into an opportunity, you may not feel 100 percent prepared for, because the reality is you're probably as prepared as anyone else is going to be.

- Giving yourself the benefit of the doubt because other people who know your work believe in your ability to handle a new situation.

- Knowing that even if things don't work out, you made the best decision with the information you had at the time, and you will have learned valuable lessons as part of the process (because you've committed to do so).

These are some of the hallmarks of a resilient individual and an adaptable professional, one able to embrace change and its frequent opportunities with positive energy.

## Freedom to Choose

We alone choose how we frame reality. As Martin Seligman pointed out in *Learned Optimism* (Knopf, 1991), how you explain to yourself why the events of your life have happened—your explanatory style—to a great degree determines whether or not you feel able to shape your outcomes.

In the LIS profession, we have the option to decide which stories to embrace: the ones where your opportunities are already defined and determined for you within a set range of expectations, or the ones where you're tap dancing as fast as you can to bring your incredible skills into an increasing range of information spaces. Your stories can be about what the world did or didn't do for you, or about what you did for yourself and for others.

If we rethink information work, we can blow away boundaries that say "that's not what we do" and instead with confidence say "I think I'd like to explore that." Rethinking information work frees you to improvise your responses, to create careers based on saying yes to opportunity and seeing where it leads. It's what allows you to have a career of no limits, one where you alone define the universe of opportunities. It's what leads to a resilient career, a lifetime of professional independence.

You now possess strategies, tactics, and tools, as well as a career journal rich in ideas and potential pathways. You've mapped an action plan to move you from today's circumstances to tomorrow's opportunities.

You're part of one of the smartest, most passionate, most supportive professional communities in existence. You work with the two most important resources of the twenty-first century—information and knowledge. You have a skill set whose applicability across all types of organizations, industries, and communities is limited only by your imagination.

You are poised for a terrific career as an LIS professional. What choices will you make?

# Resources

## Books

Bateson, Mary Catherine. *Composing a Life.* Grove Press, 2001. 256p. ISBN 0802138047.
  An exploration of the lifetime experiences of five women who managed to overcome a diverse range of challenges to "compose" highly meaningful and personally successful lives.

Flach, Frederic. *Resilience: Discovering a New Strength at Times of Stress.* Hatherleigh Press, 2004. 240p. ISBN 1578261481.

Graham, Linda. *Bouncing Back: Rewiring Your Brain for Maximum Resilience and Well-Being.* New World Library, 2013. 464p. ISBN 1608681297.
  A fascinating exploration of the neurobiology of resilience—that is, how the brain does or doesn't develop resilience. Fortunately, our emerging understanding of the brain's neuroplasticity or ability to learn new behaviors is providing tools and techniques for growing or strengthening our resilience neural pathways.

Huffington, Arianna. *Thrive: The Third Metric to Redefining Success and Creating a Life of Well-Being, Wisdom, and Wonder.* Harmony, 2014. 352p. ISBN 0804140847.
  I expected to hate this book (what can most of us learn from a multimillionaire media queen?), but found Huffington's message to be surprisingly down to earth and resonant. Her third metric is based on

well-being, wisdom, wonder, and giving of yourself and your talents in ways that provide meaning to your life while nourishing those around you. She is clear that this is a luxury for those pressed daily with the logistics of sheer survival and encourages the rest of us to (1) appreciate the goodness in our lives and (2) help create a path for a less soul-grinding definition of success.

Maddi, Salvatore R. and Deborah M. Khoshaba. *Resilience at Work: How to Succeed No Matter What Life Throws at You*. American Management Association, 2005. 213p. ISBN 0811472605.
Maddi and Khoshaba equate resilience with "hardiness," or the ability to survive if not thrive despite stressful circumstances. Emphasizing that resilience is a skill that can be learned, the authors focus on information, motivational insights, processes, and tools to help readers master this important capability.

McKnight, Michelynn. *The Agile Librarian's Guide to Thriving in Any Institution*. Libraries Unlimited, 2009. 201p. ISBN 1591586685.
Agility is a defining skill of career resiliency, and McKnight's practical guide will help you develop both an agility mind-set and the professional tools to keep you on top of your game. The author's breadth of experience (school, public, academic, hospital librarianship, and now MLIS faculty) brings first-hand experience to her coverage of such topics as understanding and "positioning" your value to the organization, expanding political influence, and working effectively (and strategically) with key decision makers. Useful information for those new to the profession as well as for LIS professionals wanting to have greater impact (and agility) within their organizations.

Pink, Daniel. *Drive: The Surprising Truth about What Motivates Us*. Riverhead Books, 2011. 272p. ISBN 1594484805.
A landmark book in the field of individual motivation, *Drive* asserts that what motivates us (especially in a work setting) is the triad of autonomy, mastery, and purpose. His research-based findings are as important to individuals as to employers because individuals will probably need to take the lead on starting to restructure their jobs to reflect these three elements. (Key resource)

Reivich, Karen and Andrew Shatté. *The Resilience Factor: 7 Keys to Finding Your Inner Strength and Overcoming Life's Hurdles*. Three Rivers Press, 2002. 352p. ISBN 0767911911.

Salmansohn, Karen. *The Bounce Back Book: How to Thrive in the Face of Adversity, Setbacks, and Losses*. Workman Publishing, 2008. 192p. ISBN 076114627X.
Salmansohn is known for upbeat, if quirky, self-help books, and *The Bounce Back Book* reflects her usual brand of serious intent but humorous, graphically beautiful delivery. An easy book to pick up, read for a bit, and then return to on a regular basis.

Seligman, Martin E.P. *Flourish: A Visionary New Understanding of Happiness and Well-being*. Atria Books, 2011. 368p. ISBN 1439190763.
Seligman, former president of the American Psychological Association and founder of the Positive Psychology movement within psychology studies, has written several highly regarded works on the pursuit, meaning, and characteristics of happiness and well-being, most notably *Learned Optimism: How to Change Your Mind and Your Life* (Knopf,

1991). *Flourish* represents his most recent thinking, which is a more nuanced and balanced treatment of what constitutes a good life. (Key resource)

Shell, Richard G. *Springboard: Launching Your Personal Search for Success.* Portfolio, 2014. 320p. ISBN 1591847007.
*Springboard* stands out for not only strategies and tactics, but also the importance of first identifying, understanding, and/or creating a definition of success that truly resonates with your personal passions and values. A thoughtful and useful work for those seeking a better understanding of what choices—in career and life—will bring them the most personal fulfillment.

Siebert, Al. *The Resiliency Advantage: Master Change, Thrive under Pressure, and Bounce Back from Setbacks.* Berrett-Koehler, 2005. 225p. ISBN 1576753298.
Although now more and more individuals, researchers, organizations, and education and health professionals are realizing the incredible value of personal resiliency, Siebert's was one of the first consumer-focused books to identify its core elements and how they could be integrated into your daily life. A classic work and a great starting point for understanding resiliency, while also an important complement to self-leadership. (Key resource)

## Articles

Coutu, Diane L. "How Resilience Works." *Harvard Business Review* 80, no. 5 (May 2002): 46–52. Accessed at https://hbr.org/2002/05/how-resilience-works.
Coutu's research-based article was one of the first to identify the importance and elements of personal resiliency. Based on organization behavior research and numerous interviews with human resource professionals, she identified three characteristics found in resilient individuals: (1) an ability to understand and accept reality, (2) an ability to find meaning in the aspects of one's personal and professional life, and (3) an ability to improvise as circumstances change.

Drucker, Peter. "Managing Oneself." *Harvard Business Review* 83, no. 1 (January 2005): 100–109. Accessed at https://hbr.org/2005/01/managing-oneself.
Intended for all knowledge workers, this classic article expands on Drucker's assertion that "success in the knowledge economy comes to those who know themselves—their strengths, their values, and how they best perform." Although not specifically focused on information professionals, Drucker's take on the information economy and those who will work in it has relevance to all in our profession. Available for purchase at the website, or free to HBR subscribers.

## Periodicals

*Note: A large part of developing your personal career resiliency is made up of looking outside the profession to monitor emerging trends, potential developments, societal dynamics, science and technology advances, and similar types of change indicators. The periodicals that follow are representative of the types of publications likely to surface this type of information.*

*Fast Company.* Fast Co., Inc., 1995–. Monthly. ISSN 1085–9241.
www.fastcompany.com
One of the best resources for identifying what's new, what's excellent, and a bit of what's just plain weird. The writing is generally quite good, and the website is a content-rich source of articles, blogs, and insights.

*The Futurist.* World Future Society, 1967–. Bimonthly. ISSN 0016–3317.
www.wfs.org/node/765
A fascinating collection of research results, prognostications, scientific musings, and social predictions. The January 2015 issue included articles on "Trends at Work: An Overview of Tomorrow's Employment Ecosystem" and "Library Futures: From Knowledge Keepers to Creators," both of potential interest from a resilient career perspective.

*Harvard Business Review.* Graduate School of Business Administration, Harvard University, 1922–. Monthly. ISSN 0017–8012.
https://hbr.org
One of the most respected business publications, *HBR* publishes cutting-edge, long-form articles by thought leaders, scholars, and researchers from all areas of business and related topics (such as resiliency, career development, leadership, emerging technologies, and other areas of interest to LIS professionals considering career options). The website provides some free content, mostly derived from the print publication.

*Inc.* Inc. Publishing Co., 1979–. Monthly. ISSN 0162–8968.
www.inc.com
Focusing on an audience of small- to mid-sized businesses, *Inc.* covers a fascinating mix of entrepreneurial initiative and success stories, while also charting trends such as developments in materials science, social-good players, microfinancing, and similar types of innovative ways in which business is creating change around us. A great way to practice your "identifying opportunities" skills is to cruise issues of *Inc.* and strategize ways you could be contributing your information skills to the various initiatives described.

*The Intelligent Optimist.* Global Light Media, 1995–. Bimonthly. ISSN 2168–8001.
http://theoptimist.com/
Formerly named *Ode, The Intelligent Optimist* describes itself as "an independent international media platform focused on solutions, possibility and inspiration." Besides just being fascinating to read, the issues often describe unusual ways to contribute to the social good. A great resource for thinking about new ways that information professionals could contribute skills or create new social-impact career paths.

*Psychology Today.* Sussex Publishers, 1967–. Monthly. ISSN 0033–3107.
www.psychologytoday.com
Broad coverage of psychological topics and issues, including such career-relevant ones as personal motivation, change management, risk assessment, dealing with difficult personalities, understanding personality types, bridging different communication styles, and more. Check the website for hundreds of contributed blogs.

*Scientific American.* Scientific American, Inc., 1921–. Monthly. ISSN 0036–8733.
www.scientificamerican.com
Accessible writing and reputable science make *Scientific American* a great read even for those of us who were humanities majors. See especially the Mind special issues, which you can subscribe to separately from the main Scientific American publication.


## Online Resources

*How to Be a Leader in Your Field: A Guide for Students in Professional Schools*
http://polaris.gseis.ucla.edu/pagre/leader.html
Philip E. Agre, an associate professor of information studies at UCLA, has written what he describes as "detailed instructions for students on the process of becoming an intellectual leader in your profession." Excellent, thoughtful, and practical advice that will serve you well during both your graduate school tenure and subsequent career.

*How to Build a Meaningful Career*
https://hbr.org/2015/02/how-to-build-a-meaningful-career
From *Harvard Business Review* blogger and contributing editor Amy Gallo, this February 2015 *HBR* post is a practical exploration of an increasingly important career concept, that is, meaning and purpose as it relates to the work we choose to do, how we do it, and how it does (or doesn't) support our human need for meaning and purpose in our lives.

*The Impostor Syndrome: Or How I Learned to Get Over My Panic Attack, Love My Promotion, and Make My To-Do List*
http://bit.ly/1CtadeA
This post addresses a phenomenon often experienced by individuals (predominantly women) who are promoted to positions of leadership or authority. "The impostor syndrome" is a feeling that despite your promotions and increasing levels of responsibility, you're actually faking it and/or incapable of doing high-level work, and people will discover at any moment that in truth you've no idea what you're doing. This is an especially important concern if you're trying to build confidence and courage, so worth investing the time to address.

*Personal SWOT Analysis: Making the Most of Your Talents and Opportunities*
www.mindtools.com/pages/article/newTMC_05.htm
From the career site MindTools, this article and accompanying worksheet help you identify the key questions to ask yourself in order to unearth the information most useful for making career decisions. A great tool for making strategic decisions as you grow your career.

*SmartBrief on Your Career*
*www.smartbrief.com/yourcareer/*
Daily newsletter that aggregates career articles, columns, and blog posts from multiple online sources such as the *Wall Street Journal, Harvard Business Review,* Forbes.com, and CareerRocketeer. Useful resource for monitoring emerging career trends and broadening your thinking about career possibilities.

*What Is This Thing Called Resilience?*
http://bit.ly/1BEjooj

A *Strategy+Business* post from Eric J. McNulty, this assessment of resilience is focused on organizations but has relevance to LIS professionals and their careers as well. Drawing a distinction between robustness ("the ability to withstand disruption") and resilience, McNulty argues convincingly that in many cases being resilient isn't the ability to bounce back (since there is no longer a "back" to move toward) but rather to bounce *forward*. His assertion is that "resilient individuals, organizations, cities, nations, and species survive, learn, adapt, and grow stronger as a result." An apt prescription for the LIS profession as well.

# Appendix A
## Special Interest Groups

Membership in professional organizations can be an effective way to extend the breadth and depth of your professional community, especially if you join one of the many special interest groups (SIGs) hosted by the major associations. Looked at this way, ALA, SLA, and other LIS organizations offer a rich and varied community of communities, at least one of which may align with your interests.

SIGs are an excellent way to connect with others who share your professional interests, to learn more about a specific practice area, and to create a personal connection within what can often feel like an overwhelmingly large and somewhat distant organization. SIGs are also a great place to start volunteering and begin building a national community of colleagues.

Depending on the structure and activities of SIGs, they may be called sections, roundtables, discussion groups, caucuses, forums, or simply special interest groups. Almost all of the SIGS also have electronic discussion groups that address their topic area or several of its subtopics. Also, new SIGs are formed on a regular basis, so be sure to check with the association to see whether new ones have been added since this list was compiled.

## American Library Association

www.ala.org

### Divisions

*American Association of School Libraries (AASL)*
www.ala.org/aasl/sections; www.ala.org/aasl/sigs

*Sections*

Educators of School Librarians

Independent Schools

Supervisors. Special Interest Groups include Retirees and Students.

*Association for Library Collections & Technical Services (ALCTS)*
www.ala.org/alcts/mgrps/ig
Check site for nearly four dozen special interest groups.

*Association for Library Service to Children (ALSC)*
www.ala.org/alsc/
Check site for special initiatives.

*Association of College & Research Libraries (ACRL)*
www.ala.org/acrl/aboutacrl/directoryofleadership/sections

*Sections*

African American Studies Librarians (AFAS)

Anthropology and Sociology (ANSS)

Arts

Asian, African, and Middle Eastern (AAMES)

College Libraries (CLS)

Community and Junior College Libraries (CJCLS)

Distance Learning (DLS)

Education and Behavioral Sciences (EBSS)

Instruction (IS)

Law and Political Science (LPSS)

Literatures in English (LES)

Rare Books and Manuscripts (RBMS)

Science and Technology (STS)

Slavic and East European (SEES)

University Libraries (ULS)

Western European Studies (WESS)

Women and Gender Studies (WSS)

*Association of Specialized and Cooperative Library Agencies (ASCLA)*
www.ala.org/ascla/asclaourassoc/asclainterest/list

*Interest Groups*

Alzheimer's & Related Dementias

Bridging Deaf Cultures @ Your Library

Collaborative Digitization

Consortial eBooks

Consortium Management Discussion

Future of Libraries

Interlibrary Cooperation

Library Consultants

Library Services to the Incarcerated and Detained

Library Services to People with Visual or Physical Disabilities That Prevent Them from Reading Standard Print

Library Services for Youth in Custody

LSTA Coordinators Interest Group

Physical Delivery Interest Group

State Library Agencies—Library Development

Tribal Librarians

Universal Access

Youth Services Consultants

*Library & Information Technology Association (LITA)*
www.ala.org/lita/igs

*Interest Groups*

Accessibility

Altmetrics and Digital Analytics

Authority Control (LITA/ALCTS)

Distance Learning

Drupal4Lib

Electronic Resources Management (LITA/ALCTS)

Game Making

Heads of Library Technology

Imagineering

Library Code Year (LITA/ALCTS)

Library Consortia Automated Systems

Linked Library Data

LITA Instruction Technologies

MARC Formats Transition (LITA/ALCTS)

Mobile Computing

Next Generation Catalog

Open Source Systems

Patron and Privacy Technologies

Public Library Technology

Search Engine Optimization

User Experience

*Library Leadership Administration and Management Association (LLAMA)*
www.ala.org/llama/committees/sections

*Sections*

Buildings and Equipment (BES)

Fundraising and Financial Development (FRFDS)

Human Resources (HRS)

Library Organization and Management (LOMS)

Measurement, Assessment, and Evaluation (MAES)

New Professionals (NPS)

Public Relations and Marketing (PRMS)

Systems and Services (SASS)

*Public Library Association (PLA)*
www.ala.org/PLA/about/committees

Check the site for committees, task forces, advisory groups, and awards juries.

*Reference and User Services Association (RUSA)*
www.ala.org/rusa/sections

*Sections*

Business Reference and Services (BRASS)

Collection Development and Evaluation (CODES)

History

MARS: Emerging Technologies in Reference

Reference Services (RSS)

Sharing and Transforming Access to Resources (STARS)

*Young Adult Library Services Association (YALSA)*
www.ala.org/yalsa/workingwithyalsa/discussion

Interest Group: Intellectual Freedom

## Roundtables

Ethnic and Multicultural Information Exchange (EMIERT)

Exhibits (ERT)

Federal and Armed Forces Libraries (FAFLRT)

Games & Gaming (GAMERT)

Gay, Lesbian, Bisexual, and Transgender (GLBTRT)

Government Documents (GODORT)

Intellectual Freedom (IFRT)

International Relations (IRRT)

Learning (LearnRT, formerly CLENERT)

Library History (LHRT)

Library Instruction (LIRT)

Library Research (LRRT)

Library Support Staff Interests (LSSIRT)

Map and Geospatial Information (MAGERT)

New Members (NMRT)

Retired Members (RMRT)

Round Table Coordinating Assembly

Social Responsibilities (SRRT)

Staff Organizations (SORT)

Sustainability (SustainRT)

Video (VRT)

# Association for Information Science and Technology (ASIS&T)

www.asis.org/sigschapters.html

## Special Interest Groups

Arts & Humanities (AH)

Classification Research (CR)

Digital Libraries (DL)

Education for Information Science (ED)

Health Informatics (HLTH)

History & Foundations of Information Science (HFIS)

Information Needs, Seeking and Use (USE)

Information Policy (IFP)

International Information Issues (III)

Knowledge Management (KM)

Management (MGT)

Metrics (MET)

Scientific & Technical Information Systems (STI)

Social Informatics (SI)

Visualization, Images & Sound (VIS)

## Virtual SIGS

Bioinformatics (BIO)

Blogs, Wikis, Podcasts (BWP)

Critical Issues (CRIT)

Human Computer Interaction (HCI)

Information Architecture (IA)

Library Technologies (LT)

# Special Library Association (SLA)

www.sla.org

## Caucuses

Archival & Preservation

Association Information Services

Baseball

Gay & Lesbian Issues

Information Futurists

International Information Exchange

Labor Issues

Natural History

Nontraditional Careers

Retired Members

Women's Issues

## Communities of Practice

Biomedical & Life Sciences

Cataloging

Chemistry

Competencies

Competitive Intelligence

Emerging Leaders Network

Government Information Section

Government Libraries

Information Literacy Committee

Information Systems Section

Information Technology

Insurance, Risk Management & Employee Benefits

Medical Section/Biomedical & Life Sciences

Military Librarians

Risk Management Network

Solo Librarians

Technical Services Section

Terrorism/Homeland Security

Webmaster Section

## Divisions

Academic

Biomedical & Life Sciences (DBIO) (Medical Section)

Business & Finance (Advertising and Marketing, Corporate Information Centers, College and University Business Libraries, Financial Services)

Chemistry

Competitive Intelligence

Education

Engineering (Aerospace, Architecture, Building Engineering, Construction & Design)

Environment & Resource Management (Forestry & Forest Products)

Food, Agriculture, & Nutrition

Government Information

Information Technology (Communications and Social Media, Information Systems, Technical Services, Web Management)

Insurance & Employee Benefits

Knowledge Management (Records Management)

Leadership & Management (Consulting, Content Buying, Marketing)

Legal

Military Librarians

Museums, Arts, & Humanities

News

Petroleum & Energy Resources

Pharmaceutical & Health Technology (Medical Devices & Diagnostics)

Physics-Astronomy-Mathematics

Sciences-Technology

Social Science (Geography & Map, International Relations, Nonprofit Sector, Public Policy, Labor Issues)

Solo Librarians

Taxonomy

Transportation

# Ethnic Group Organizations

*American Indian Library Association*
http://ailanet.org/

*Asian / Pacific American Librarians Association*
www.apalaweb.org/

*Black Caucus*
www.bcala.org/

*Chinese American Librarians Association*
www.cala-web.org

*REFORMA: The National Association to Promote Library & Information Services to Latinos and the Spanish Speaking*
www.reforma.org

# Appendix B
## Career and Employment Resources

### LIS Job Listing Sites

*Note: Many associations—and divisions and other special interest groups—have their own job boards; sometimes these are available to members only, other times to the public. A wise strategy would be to check out any and all associations that correspond to your career interest (start with the lists in Chapter 4 and Appendix A), and then check to see (1) if they post job openings, (2) if you have to be a member to access them, and (3) roughly how many new job openings they post per month (to see whether this is a resource worth monitoring). In addition to the resources listed in the following, several of the MLIS programs and nearly all of the state libraries post job listings.*

#### Academic Employment Network (AEN)
www.academploy.com/
Lists higher education positions for faculty, staff, and administrative professionals.

#### ALISE Job Postings
www.alise.org/job-placement-2
Listing of faculty openings in LIS graduate programs. ALISE also does placement outreach at its annual conference.

## The Chronicle of Higher Education
https://chroniclevitae.com/job_search/new
Leading publication of the higher education community, lists thousands of faculty and other job postings, including library positions.

## Higher Ed Jobs
www.HigherEdJobs.com
Faculty and staff positions listed for hundreds of higher education institutions.

## I Need a Library Job (INALJ)
http://inalj.com
Librarian Naomi House, working with a dedicated team of volunteers, had as her goal to aggregate every single LIS job posting not only in North America but globally as well. House has since moved on to a new opportunity, but the site remains a terrific resource for LIS job hunters. Updated daily; sign up for the e-mail alerts to be apprised of an ongoing flow of new job opportunities.

## Job Zone/Library Journal
http://jobs.libraryjournal.com/?ref=menu
Search jobs by category (academic libraries, children's/young adult, management, public libraries, school libraries, technical). Postings include title, company/organization, location, and job description, often including salary.

## Joblist/ALA
http://joblist.ala.org/
Approximately 340 job listings primarily in traditional libraries. Check out the FAQs for using the search function most effectively, and the Career Resources section for helpful job-hunting and landing tips. Unfortunately, there's no way to save a search or set up an alerting service.

## LibGig
www.libgig.com
Sponsored by LAC, the staffing, consulting, and placement firm specializing in information curation and knowledge management, LibGig is a content-rich source of information about the profession, include a career Q&A section, several excellent blogs, news, career profiles, events, newsletters, and links to LIS schools. Of special interest for job-seekers, however, are its job board and job alerts.

## Libjobs.com
www.libjobs.com/
Post your resume (or resumes—up to five), and/or search job postings by keyword, category (e.g., administration, information services, reference, sales, training), employer, location, and date. A commercial site maintained by WebClarity Software, Inc., the job listings here are for public, academic, and school library positions. This site is clearly in "build-up" mode, but can be worth checking into.

# General Job Listing Sites

*Note: An important part of exploring how many different ways your LIS skills might be applied is to understand how they match up with non-LIS jobs. The following sites provide plenty of jobs to explore; try running some of the job titles listed in Chapter 4 in their search engines to see what you find.*

## Careerbuilder
www.careerbuilder.com
Find jobs, set up job alerts, post a resume, explore by location of job type within category (e.g., college, human resources, information technology, non-profit). Other search options include searching by company, by industry, in Spanish, and by international jobs. Register to receive e-mailed job opening alerts.

## Idealist
www.idealist.org
Central clearinghouse for social-good organizations and the jobs and internships they have available. Searchable by type (all types, jobs, internships, volunteer opportunities, action opportunities, people, organizations, events, blogs); keyword, skill, or interest; and location.

## Indeed
www.indeed.com
Post resumes, search jobs by job title, keywords, or company location filtered by city, state, or zip code. Indeed scrapes job sites, newspapers, associations, and company career pages to compile its listings.

## Jobshark
www.jobshark.ca
Job aggregator for open positions in Canada, supplemented by additional services like a salary calculator, connections with volunteer opportunities, and resume writing services.

## LinkedIn > Jobs
www.linkedin.com/jobs?displayHome=&trk=hb_tab_findjobs
Job listings posted by the hundreds of companies with a LinkedIn presence. Search by company name, keywords, or industry, and/or sign up to start following specific companies to receive alerts about recent developments, employees who have recently joined, left, or been promoted, and receive information about job openings. (Requires you to have a LinkedIn profile, which is free.)

## LinkedIn > Companies
www.linkedin.com/companies?trk=hb_tab_compy
An alternative route for signing up to follow companies that have a Linked In presence. Monitor information updates, press releases, new job postings, etc. (Requires that you have a LinkedIn account as well.)

## Monster.com

www.monster.com

Similar in scope to Careerbuilder, Monster's primary focus is job listings and resume posting, but it has also branched out with education partners, career networking, and career advice message boards. If you're interested in the broader aspects of career exploration, consider signing up for Monster Career News, their online e-newsletter.

## The Riley Guide

www.rileyguide.com

The Riley Guide doesn't post jobs itself but links to hundreds of sites that do (unannotated, listed alphabetically). In addition, it lists all sorts of career how-to resources on topics like business etiquette, changing careers, and internships, fellowships, and work exchange programs. An extensive, content-rich, very useful career resource.

## Simply Hired

www.simplyhired.com/

Search by job title, skills, or company; city, state, or zip code; category; and advanced search. Simply Hired "scrapes" job listings from company sites, job boards, and the web. See also the site's Job Salaries, Job Trends, and Job Search/Career Tips.

## USAJobs

www.usajobs.gov

The starting point for exploring federal jobs. See the Resource Center for pretty much everything you ever needed to know about applying for a federal government job. A search on the keyword "libraries" brought up 52 open positions at the end of 2015, but it would be useful to search by several terms to see what other opportunities might be available though not listed under the libraries search term. Bonuses: you can save your search, set up an RSS feed, and see in the job posting what the pay is.

## Workopolis

www.workopolis.ca

Search job by keyword/title and city or province, plus browse jobs by broad category (administrative, finance, healthcare, retail, technology, etc.). In addition, post resumes and check out multiple additional career resources such as articles, salary calculators, resume advice, and further education resources. A key resource for Canadian jobs.

# LIS Employment/Placement/Contract Firms

*Note: The firms listed below have a national presence; for recruiting, placement, and temporary-job firms that focus on a specific geographic area (e.g., a state or city), try searching online using variations of terms such as "recruiter,"* "placement," "project work," "contract work," and "temporary job," your target location, and the type of LIS work you're interested in, for example, cataloging or records management.

## AIM Library & Information Staffing
www.aimusa.com/
A library and information staffing firm, AIM states that it "specializes in placing librarians and support staff to work in a wide variety of library jobs in special, public, academic, school, government libraries and information centers" throughout the United States. You can subscribe to e-mail updates based on the geographic area you're interested in and your career level (professional MLIS, information professional/MLIS equivalent, library technician/support staff).

## Bradbury Associates/Gossage Sager Associates
www.gossagesager.com
Formerly known as Gossage Regan Associates, this company specializes in executive searches for all types and locations of libraries.

## Cadence Group
www.cadence-group.com/
The Cadence Group specializes in searches for "C-Suite officers with compliance, collaboration or communication responsibilities, as well as the records, library and creative managers who report to them." The company's primary focus is all aspects of information management, including contract staffing.

## Corbus Library Consultants
www.libraryjobs.com
Works with client libraries and library boards to recruit library directors as well as providing additional library management consulting services.

## InfoCurrent
www.infocurrent.com
InfoCurrent specializes in library and records management staffing, on both a project and permanent basis. At the website, check Job Categories for a listing of the types of positions being filled. InfoCurrent is now identified as "a dedicated business sector within CORESTAFF Services."

## Information International Associates (IIa)
www.iiaweb.com/
IIa's focus is in the four areas of knowledge management, information technology, "data exploitation," and strategic planning and consulting; clients include government agencies, academia, nonprofit organizations, private entities, and international organizations. For potential work opportunities, see Careers > Careers at IIa and Job Openings on its website.

## John Keister & Associates

www.johnkeister.com/library/
Executive search firm specializing in library executive directors as well as C-level business and technology candidates for corporations.

## LAC

www.libraryassociates.com/index.php
Formerly known as Library Associates, LAC describes itself as "The Leader in Information Curation and Knowledge Management" and has built a national reputation as an information-focused organization providing staffing and information management solutions to libraries, corporations, archives, museums, academia, hospitals, law firms, and government agencies. Areas of specialization include research services, digital asset management, knowledge management, spend management (that is, helping clients control/reduce expenditures), library outsourcing, and film preservation and curation.

## Pro Libra Associates, Inc.

www.prolibra.com
Library services company providing experienced personnel specializing in all facets of library service and maintenance to corporations, public entities, and individuals. Focus is on consulting services, personnel staffing (direct hire/temp/temp-to-hire), and project management.

## PTFS

www.ptfs.com
PTFS (Progressive Technology Federal Systems) is a contract information services firm providing expertise and project staffing for enterprise (i.e., company-wide) content management, primarily to federal, civilian, defense, and intelligence agencies. See the site's Careers section (bottom of the page) for employment opportunities.

## USIS | Labat

www.usis.com/Information-Management-Support-Services.aspx
Provides many types of specialized contract expertise to clients, including information management and support services. Perusing their website provides an interesting snapshot of information career opportunities in the "confidentiality and security" side of information management (e.g., construction surveillance, intelligence analysis, and litigation support).

# LIS Job and Career Resources

## Career Q&A with the Library Career People

http://librarycareerpeople.com/
A monthly career question-and-answer session with two exceptionally knowledgeable LIS professionals, Tiffany Allen (director of Library HR, University of North Carolina, Chapel Hill University Library) and Susanne Markgren (digital services librarian, Purchase College, State University of New York). Terrific, down-to-earth advice; see also the wealth of archived responses browsable by category (e.g., burnout, getting started, job seeking).

## The Digital Shift
www.thedigitalshift.com/
From *Library Journal* and *School Library Journal*, The Digital Shift provides an ongoing stream of information about current activities and advances in the library world related to the role of digitization and digital content. If you're interested in a career involving digital librarianship, this is a great resource for staying current.

## Hiring Librarians
http://hiringlibrarians.com/
A practical resource from Emily Weak that fields questions from LIS job-hunters and seeks out answers from (mostly anonymous) hiring managers. In addition, the site offers a number of "special collections," including Authors' Corner: A Booklist for Job Hunters, Job Hunters Web Guide, and Researchers' Corner: A Guide for the Evidence-Based Job Hunter.

## Job-Hunting Tips & Links
http://mrlibrarydude.wordpress.com/nailing-the-library-interview/advice-job-hunting-tips-links/
A very useful resource from Mr. Library Dude (a.k.a. Joe Hardenbrook), this collection of LIS job-hunting links should be your starting point for exploring job opportunities for librarians and other information professionals.

## Job Searching Articles/LIScareer.com
www.liscareer.com/jobhunting.htm
More than 50 job-search advice and coaching articles from the LIScareer. com archives. Covers a wide range of topics, including crafting effective resumes, punching up your portfolio, considering international librarianship options, and multiple articles on resumes and interviewing.

## Librarians in the Job Market
www.linkedin.com
Created in 2010 by Jason Mulack, this popular LinkedIn group has over 14,000 members—a testament to the substantial (and ongoing) interest in finding, landing, changing, or creating LIS jobs. To access, from the LinkedIn home page search box, search on "Groups" and the title of this group.

## Librarianship Job Search and Careers
www.linkedin.com/
Created by David M. Connolly and ALA JobList as an ALA subgroup with this mission: "Discuss current events, best practices, and industry trends related to library jobs, and network with your professional peers." To access, you must first join the ALA LinkedIn group (but not necessarily ALA), then go to the "More" tab at the top of the page, select "Subgroups," and then this group.

## Library Interview Questions
https://mrlibrarydude.wordpress.com/nailing-the-library-interview/library-interview-questions/
This post has two parts: the first is a list of 23 sites dedicated to helping you identify, prepare for, and navigate tricky interview questions, and the second

is a list of some 50 job questions Mr. Library Dude has himself fielded during his career.

## Library Job Search

www.ala.org/tools/library-job-search
From ALA's Office of Human Resource Development and Recruitment (HRDR), this page aggregates dozens of library job-search resources. The collection of articles and books listed under "Library Job Search Skills" is about seven years out of date, but is still somewhat useful.

## LIScareer.com: Career Strategies for Librarians

http://liscareer.com
Hundreds of articles written by LIS practitioners on a wide range of career topics (e.g., career exploration, job searching, and work/life balance), many of which touch on topics related to career transitions. Although the site is no longer posting new content, the archive is nevertheless a trove of still-relevant insights and information.

## New Academic Librarians: Networking to Success

www.linkedin.com/
LinkedIn group created by Sarah Forbes with this mission: "Entering into a new job can be a very daunting period in a librarian's life. This interactive forum will discuss avenues and techniques that new librarians can use when they are looking for or starting a new position in an academic library." To access, from the LinkedIn home page search box, search on "Groups" and the title of this group.

## The New Librarian's Listserv (NEWLIB-L)

http://walternelson.com/dr/newlib-l
A discussion list intended for "librarians new to the profession who wish to share experiences and discuss ideas, issues, trends, and problems faced by librarians in the early stages of their careers." The list is open to all and currently includes more than 1,300 subscribers (from North America as well as globally) representing all aspects and types of librarianship. Those contemplating but not yet pursuing an LIS career are encouraged to participate as well.

## Placements and Salaries [year]

http://features.libraryjournal.com/placements-and-salaries/
Undertaken annually by *Library Journal,* this survey reports on who's getting jobs, where, and at what salary. This will help you identify what salary range to target for specific jobs.

## Resume Review Service/New Members Round Table

www.ala.org/ala/mgrps/rts/nmrt/oversightgroups/comm/resreview/resumereview.cfm
For members of the NMRT, this service is based on volunteers from all types of libraries reviewing and critiquing submitted resumes. In addition, the (conference-based) onsite Resume Review Service is open to any job-seeker attending either the ALA annual or midwinter conferences (for more information, see the website).

## Retirement and Second Careers

http://bit.ly/1Hgy4uL

A special issue of *Feliciter*, the Canadian Library Association's bimonthly professional publication, whose articles focus on what to consider regarding retirement, career-continuation options post-retirement, and creative ways LIS professionals are approaching their retirement lives.

# General Job Resources

## Craft

https://craft.co/

Using an increasingly popular approach to information gathering, the Craft site "scrapes" and aggregates data of all sorts from social media sites such as Twitter, Facebook, and LinkedIn; Google; and hundreds of blogs and news outlets. The Craft folks state that so far they've gathered information on about 250,000 organizations, so this will be most effective as a way to gather more information on large firms. Companies also have the option of creating their individual About Us pages on the site in order to reach out more directly to potential hires (and let you know how great they'd be to work for).

## Glassdoor

www.glassdoor.com

Glassdoor's mission is to help job-seekers "find jobs and see company salaries, reviews, and interviews—all posted anonymously by employees." Information provided includes North American companies as well as those outside North America and is drawn from both current and former employees. Searchable by company, industry, and highest-rated company. Also includes "best places to work" rankings. One caveat: assume that disgruntled employees are much likelier to take the time to post than are happy ones.

## Hoover's Online

www.hoovers.com/

Hoover's company and industry information is primarily available as an online database through academic and/or large public libraries, since its primary market is large companies doing market or competitive research. But if available to you, Hoover's can be a good source for descriptions of key companies in a given industry, as well as for overviews, analysis, and forecasts for those industries themselves.

## Industries at a Glance

www.bls.gov/iag

This Bureau of Labor Statistics (BLS) resource provides "a 'snapshot' of national data obtained from different BLS surveys and programs" as well as additional industry detail, including state and regional data, when available. Searchable by alphabetical industry index or by industry numerical order (North American Industry Classification System/NAICS), this is a good place to start gathering information about industries of potential interest for employment purposes.

## Job Hunters Bible>Counseling, Testing & Advice
www.jobhuntersbible.com/counseling/sec_page.php?sub_item=047
The online component of John Bolles's classic job-exploration manual, *What Color Is Your Parachute*. Within the Counseling, Testing & Advice section, see especially the "Online Personality & Traits Tests" and the "Online Careers Tests" entries.

## Job Seekers Guide
http://learn.linkedin.com/job-seekers/
LinkedIn's online tutorial for job-seekers. Addresses how to complete your profile, seek connections, search the LinkedIn job listings, message your contacts, and build visibility for your expertise.

## Job Seekers Salary Calculator
www.jobsearchintelligence.com/NACE/jobseekers/salary-calculator.php
From the National Association of Colleges and Employers (NACE), this salary calculator is one of several reliable sources to check when gathering salary comparables in preparation for negotiating your compensation.

## Mindtools: Essential Skills for an Excellent Career
www.mindtools.com/
A collection of more than 900 "tools" in the areas of management, career, and thinking skills. Although a fee-based membership is encouraged, many of the site's excellent resources are available for free.

## Payscale
www.payscale.com/
One of the best-known salary calculators, based on "salary and career data from more than 30 million people, covering 12,000 job titles and 1,100 distinct industries in 150 countries."

## Plunkett Research
www.plunkettresearch.com
Like the Hoover's information, Plunkett's profiles are now primarily available as an online database via academic or large public libraries. Although Plunkett does publish print industry guides, their cost is generally prohibitive for the average job-seeker, so best bet is to check your local libraries to see whether any of them include Plunkett among their online resources. If so, check out their industry overviews, company write-ups, and trends and forecast information.

## Salary.com
www.salary.com
Search by title and location to see a list of relevant options (e.g., a search on "librarian" in a specific zip code brought up information for "Librarian," "Librarian—Higher Ed," "Librarian Assistant," "Chief Medical Librarian," and "Database Librarian," among others). The site provides both free information and more detailed fee-based information.

## SmartBrief on Your Career
www.smartbrief.com/yourcareer/
Daily newsletter that aggregates career articles, columns, and blog posts from multiple online sources such as the *Wall Street Journal, Harvard Business Review,* Forbes.com, and CareerRocketeer.

## Vault Career Intelligence [Vault Reports]
www.vault.com
Most of the Vault content is fee based, so your best option if you are a student or recent grad is to check to see whether your college career center offers access. You can read the site blogs and a substantial number of well-done career articles for free, but generally Vault is in the business of selling special reports on key industries and job-search topics (or signing up college career centers for their full online offerings).

## WetFeet
www.wetfeet.com
With a mission of equipping "job seekers...with the advice, research, and inspiration you need to plan and achieve a successful career," WetFeet provides a wealth of articles, blog posts, insider tips, employee profiles, and industry overviews to help you accomplish that goal. Like Vault, WetFeet is in the business of selling career overviews (e.g., "Careers in Marketing"), but they are generally current and very reasonably priced. While WetFeet doesn't offer a guide on the library profession, it does offer insights into non-LIS career paths that may have relevance to alternative LIS options.

# Insights from the Experts

*Note: The following articles, blog posts, and similar resources address many of the job-hunting and career-transition issues LIS professionals face throughout their careers. Not all are written by individuals from the profession, but all should have relevance.*

## Finding a Library Job—Updated
http://lj.libraryjournal.com/2009/09/careers/finding-a-library-job-updated/
From one of the experts in library job searching, this online article by Rachel Singer Gordon provides a great overview of the steps needed to break into the library profession for those new to the LIS job market. Although somewhat out of date, the advice remains practical and realistic.

## Finding the Right Library Job Is Kind of Like Dating
http://inalj.com/?p=46707
An unusual but fun (and smart) approach to finding the right library job for you, from Kathleen Kosiec. An especially great read when you're getting bogged down by taking the career questions too seriously.

## From Temporary to Permanent—Making the Best of Your Time as a Temp
http://liscareer.com/bridgewater_temp.htm
Although author Rachel Bridgewater's experience was with academic libraries, her wise advice on using a "temp" job to position yourself for

permanent opportunities is applicable across all temporary employment situations.

### How to Become a 21st Century Librarian

http://lj.libraryjournal.com/2013/03/careers/how-to-become-a-21st-century-librarian/
This terrific article starts out with the wise advice that "if you want quiet and lots of time to read, think again." It's not only a great resource (and reality check) for those considering traditional librarianship, but also an equally great reminder of why library work can be so rewarding. (Per *LJ*, "a version of this article by Rachel Singer Gordon was originally published June 1, 2005, under the title 'How to Become a Librarian.' It has been updated a number of times over the years with new information and resources, most recently [March 2013] by *LJ* News Editor Meredith Schwartz.")

### How to Land a Library Job

http://bit.ly/1GQ0kcu
From *Publishers Weekly* contributing editor and librarian Brian Kenney, this 2013 post provides a realistic overview of job opportunities in the library field—that is, although an improving economy may somewhat expand the number of library job openings, you're likely to face increasing competition for them. Nevertheless, as Kenney points out, it is possible to land a spot—as he should know, since he tended to change library jobs every two or three years in the first 20 years of his career.

### The Info Pro's Survival Guide to Job Hunting

www.infotoday.com/searcher/jul02/mort.htm
Written in summer 2002, this *Searcher* article by Mary-Ellen Mort still provides an excellent overview of how to approach job hunting for LIS professionals, whether just starting out or as someone well into his or her career. Although some of the resources are dated, the advice is not; this is a timeless and useful resource for all LIS job hunters.

### Job-Hunt: Your Guide to Smarter Job Search

www.job-hunt.org/company_research/research-start-ups.shtml
See especially the information on how to research companies (e.g., the post on how to research early-stage start-ups at http://bit.ly/1EuF0HB). One of the best (if not the best) sources of information on how to research prospective employers, especially helpful for those considering nontraditional LIS paths.

### Job Interview Collections for Job Seekers

www.quintcareers.com/interview_question_collections.html
Tons of interview preparation questions from Quintessential Careers, a content-rich site geared toward helping job-seekers navigate their careers and career change.

### Job Interviewee Questions

http://annoyedlibrarian.blogspot.com/2008/02/job-interviewee-questions.html
A terrific and highly entertaining discussion about what questions or other "problematic signals" library job applicants should be on the look out for

that may indicate a dysfunctional work environment (translation: excuse yourself from further consideration as a potential job candidate as quickly and gracefully as possible!). Be sure to read the comments . . ..

## Job Loss: How to Cope
http://careerplanning.about.com/od/jobloss/a/job_loss.htm
By Dawn Rosenberg McKay, About.com guide for Career Planning, this is a collection of articles about all the things to think about if you get laid off or anticipate it happening. Lots of practical information about unemployment compensation, COBRA policies, etc.

## Making the Move
www.wetfeet.com/advice-tools/job-search/making-the-move
The five factors you'll want to consider when evaluating a possible career relocation decision. By WetFeet writer Liz Seasholtz. Especially relevant to academic librarianship careers, which often involve moving to a new location.

## Making the Shift: Using Transferable Skills to Change Career Paths
http://liscareer.com/taylor_transferable.htm
A very practical overview from LIS practitioner Deborah Taylor on using transferable skills (which she helps you identify) to create career path options.

## Mind the Gap: 8 Ways to Handle Gaps between Jobs
http://blog.rezscore.com/2011/09/mind-the-gap-8-ways-to-handle-gaps-between-jobs
Transition points often result in periods of unemployment. If your plans involve moving from one employer to another with an interim phase of unemployment, this article will help you frame that interim period in a positive way during job interviewing or on resumes and cover letters.

## Move Along: Relocation for Librarians
http://liscareer.com/gertz_relocation.htm
A thorough overview of relocation considerations where, instead of envisioning a sequence of linear steps, readers are encouraged to think about the job hunt "as a holistic and integrated process by which actions taken at any time will move you closer to your ultimate goal." From Christine Gertz, library and information specialist at Career and Placement Services, University of Alberta.

## Navigating the Salary Question
http://slisapps.sjsu.edu/blogs/career/?p=103
Q&A follow-up to one of San Jose State University's SLIS program career development workshops. Excellent source of specific language to use when attempting to navigate the salary question during the initial interview.

## New City, New Job: How to Conduct a Long-Distance Job Search
www.quintcareers.com/long-distance_job-search.html
Eighteen smart strategies for laying the groundwork to land a job in your new locale, from Quintessential Career experts Katharine and Randall Hansen.

## An Open Letter to New Librarians
www.thedigitalshift.com/2011/02/roy-tennant-digital-libraries/an-open-letter-to-new-librarians/
An outstanding and honest response from technologist and LIS thought leader Roy Tennant on dealing with the frustrations facing many recent graduates and others new to the library profession. From his *Library Journal* blog.

## A Permanent Alternative: Temporary, Part-Time Library Work
http://liscareer.com/johnston_temporary.htm
Written in 2004 by academic librarian Jennifer Johnston, this helpful article explores the pros and cons of temporary positions, how to find them, and how to make the most of them. Probably has even more relevance for today's job-seekers than when first written.

## Personal SWOT Analysis: Making the Most of Your Talents and Opportunities
www.mindtools.com/pages/article/newTMC_05.htm
From the career site MindTools, this article and accompanying worksheet help you identify the key questions to ask yourself in order to unearth the information most useful for making career decisions. A great tool for making strategic choices as you grow your career.

## Relocating: The Beginning of a Great Adventure
http://liscareer.com/dickinson_relocation.htm
A thorough and practical guide for picking up your LIS career and relocating to a new location, written by Thad Dickinson, who's relocated numerous times and generously shares his "lessons learned."

## The Starter Job: Or, Why You Should Consider That Job in Smalltown, USA
http://infonista.com/2011/the-starter-job-or-why-you-should-consider-that-job-in-smalltown-usa/
Many new MLIS graduates assume that an entry-level job at a small library in an out-of-the-way locale would have little to offer from a career-building perspective, but in fact, just the opposite may be true.

## Telling Stories to Get the Job
www.liscareer.com/glover_stories.htm
Being able to recount stories that demonstrate and showcase your outstanding professional strengths is quickly becoming a key interview strategy. In this article, John Glover discusses why this can be a valuable tool for you and how to prepare your best stories using the STAR method: Situation, Task, Action, Result.

## They Hired the Other Candidate—Now What?
http://infonista.com/2011/they-hired-the-other-candidate---now-what/
How to turn a disappointment—losing a job to the competition—into an opportunity to potentially create additional job possibilities.

## Top Ten Questions to Ask in a Job Interview

www.libgig.com/toptenquestionstoask

Most interview job prep focuses on preparing to answer questions that interviewers will shoot at you, but it's just as important to ask thoughtful questions of your interviewer. This article identifies 10 questions to ask and why.

## What Is an Informational Interview and How It Can Help Your Career

http://jobsearch.about.com/cs/infointerviews/a/infointerview.htm

An About.com article written by Alison Doyle, this article from her *Job Searching* guide discusses what an informational interview is, how to conduct one, what questions to ask, and follow-up etiquette. See also the related articles on informational interviews.

## Your Job Search Toolkit

http://career-advice.monster.com/

This career-advice section of the well-known job search site offers useful information for any job exploration or search strategy, both within and outside of the LIS field. Check here for multiple articles on finding your best job match, writing cover letters and resumes, acing interviews, and more.

# Appendix C
## LIS Blogs and Social Media

Blogs and social media feeds are at best a tremendous source of ongoing insightful information about a given topic (in this case, the LIS profession) and at worst, an ephemeral source of trending topics whose authors end up abandoning them when other personal or professional priorities intervene (an observation based on my own temporary but nevertheless embarrassing absence from both my Infonista blog and the LIS Career Options LinkedIn group I started in 2010). In addition, any list of recommended resources here will necessarily be incomplete (a May 27, 2014, Hack Library School post by Michael Rodriguez noted there are "5,000 librarylanders on Twitter"[1]) and undoubtedly out of date at some point.

Your best approach is to simply start exploring the various social media channels and the blogosphere using the terms that are most relevant to career interests, for example, digital asset management, content curation, school libraries, or similar terms. Or start by finding out what blogs thought leaders (or the smartest professionals you know) are reading, what tweet feeds they're following, what LinkedIn groups they belong to, and/or what other online sources they tap into.

If you're not (yet) comfortable with the blogosphere and social media space, now's the time to jump in. These types of online commentary are an increasingly important way of communicating across the profession and its specializations, so the highly selective list that follows identifies some of the leading blog and social media resources simply to help you get started. The real goal is to encourage you to start creating your own personally curated list or professional information sources, based on your career focus and your preferred social media channels.

# Lists and How-To Resources

**75 of the Coolest Librarians to Follow on Twitter**
http://librarysciencelist.com/75-of-the-coolest-librarians-to-follow-on-twitter/

**100 Libraries to Follow on Facebook**
www.mattanderson.org/blog/2013/01/31/100-libraries-to-follow-on-acebook/

**100 Libraries to Follow on Twitter**
www.mattanderson.org/blog/2013/01/11/100-libraries-to-follow-on-twitter/

**200 Librarians to Follow on Twitter**
www.mattanderson.org/blog/2014/12/13/200-librarians-to-follow-on-twitter/

**Top Twitter Hashtags for Librarians**
http://hacklibraryschool.com/2014/05/27/hashtags/

**Tumblrarian 101: Tumblr for Libraries and Librarians**
www.thedigitalshift.com/2012/08/social-media/tumblrarian-101-tumblr-for-libraries-and-librarians/

# Blogs

**ACRLog**
http://acrlog.org

**The Adventures of Library Girl**
www.librarygirl.net/

**Against the Grain News Channel**
www.against-the-grain.com

**Agnostic Maybe**
http://agnosticmaybe.wordpress.com/

**ALA TechSource**
www.alatechsource.org/blog

**Annoyed Librarian**
http://lj.libraryjournal.com/blogs/annoyedlibrarian/

**Blended Librarianship**
www.scoop.it/t/blended-librarianship

**Code{4}Lib**
http://planet.code4lib.org/

**Confessions of a Science Librarian**
http://scienceblogs.com/confessions/

**The Daring Librarian**
www.thedaringlibrarian.com/

**David Lee King**
www.davidleeking.com/

**Designing Better Libraries**
http://dbl.lishost.org/blog/#.VMR7QSvF-Co

**The Digital Shift**
www.thedigitalshift.com/

**Disruptive Library Technology Jester**
http://dltj.org/

**Free Range Librarian**
http://freerangelibrarian.com/

**From the Bell Tower**
http://lj.libraryjournal.com/category/opinion/steven-bell/

**Hack Library School (hls)**
http://hacklibraryschool.com/

**Higher Education in the Future**
www.scoop.it/t/higher-education-in-the-future

**Hiring Librarians**
http://hiringlibrarians.com/

**iLibrarian Blog**
http://oedb.org/ilibrarian/

**In the Library with the Lead Pipe**
www.inthelibrarywiththeleadpipe.org/

**InfoDocket**
www.infodocket.com/

**Infonista**
www.infonista.com/

**Information Wants to Be Free**
http://meredith.wolfwater.com/wordpress/

**Inkdroid**
http://inkdroid.org/journal/

**Latest Library Links**
www.americanlibrariesmagazine.org/blog/

**Letters to a Young Librarian**
http://letterstoayounglibrarian.blogspot.com/

**Librarian by Day**
http://librarianbyday.net/

**Librarian in Black**
http://librarianinblack.net/librarianinblack/

**Librarian.net: Putting the Rarin Back in Librarian Since 1999**
www.librarian.net/

**Library Babel Fish**
www.insidehighered.com/blogs/library-babel-fish

**The Library Career People**
http://librarycareerpeople.com/

**Library Hat**
www.bohyunkim.net/blog/

**Library Juice: On the Intersection of Libraries, Politics, and Culture**
http://libraryjuicepress.com/blog/

**Library Link of the Day**
www.tk421.net/librarylink/2014/12.html

**Library Tech Talk**
https://libtechtalk.wordpress.com/

**LibraryScienceList.com—A New Social Community for Librarians Worldwide**
http://librarysciencelist.com

**Lipstick Librarian**
www.lipsticklibrarian.com/

**LISNews**
http://lisnews.org/

**LITA Blog**
http://litablog.org/

**The 'M' Word—Marketing Libraries**
http://themwordblog.blogspot.com/

**A Media Specialist's Guide to the Internet**
http://mediaspecialistsguide.blogspot.com/

**Mr. Library Dude: Blogging about Libraries, Technology, Teaching, and More**
http://mrlibrarydude.wordpress.com/

**Musings about Librarianship**
http://musingsaboutlibrarianship.blogspot.com/

**No Shelf Required**
www.libraries.wright.edu/noshelfrequired/

**Pegasus Librarian**
http://pegasuslibrarian.com/

**Public Library News**
www.publiclibrariesnews.com

**R. David Lankes Blog**
http://quartz.syr.edu/blog/?page_id=6070

**Research Buzz**
http://researchbuzz.me/

**Resource Shelf**
www.resourceshelf.com/

**Screwy Decimal**
www.screwydecimal.com/

**SearchReSearch**
http://searchresearch1.blogspot.com/

**The Shifted Librarian**
http://theshiftedlibrarian.com/

**Stephen's Lighthouse**
http://stephenslighthouse.com/

**Swiss Army Librarian**
www.swissarmylibrarian.net/

**Tame the Web**
http://tametheweb.com/

**Techsoup for Libraries**
www.techsoupforlibraries.org/blog

**Teleread**
www.teleread.com

**Walt at Random: The Library Voice of the Radical Middle**
http://walt.lishost.org/

# Representative LinkedIn LIS Groups

American Association of School Librarians
Association of Canadian Archivists
Children's Librarians
Corporate Librarians
Digital Asset Management
Digital Libraries
Electronic Documents and Records Management Professionals
Health Care Informatics
International School Librarians
Law Librarians
Librarians Emerge as Project Managers
Librarians in the Job Market
Libraries & Librarians
Librarians' Problems and Guidance
Librarians Sans Libraries
Music Librarians
New Academic Librarians: Networking to Success
Patent Researchers
School Librarians
SLA Solo Librarians Division
Special Libraries Association
Strategic Librarians
Sustainability Librarians
Taxonomy Community of Practice

# Note

1.  Michael Rodriguez. "Top Twitter Hashtags for Librarians." Hack Library School, May 27, 2014. http://hacklibraryschool.com/2014/05/27/hashtags/

# Index

## About the Author

G. KIM DORITY is the founder and president of Dority & Associates, Inc., an information and content development consulting company. She is also an adjunct faculty member for the University of Denver MLIS program, where she created and has taught a course, Alternative LIS Careers for Students and Professionals, for 16 years.

In addition to her Dority & Associates client work, Kim has been the chief content officer for WebPsychology, an online start-up focusing on mental health and positive psychology resources, and vice president of Content and Development for Disaboom, an online resource  for people with disabilities. She previously led the team that designed and created the first virtual academic library, e-global library, for Jones International University. In addition, Kim has served as the interim director of the University of Denver's MLIS program, created and provided executive information services to several CEOs, and presented numerous webinars and workshops on all aspects of building a resilient LIS career, whether traditional or nontraditional.

Kim's passion is helping others discover how versatile and dynamic an information professional's career can be; she blogs on this topic at Infonista.com.